Race, Religion, and Civil Rights

Asian American Studies Today

This series publishes scholarship on cutting-edge themes and issues, including broadly based histories of both long-standing and more recent immigrant populations; focused investigations of ethnic enclaves and understudied subgroups; and examinations of relationships among various cultural, regional, and socioeconomic communities. Of particular interest are subject areas in need of further critical inquiry, including transnationalism, globalization, homeland polity, and other pertinent topics.

Series Editor: Huping Ling, Truman State University

Stephanie Hinnershitz, *Race, Religion, and Civil Rights: Asian Students on the West Coast, 1900–1968*

Jennifer Ann Ho, *Racial Ambiguity in Asian American Culture*

Jun Okada, *Making Asian American Film and Video: History, Institutions, Movements*

David S. Roh, Betsy Huang, and Greta A. Niu, *Techno-Orientalism: Imagining Asia in Speculative Fiction, History, and Media*

Race, Religion, and Civil Rights

. . . .

Asian Students on the West Coast, 1900–1968

STEPHANIE HINNERSHITZ

Rutgers University Press

New Brunswick, New Jersey, and London

Library of Congress Cataloging-in-Publication Data
Hinnershitz, Stephanie, 1984–
    Race, religion, and civil rights : Asian students on the West Coast, 1900–1968 / Stephanie Hinnershitz.
        pages cm. — (Asian American studies today)
    Includes bibliographical references and index.
    ISBN 978-0-8135-7179-9 (hardcover : alk. paper) — ISBN 978-0-8135-7178-2 (pbk. : alk. paper) — ISBN 978-0-8135-7180-5 (e-book (web pdf) — ISBN 978-0-8135-7536-0 (e-book (epub)
    1. Asian Americans—Civil rights—Pacific States—History—20th century. 2. Civil rights movements—Pacific States—History—20th century. 3. Asian American college students—Political activity—Pacific States—History—20th century. 4. Pacific States—Race relations—History—20th century. I. Title.
    F855.2.A75H56 2015
    323.1195'0730790904—dc23
    2014046334

A British Cataloging-in-Publication record for this book is available from the British Library.

Visit our website: http://rutgerspress.rutgers.edu

Manufactured in the United States of America

Contents

Acknowledgments

This book is the product of many individuals who have assisted me along the way. I am forever grateful to those who contributed to this project, and although I cannot list everyone here, I want all of my friends, family, and colleagues to know how important their love and support are to me.

The team at Rutgers University Press offered guidance throughout this process, and I could not have asked for better mentors than the series editors, Huping Ling, Katie Keeran, and Lisa Boyajian. Molan Goldstein significantly improved the manuscript with her careful and thoughtful editing. I am also grateful for the recommendations from readers at both Rutgers University Press and Temple University Press for making this a stronger book.

This work would not exist without the input of scholars and friends from Lock Haven University, Temple University, and the University of Maryland. My undergraduate advisor, Dr. Janet Irons, helped me become a better historian, and Todd Shepard and Petra Goedde provided advice when this was just a master's thesis about Filipino students. At the University of Maryland I found a wonderful, kind, and nurturing advisor in Julie Greene, and Lisa Mar provided me with a strong grounding in Asian American history and pushed me to think theoretically about my work. Eiichiro Azuma, Janelle Wong, and Robyn Muncy also assisted with the final product, and I am thankful for their help. Josh Bearden, Will Burghardt, Reid Gustafson, Jon Shelton, Stephen Duncan, and Scott Heerman all read drafts of this work and offered honest and excellent critiques. Melissa Borja, Scott Manguno, Kirsten Eckley, Melissa Adler, Angela Ju, Kate Jirik, and Trevor Hoppe have also been crucial in shaping this book by allowing me to ramble about cultural bridges and Asian American students. My Valdosta State University colleagues Owen Jones, David Williams, Dixie Haggard, Mary Block, Tom Aiello, Lorna Alvarez-Rivera, John Dunn, Melanie Byrd, Jay Rickman, and Cathy Oglesby also contributed to this book with their friendship and laughter. The department head, Paul Riggs, made reduced teaching loads possible so I could devote time to writing and revising.

As with any undertaking, money, time, and resources are needed to complete a book, and I am grateful to the institutions and individuals who made this possible. The University of Maryland, the Kautz Family YMCA Archives, the Charles E. Young Library at UCLA, the Social Science Research Council, the American Council of Learned Societies, the Library of Congress, and Valdosta State University provided much needed support for travel and writing in the early stages of this project, and archivists at the University of Washington Special Collections Department, the Kautz Family YMCA Archives, Valdosta State University, the Hoover Institution Archives, the Bancroft Library, the Filipino American National Historical Society in Seattle, and the Library of Congress all assisted in locating various records and sources.

Parts of chapter 3 of this book were previously published in the *Journal of Social History*, and I thank the editors for allowing reproduction, as well as for providing an early venue for some arguments presented herein.

And last but certainly not least, I'd like to thank my husband, Rob. I've heard that being married to another academic can be challenging, but our relationship has been the opposite. I could not have completed this book without his love and support along the way (as well as his editing and advice) and I thank him with all of my heart (and hope that he will forgive me for not discussing the Fourteen Points in chapter 1—maybe in the next book).

Abbreviations

AFSC	American Friends Service Committee
CFR	Committee on Friendly Relations among Foreign Students
CFRE	Christian Friends for Racial Equality
CRJA	Committee on Resettlement of Japanese Americans
CSCA	Chinese Students' Christian Association of North America
CWFLU	Cannery Workers' and Farm Laborers' Union
FSCM	Filipino Students' Christian Movement
JSCA	Japanese Students' Christian Association in North America
NJASRC	National Japanese American Student Relocation Council
WRA	War Relocation Authority
WSCF	World Student Christian Federation

**Race, Religion,
and Civil Rights**

Introduction

• •

On a spring afternoon in 1938, foreign-born Chinese, Filipino, and Japanese students joined with other classmates at the University of Washington in Seattle to discuss America's problems with racial discrimination. The atmosphere was electric: students were excited yet wary of sharing their experiences with one another on a campus and in a city beset with often rocky race relations. Sponsored by the campus Young Men's Christian Association as well as the campus chapters of the Chinese Students' Christian Association, the Filipino Students' Christian Movement, and the Japanese Students' Christian Association, the university's first large-scale interracial conference drew attendees from a variety of racial and ethnic groups, including white, black, and Asian American students. The trepidation students may have felt, however, gave way to fruitful and passionate conversations. During their meeting, students debated the place of nationalism in a Christian world, the "toxic presence" of American military, economic, and political domination in Asia, and the negative effects of these unchristian forces on racial equality and Christian fellowship.[1] The students strategized to fight prejudice and racism on campus, in Seattle, and along the West Coast. Concerns over the oppression of colonized peoples and resulting racial and ethnic tensions brought politically and socially active students together at the university, signaling a growing international, interracial, and panethnic movement for human and civil rights. As one Japanese Students' Christian Association member explained, the students present were "leaders of a worldly movement ... designed to overthrow racism and other evils and build a world free from prejudice beginning in America."[2]

The leadership the Protestant Christian Asian students assumed in organizing this 1938 meeting suggests that it is time to reevaluate the battle for racial justice along the West Coast and, more generally, the history of civil rights in America. What role did these students play in promoting equality in the United States, and how does an understanding of this early panethnic (or, considering the time period, pan-"Oriental") and interracial cooperation change how we approach the history of race relations during the twentieth century? These questions form the foundation of this book, which explores the reactions of leaders, members, and supporters of the Chinese Students' Christian Association of North America (CSCA), the Japanese Students' Christian Association in North America (JSCA), and the Filipino Students' Christian Movement (FSCM)—three of the largest Asian Christian associations, with vast membership on the West Coast—to racism and prejudice in the United States. The students' response to racial discrimination on and off campus challenges the long-held perceptions of Asian Americans as intraethnic activists removed from larger social and political movements prior to the late 1960s. Foreign students were the early leaders of these organizations, which later grew to encompass American-born Chinese, Filipinos, and Japanese as well. A close study of the CSCA, FSCM, and JSCA members also adds to our understanding of the place of Christian-inspired activism in interracial/interethnic movements during the early twentieth century. Although there were limits to the forms of activism the students engaged in, the Christian networks contributed to and shaped a growing West Coast civil rights movement through the interwar years and into the post–World War II era.

The students' early participation in campus Christian associations and their later activism in postwar community organizations present a nuanced narrative of the struggle for racial equality. Methodologically, this book blends the historiographies of Asian American, civil rights, immigration, and ethnic history to offer a new view of activism on the West Coast, illuminating what the historian Mark Brilliant describes as a "wide" as well as a "long" civil rights movement. I argue that these students interpreted the racial climate and the discrimination in America as violations of Christian ethics and responded with influential social, cultural, and later political tactics requiring interracial and interethnic solidarity.[3]

Race, Religion, and Civil Rights is part of a growing body of work that examines the transnational experiences of foreign Asian students who study abroad in the United States, but I dig deeper into the impact of these students on American social movements and the politicization of Asian American students. Chih-ming Wang's recent book on the "transnational mode of being" of Chinese students who came to the United States provides a framework for my analysis. Wang convincingly argues that the "foreign student is a figure of articulation in that he or she brings together Asia and America through multiple crossings and engagements," a concept that helps in explaining the role of foreign-born students in connecting with Asian American students and building large, Christian-based organizations.[4] Whereas Wang's focus is on the transpacific/transnational writings of Asian students and their place in contemporary Asian American studies, my work argues for a greater understanding of the historical relationship of foreign students to Asian Americans and the racial and civil rights trajectory of the United States. While Chinese, Filipino, and Japanese students were, as the historian Eiichiro Azuma explains, often caught between the politics of their homelands and their lives as racial "others" in the United States, scholars of Asian America have often overlooked their demands for racial justice and interracial cooperation.[5] These students brought their Christian ideas with them to the United States and called on Americans to address the suffering of migrants and Asian Americans along the West Coast and across the nation. The imprint of the Chinese, Filipino, and Japanese students' Christian movement on race relations in the United States challenges historians to recognize the variety of ideas and actors that influenced the struggle for civil rights. By analyzing association materials, English-language publications, members' writings, and other archival sources, the undeniable impact of Asian American and Christian-based activism on broader social and political movements becomes clear.

In order to demonstrate the broad influence of foreign-born Christian students on the United States, students from China, Japan, and the Philippines share the pages of this book with their American-born classmates. Membership lists compiled by the student associations often listed the place of origin for students, providing an opportunity to identify which students were foreign-born and which were American citizens. The term "foreign student" is, as Wang argues, a transitory term rather than a set identity. Indeed, many foreign-born students returned to their homelands after their education, but many did not, and many more crisscrossed the boundaries between student and worker, scholar and layperson during their time in America.[6] This fluctuating status is what makes the Christian associations and Christian ideas central to this portrait of Asian American activism. Maintaining cohesion as well as commitment to the goals of interracial, panethnic, and Christian brotherhood were challenges for the students as graduation, return migration, and changes in internal leadership posed threats to the stability of the organizations. However, the foreign students who initially established the CSCA, FSCM, and JSCA created lasting relationships with members of the second generation of Asian American students. These connections allowed the associations to continue to operate for approximately twenty years and inspired former foreign-born and American-born members to seek opportunities for interracial activism in larger communities after leaving school. I frequently use the term "Asian students" throughout the book in describing the activities of the Christian student associations (unless specified otherwise) to argue that these students established networks that blurred national, racial, and ethnic status. Because of the students' groundbreaking work in forging connections between various members of Asian America, the historian Yuji Ichioka's phrase "Asian American" (coined during the late 1960s to describe changes in the makeup of ethnic groups and activists) more accurately describes the student dynamics during the early twentieth century and highlights the long history of this term in practice.[7] While Americans and the students themselves often used the term "Oriental" to reference their common identity, their early "pan-Oriental" groups suggest that Asian American identity is a powerful one with a lengthy past. The unique foreign-born/American-born memberships found in the Christian associations as well as the panethnic and interracial networks they established make *Race, Religion, and Civil Rights* central to understanding the relationship of Asian American experiences to the emergence of social movements on the West Coast.

The Arrival of Asian Students: A Brief History

The story of Asian Christian students in West Coast and American social history is part of a larger narrative of scholarly migration across the Pacific. Chinese scholars composed the earliest "wave" of student migration to America. During the middle to late nineteenth century, a small number of Chinese students traveled to the United States as an extension of their formal education, with the encouragement of Protestant missionaries. During the early twentieth century, however, the Boxer Rebellion of 1900 (an antiforeign, anti-imperialist, and anti-Christian movement) created a new opportunity for more students to seek an education in America. The US government used the monetary restitution it received for damages during the uprising to create the Boxer Indemnity Fund, a program that provided financial assistance to Chinese students. The financial aid made available by the indemnities, coupled with the Qing dynasty's promotion of modernity and knowledge of Western ideas and innovation, resulted in an increase in Chinese student migration to the United States. Without indemnity funds, self-supporting students also came to American universities and colleges with the guidance of Christian organizations such as the YMCA and other missionary efforts.[8]

Likewise, a relatively small group of Filipino students also benefited from American educational "benevolence" and colonialism during the early twentieth century. In 1903, Philippines Governor-General Howard Taft passed the Pensionado Act, which provided one hundred Filipino students that year with full government-sponsored scholarships to any college or university in the United States of their choosing. American officials and legislators designed the program to invite Filipinos from elite families to gain an American education and return home to begin careers as colonial administrators. High-ranking Filipinos also benefited from sending their sons, and in some cases daughters, to the United States to prove the dignity and respectability of Filipinos to Americans. By 1912, more than two hundred *pensionados* had graduated from American universities and returned home, with many becoming teachers or colonial bureaucrats and leaders. During the 1920s, more self-supporting Filipino students arrived in the United States eager to begin college and take advantage of their exceptional status as American nationals, an identity that allowed Filipinos to enter the United States despite the restrictions on other Asian groups under the Immigration Act of 1924. The imperial relationship of the Philippines to America created educational opportunities based on colony/metropole connections.[9]

For Japan, sending students abroad was also a way to ensure that Americans were exposed to the best and brightest Japanese immigrants.

Following rising anti-Japanese sentiment among white Californians who identified Japanese laborers as unfair competition, the San Francisco Board of Education mandated that Japanese students attend segregated schools. The segregation decision prompted fear from Japanese officials that continued discrimination against Japanese immigrants would ultimately lead to policies similar to the Chinese Exclusion Act, which prevented Chinese laborers from entering the United States. The Japanese government agreed to self-impose emigration restrictions on citizens in return for a guarantee from President Theodore Roosevelt that Japanese émigrés would receive equal protection and basic rights. The resulting Gentleman's Agreement of 1907 prohibited Japanese labor migration to America, while a steady stream of Japanese students continued to enter colleges and universities in the United States and particularly along the West Coast. Overall, the Gentleman's Agreement represents the impact of foreign policy on opportunities for Asian students during the late nineteenth and early twentieth centuries.[10]

In West Coast states, Asian students outnumbered those from other nations during the early to mid-twentieth century, and those from China, Japan, and the Philippines formed the largest groups of foreign students on many college campuses. By the 1920s, more than three thousand mostly male Asian students were studying along the West Coast, with Chinese students being the most numerous.[11] Although many foreign-born students attended elite schools along the East Coast in the 1920s to avoid the increasingly racist atmosphere in the West, more Chinese, Filipino, and Japanese students traveled to the often more affordable schools in California and Washington.

As a result of the political nature of student migration from Asia, existing works on Asian students in the United States during the early to mid-twentieth century focus almost exclusively on their ties to Asia and rarely shed light on the students' relationships with American social movements.[12] Although the students were important actors in the development of various institutions and programs in their home countries, historians and other scholars have built their studies of these groups on the concepts of "in-betweenness" and transnational political identities. Undeniably, students from China and Japan often came to America with the responsibility of representing their respective governments as well as learning the ways of American life and society in order to benefit their own nations. Weili

Ye explains in her work that Chinese officials expected students to gain knowledge and experience abroad and then return to "modernize" China, while Eiichiro Azuma argues that Japanese students served their nation as exploratory agents, venturing into the American "frontier" and helping to establish transpacific communities. Similarly, Filipino students often described themselves as unofficial diplomats responsible for proving to Americans that the people of the Philippines were ready for and deserving of their independence. Arriving with the goals of representing and serving their homelands, Chinese, Filipino, and Japanese students often engaged in conversations and activities with other foreign and American students on their campuses in order to build a "cultural bridge" between America and Asia. Such goals reinforce Ye and Azuma's interpretations of the students as transnational political and cultural agents. This focus on the ties of Asian students to the politics of their homelands, however, leaves little room for an in-depth discussion of how these transnational agents are also important for constructing the broad narrative of American social and civil rights movements during the twentieth century and their interaction with Asian Americans.

Rather than downplay the transnational influence of Asian students, *Race, Religion, and Civil Rights* connects the international ideas of the CSCA, FSCM, and JSCA members to their goals of ending prejudice and promoting equality in the United States. My purpose here is not to deny that Asian Christian students held political and cultural importance for their homelands but to intertwine their experiences with race and identity in the United States with those of Asian Americans. Doing so allows for further integration of Asian American and civil rights history. I posit that Protestant Asian students applied Protestant Christian principles to the problems with race and discrimination they encountered in America, bridging their identities as Asians, students, and transnational agents. Protestant Asian students present an opportunity for historians and scholars to examine the influence of their political and religious backgrounds on concepts of equality, rights, and citizenship in the United States. As the historian Derek Chang has compared the relations between black and white Protestants in the South with relations between Chinese missionaries and white Protestants in the West to examine concepts of citizenship and belonging, *Race, Religion, and Civil Rights* uses a similar method to analyze the students' panethnic connection to civil rights in the twentieth century.[13]

Christian Activism and Civil Rights

Before arriving in the United States, many Chinese, Filipino, and Japanese students were already acquainted with Protestant Christianity and its ideas. The students' religious knowledge was the product of a historical relationship between Western missionaries and Asians during the nineteenth and early twentieth centuries. Beginning in the mid-nineteenth century and corresponding with America's overseas expansion, American missionaries from Protestant churches, including Lutherans, Baptists, Methodists, and Presbyterians, traveled to Asia to convert its populations to an "American" type of Protestant Christianity. Guided by the concept of liberal Protestantism and its focus on using Christianity to promote modernization and ethics in an industrializing society, the YMCA and YWCA were also active organizations in Asia. As a result, before they came to the United States, Chinese, Filipino, and Japanese students already participated in fellowship missions and identified as Presbyterians, Methodists, Baptists, and so forth, or embraced the nondenominational status of the YMCA. As many scholars of religious development in Asia have noted, Protestant Christianity offered a medium for political and cultural leaders in China, Japan, and the Philippines to create movements for modernity and revitalization. Both white and Asian leaders preached the Social Gospel, using Christianity to cure the ills of industrializing and urbanizing nations and communities. These leaders attracted acolytes by cleaning up the impoverished, underdeveloped areas of cities like Tokyo, Yokohama, and Manila and promoted modern or Western practices of education and hygiene. Through such programs, organizations such as the YMCA and other Protestant groups appealed to many Asian students and their passion for social reform. As authors Albert Park and David Yoo argue, Asian students were influenced by "the ways in which followers of Protestant Christianity pursued political, economic, and social reforms and the establishment of a heaven on earth as means for advancing the principles and objectives of their religion."[14]

But an atmosphere of racism and prejudice in America challenged the faith in Christian social progress among those students who crossed the Pacific. During the early to mid-twentieth century, anti-Asian sentiments created a hostile atmosphere for the students when they arrived on the West Coast. Many white Americans and elected officials channeled their anger at the labor competition from Chinese arriving for railroad and

mining work during the mid-nineteenth century into legal action, resulting in the Chinese Exclusion Act of 1882 (renewed indefinitely in 1902).
While the flow of Chinese to America was reduced because of exclusion,
more Japanese immigrants arrived on the West Coast during the early
1900s. These settlers engaged in truck farming and other forms of agriculture in the central and southern regions of California, but they also
opened businesses in cities like Tacoma and Seattle, prompting more backlash from anti-Asian activists. Later during the 1920s, after the Immigration Act of 1924 excluded virtually all Asian immigrants, white residents
were shocked at the perceived voracious sexual appetites of male Filipino
laborers (who were still allowed to enter the United States under their
status as colonial nationals) for white women. Although, as the historian
Charlotte Brooks explains, the rampant anti-Asian sentiments of the late
nineteenth and early twentieth centuries quieted following the exclusion
acts, the West Coast was still a largely segregated and generally unwelcom-
ing region for both Asian immigrants and Asian Americans, a "Mississippi
with palm trees."[15] A general suspicion of the traditions, customs, and overall unassimilable "Oriental-otherness" of Asians who, by definition, could
never become citizens (stipulated in the Naturalization Act of 1790 and
reaffirmed in the 1922 Supreme Court decision *Ozawa v. United States*)
preserved anti-Asian reactions and ideas.[16] This West Coast brand of anti-
Asian nativism manifested itself in a variety of ways, including social prejudice, segregation, land-ownership restrictions, anti-miscegenation laws,
and violence.

Christianity and American Racism

The relationship of the Asian student-migrants to West Coast prejudice
was unique compared with other Asian communities. While many Asian
students were spared from the more violent outbursts by staying close to
their college campuses, they still experienced less-than-welcoming receptions from their white American classmates and administrators. When students did venture off campus, which occurred frequently for students who
worked or lived outside the confines of their colleges or universities, they
came face-to-face with virulent anti-Asian hatred. From racial slurs to discrimination and segregation in housing, employment, and services, Asian
students (despite their elite backgrounds or education) were not immune

from the prejudices that others faced in the United States. The reality that so many Americans discriminated against Asians and Asian Americans was antithetical to many students' Christian belief that all are created equal in God's image. This hypocrisy found in the supposedly Christian United States (as well as in Asia and other areas where colonizers used Christianity to support imperial and often violent projects) would shape the students' response to such incidents.

Christianity served as both a coping mechanism and a motivator for many Asian students who experienced discrimination in West Coast communities, not just as foreigners, but also as "Orientals" or Asians. Although they were technically visitors to the United States with no clear path to citizenship or American rights, these students argued in their bulletins, meetings, and larger conferences that no nation or group of rulers had the power to limit basic human rights that extended to all. There existed inalienable rights that God guaranteed to citizens of a Christian universe. This "Christian citizenship," or political identity grounded in religion, rested on respect, friendship, and peaceful relations regardless of race or immigration status. In turn, the members and leaders of the Christian student associations connected the struggle for racial equality in the United States to a global struggle against oppression caused by unchristian "isms" such as imperialism, nationalism, and racism. The students' solution to these problems was to end prejudice (the heart of racism and discrimination in the United States) by increasing interracial and interethnic exchange and building solidarity among Americans in order to bring racial justice to the world. Once Asian students came to the United States and recognized the deep hypocrisies in American religious ideas when it came to racial intolerance, Christianity became a powerful way for the students to hold a mirror to American Christians and challenge them to see their flawed interpretation of the will and words of the Lord.

Christianity serves as a lens for examining the ways in which Asian students interacted with one another as well as with other minorities both on and off campus. The YMCA, the YMCA-sponsored Student Volunteer Movement, and the Committee on Friendly Relations among Foreign Students (a branch of the Y) were large, financially strong organizations that provided administrative support to Asian students in forming their own groups. Prior to World War II, the CSCA, FSCM, and JSCA were among the largest, most diverse, and most active ethnic organizations on campuses along the West Coast, attracting large numbers of students to meetings, discussion groups, conferences, and other social and cultural events. Although other secular Asian student groups and fraternities existed on Pacific Coast campuses as well in other parts of the United States, Christian students drew on the resources of parent organizations such as the Y in order to build large interracial and panethnic networks during the interwar years and into the 1940s. The Christian student groups provide a means to uncover the complex and in-depth relationships that foreign Asian students had with one another as well as the influence they had on Asian American students through discussions of race and citizenship. The students' use of Christianity to build coalitions and fight for racial justice proves that a variety of intricately connected ideas and motives contributed to civil rights movements before the era of racial liberalism (or growing interracial activism for legal justice) in the 1940s.[17]

My study of the intersection of Asian students, Christian organization/activism, and racial politics both is influenced by and contributes to a growing body of scholarly work on religion in Asian America. The history of Chinese, Filipino, and Japanese students and their Christian associations reflects, as Park and Yoo describe, the importance of "religion as a medium for social relationships" as well as the connections between "sacred and social activism."[18] Asian Americans and Asian immigrants used religious practices and ideas to bridge class, political, and social chasms within their own ethnic communities as well as to promote and protect transpacific relations. Scholars like Yoo and Timothy Tseng have examined the influence of Protestant Christianity on the experiences and identities of Korean and Chinese students (respectively) in the United States to argue for Christianity's central place in Asian American studies. While Asian Christians were not representative of all members of their ethnic communities in the United States, their experiences are important windows into Asian American identity and activism. Asian Christian students crossed ethnic lines and contributed to the development of racial consciousness among Chinese, Filipino, and Japanese students, with the assistance of large West Coast networks. Christianity provided Asian students who came to the United States with the opportunity for exchange and panethnic discussions among themselves and Asian American students, emphasizing "religion's role in cultivating and sustaining social relationships and communities."[19] Themes of religion, identity, and transnationalism provide the framework for this book, as I expand the idea of

Christianity as an integral component of Asian American and civil rights history by placing it within a panethnic context.

For the Asian students who formed, led, and joined campus Christian associations, Christianity also conferred a "safe" political identity. Not only did shared religious ideas allow students to develop panethnic and interracial social bonds, but Chinese, Filipino, and Japanese students also used Christianity to stake a claim for recognition and basic rights. While the more radical characteristics of the left-leaning socialist or communist organizations may have deterred students from joining, Christianity was a way to voice their discontent with the American racial and political structure in a relatively unthreatening manner. At the same time, for many of the wealthier Filipinos who crossed the Pacific to enter the metropole, Christianity represented a "politics of respectability," helping them prove to American students that they represented a civilized, intelligent, and capable group of colonial people deserving of independence.[20] In general, Protestant Christianity "served as a logic and grammar for students" to make demands for equality when other options such as public protests were not as favorable or desirable.[21]

An important argument that runs throughout this book is that the Asian students and their organizations challenge the dominance of radical forms of interracial and multiethnic activism in the historiography of civil rights. A Christian-centered form of activism may not have been as far-reaching or theoretically inclusive as larger, secular organizations such as labor unions or the Communist Party, groups included in many discussions of organizing and social and political movements. Josephine Fowler's work on Japanese and Chinese communist activists during the interwar years provides examples of immigrants (including students) who applied theories of economic and class relations to problems they encountered with labor relations and racial discrimination in the United States.[22] However, it is necessary to understand the ways in which Protestant Christianity created a space for activism among those who were not attracted to more radical elements. This brand of political activism was often quite different from other forms of organizing, such as mass protests or marches, but Asian students along the West Coast were just as concerned with racial justice and equal rights in the years before and after World War II as others. Christianity served as both a national and a transnational force that made what Jacquelyn Dowd Hall refers to as the "long civil rights movement" interracial, multicultural, and interethnic.[23]

Despite their success in organizing conferences and leading groups, the students' early form of panethnic activism was often restricted to the students themselves and restrained their connections with activists off campus. Apart from FSCM members who were also active members in labor organizing as a result of their need to work, most of the students were insulated from the experiences of other Asian immigrants and Asian Americans in cities like Berkeley, San Francisco, Los Angeles, and Seattle. When students did venture off campus for errands or adventure, racism was palpable. The difference for the students, however, is that they could return to their dorms at the end of the day while other Asians remained in the center of discrimination and often violence. The association members addressed problems that directly affected their lives as students and Christians on campus, such as discriminatory Greek organizations, segregated YMCA policies, and employment difficulties after graduation, thus limiting their experiences with other forms of prejudice they did not witness on a daily basis. As self-identified Christians, these students were concerned with global incidents of prejudice, but their definition of "rights" and "liberties" were often wrapped in abstract terms of Christian citizenship and brotherhood. It was not until the challenges in race relations during the Second World War and the later postwar movements for civil rights that former students fully applied their concepts of Christian equality to segregation in housing, business, and employment.

I am not downplaying the efforts of these students in building civil rights and racial justice activism but, rather, suggesting that this early form of activism had its limits. As *Race, Religion, and Civil Rights* argues, the growing movement that the students contributed to, both during and after World War II, was different from the later forms of what Yen Le Espiritu identified as panethnic and radical activism among Asian Americans during the late 1960s.[24] My focus on the role of Asian students in promoting racial equality from the interwar years through the postwar period connects the earliest forms of Asian and Asian American activism in the United States to the later waves of student protest, offering an explanation for how Asian leadership and involvement in West Coast civil rights activities evolved through the decades. This reflects, as Gary Okihiro argues, the importance in challenging our understanding of a black/white framework for civil rights after World War II. I argue, however, that this process began well before the radicalizing and changing movements of the 1960s.[25]

Organization

In order to trace how and why Chinese, Filipino, and Japanese students evolved into racial rights advocates, *Race, Religion, and Civil Rights* moves chronologically through events and periods of the twentieth century (some of them more well known than others). The first chapter examines how foreign-born Chinese, Filipino, and Japanese students became involved in issues of racism and discrimination along the West Coast during the 1920s by challenging their parent organizations (the YMCA and the Committee on Friendly Relations among Foreign Students) to recognize the problems of Asian discrimination. Although the YMCA actively established student units in the South for African Americans during the early to mid-twentieth century, it was less interested in the racism that Asian students encountered. YMCA administrators insisted that the prejudice directed toward students was not racism so much as a generalized suspicion of foreigners, a problem that the students could easily overcome by "building a cultural bridge" with Americans, offering a social and cultural solution to the issue. The YMCA's lack of concern for racial prejudice and discrimination against Asians emphasized the problematic definition of racism as restricted to blacks and whites, but it also laid the foundation for more interaction between and among Christian Chinese, Filipino, and Japanese student organizations.[26]

Chapter 2 builds on the changing racial consciousness of the students by examining how foreign-born Chinese, Filipino, and Japanese students used the racism faced by the second generation of Asian Americans to build pan-ethnic connections. By reaching out to second-generation Asian Americans, the CSCA, FSCM, and JSCA were able to create an open dialogue on the racism and discrimination that minority groups experienced along the West Coast. In seeking to expand beyond the foreign-student population, Christianity served more as a unifying concept for association members than as a specific discussion point during the late 1920s and early 1930s. As the second-generation population grew on West Coast campuses, more American-born students joined the groups and offered their own solutions for dealing with broad problems that affected all Asians. However, as this chapter argues, the students' form of Christian activism often addressed issues that primarily affected fellow students, making their campus and larger conference meetings sites of promising, yet often narrow, goals that did not directly meet the needs of others outside of their universities or student networks.

Although Chinese, Filipino, and Japanese students were able to establish panethnic networks using the Christian associations, class and international tensions during the interwar years also created obstacles to constructing a Christian social movement in America. My third chapter follows Filipino students from campus to the Alaskan canneries and labor unions during the 1920s and 1930s. Because class tensions between FSCM members from more elite families and those who were self-supporting made the FSCM largely unresponsive to the needs of working-class members, student-workers turned to unionization to organize for rights. Many Filipino students worked during the summer break to pay their tuition in the fall, exposing them to racism, discrimination, and the push for labor and civil rights off campus. I argue that FSCM members who held powerful roles in the Cannery Workers' and Farm Laborers' Union pushed the organization in the direction of civil rights. Although many students came to the United States with the hope of returning home with an American education, this chapter examines the transition from visitor to immigrant, exposing them to more racial conflict when they moved away from school.

Chapter 4 analyzes the interactions among Chinese, Filipino, and Japanese students during the development of military and political unrest in the Pacific during the 1930s. Here I examine how Asian students in America addressed the Second Sino-Japanese War (the military and political battle between China and Japan over Manchuria) of 1937 and the beginnings of World War II. Although China and Japan were at war with each other, CSCA and JSCA members in the United States attempted (with and without success) to overlook these ethnic tensions and focus on what they perceived as the underlying causes of worldwide conflicts: aggressive nationalism and imperialism. FSCM members also participated in conversations regarding the dangers of imperialism and, with other Asian students, called attention to the connections between imperialism and racial discrimination on a global scale. CSCA, FSCM, and JSCA members globalized the American struggle for racial justice by connecting it to worldwide political and social oppression while struggling to redefine their own relationships to their homelands and their Christian principles.

Following the theme of war and disruption, chapter 5 examines the transformation of the groups during World War II a result of racial changes, migrations, and the forced removal of Japanese and Japanese Americans from the West Coast under President Franklin Roosevelt's 1942 Executive Order 9066. Social scientists and journalists described the West

Coast as a "racial frontier" during the war, a region of the United States that rapidly changed in racial and ethnic composition as a result of migrations to cities such as Seattle, Oakland, and Los Angeles for wartime work. As a result, during and after the war, Japanese, Chinese, Filipinos, Mexicans, African Americans, and whites were confronted with new neighbors, new race relations, and the opportunities and challenges that accompanied these changes in demographics. The student associations were part of this racial frontier or, as author Randi Walker describes the atmosphere on the West Coast, a transitioning "racial conscience."[27] Executive Order 9066, ethnic and racial tensions, and the difficulties in maintaining group operations during the war forced the students to apply their Christian principles to problems off campus and beyond their Christian networks. As a result, students become more active in broader Asian American rights, immigrant rights, and civil rights movements. The war challenged students to think about what interracial and panethnic Christian fellowship meant beyond conferences, discussions, and publications. This chapter argues that the students applied their theories of interracial brotherhood, a precursor to the racial liberalism of the1940s, to the growing civil rights movement.

Like many others in the United States, the war left former students and association members scattered along the West Coast and across the country. In my final chapter, I examine the activism of former students who joined post–World War II community civil rights groups and helped shape the interracial and interethnic battle for racial justice along the West Coast. While the CSCA continued to operate through the 1950s, both the JSCA and FSCM disbanded during the war, ending the era of the panethnic Christian student associations. However, former CSCA, FSCM, and JSCA members went on to use the interracial and religious tactics they embraced as students to add a social and cultural angle to the push for legal rights. This chapter also follows the former students after they graduated or withdrew from college by focusing on the continued activism of CSCA member Chingwah Lee, JSCA member Toru Matsumoto, and FSCM member Victorio Velasco (and others) in the emergent civil rights movement. However, the post–World War II period presented challenges to maintaining the panethnic coalitions the students built and affirming the place of education and outreach in a legalizing push for racial equality. Ultimately, Lee, Matsumoto, and Velasco would fall out touch with a more radicalizing movement by the late 1960s, but their work in creating interracial and interethnic activism continued to shape Christian approaches to civil rights after World War II.

As with any historical study, this book is not a comprehensive analysis of all Christian Asian students in the United States. There are other student groups (including Indians and Koreans) who are not featured in this work, not because of a lack of importance to the larger story of Asian activism on and off campus, but because of their unique relationships to colonial and imperial protest while in the United States.[28] Also, one will not find in-depth discussions of female students and their experiences in America on these pages because the majority of the members of the three associations discussed, as well as the authors of many of the articles in the student bulletins, were male. The male-dominated form of activism that characterized the student associations also reflected similar patterns in other civil rights and justice groups, leaving space for more exploration of the limits of the Christian associations' strategies and tactics. Rather than tell a complete history of Asian Christian students in America, I hope that this book will lead to useful discussions and further analysis of this important topic among historians, Asian American scholars, and others interested in the intersections of religion, racial identities, and rights.

By delving into the long-overlooked social and political activism of foreign- and American-born Asian students and the role of campus Christian organizations in creating a platform for action, *Race, Religion, and Civil Rights* offers a new approach to the study of Asian American, social, and racial history in the United States. Although these student activists did not achieve their goal of "creating a world free from racial prejudice," their devotion to their cause of promoting Christian fellowship and equality had a lasting impact on the trajectory of the broader civil rights movement in America.

1

"Western People Are Not All Angels"

•••••••••••••••••••••

Encountering Racism
on the West Coast

Upon arriving on the West Coast, Asian students often found themselves
on the receiving end of racism, even from the YMCA—the same organization that courted foreign students and preached the gospel of love and
acceptance. As the largest groups of foreign students in California, Oregon, and Washington, the Chinese, Filipino, and Japanese students joined
and formed Christian associations that were sponsored by the YMCA, the
World Student Christian Federation (WSCF), and the Committee on
Friendly Relations among Foreign Students (CFR), all Christian groups
that expanded during the ecumenical movement of the early twentieth century. Although the CSCA, FSCM, and JSCA received logistical and ideological support from these larger umbrella organizations, by the late 1920s,
the student associations began to differ from their parent groups in regard
to the appropriate response to anti-Asian racism and discrimination.

   Asian students became increasingly frustrated with the unchristian
behavior they encountered among Americans. The YMCA, with its

policies of segregated branches, came under fire from the student Christian groups, which cited its hypocrisy in claiming to promote interracial and multicultural fellowship while at the same time preventing these goals by denying admittance to white branches in cities like San Francisco and Seattle. Rather than fully addressing the problem of racism against Asians, however, the YMCA and the CFR maintained that cultural misunderstanding and Americans' parochial ignorance of foreigners were the roots of any interracial or interethnic problems. As a solution, YMCA and CFR leaders suggested that Asian students ease these misunderstandings by establishing more congenial relationships with Americans, a cosmopolitan idea that was popular among many social and cultural groups at the time. While the students initially embraced this approach, they soon realized that racism ran deep and that their problems could not be solved with an abstract bridge made of cultural good intentions.

Toward the end of the 1920s, members of the CSCA, FSCM, and JSCA argued that they had an important role to play in challenging Americans to reject the unchristian ideas of racism and prejudice. While the CFR attempted to convince foreign Asian students to bear the brunt of racial discrimination while in the United States, the students held different ideas for how they should use their time in America. The experiences of Chinese, Filipino, and Japanese students with racism shattered their preconceived view of the United States as a Christian nation of equality and forced them to come to terms with their status as racial minorities. Regardless of their class, education, or Christian and ethnic identities, their label as "Oriental" or "other" in America created despair and confusion but also laid the foundation for a growing socially and politically conscious network of Asian Christian students. As a result, throughout the 1920s, these students gradually evolved from cosmopolitan cultural advocates to crusaders for acceptance, a transformation grounded in growing Christian coalitions.

Cosmopolitanism and Growing Student Communities

During the early 1900s, Asian students did not have large-scale Christian networks to join. Although increasing numbers of Chinese, Filipino, and Japanese students traveled to the United States in the early twentieth century, many of these students did not create their own Christian organizations until after the First World War. With the exception of the CSCA

Students

(founded in 1909 by East Coast–based Chinese students), Chinese, Japanese, and Filipino students either formed small, close-knit, and ethnically based campus clubs, visited the campus branches of the YMCA or YWCA, or became members of the schools' cosmopolitan clubs, groups designed to promote cross-cultural interaction.

The students' early attempts at establishing campus associations came from a desire to have a space in which to socialize with fellow Chinese, Filipino, or Japanese. Along with a sense of marginalization from their American classmates, foreign-born Asian students were also largely disconnected from the immigrant and/or Asian American communities off-campus. Not only did language and dialect barriers exist (particularly in the case of Mandarin- or Shanghainese-speaking Chinese students, who often were not fluent in Cantonese and other dialects spoken by Chinese migrants), but socioeconomic divisions between the more educated and often wealthier students and their less-affluent fellow countrymen limited intermingling. In general, the experiences of foreign-born students often varied from those of working- or lower-class immigrants.[1]

Asian students created or joined small groups on campus to navigate the social and academic terrain of American colleges and universities. In 1902, Chinese students at Columbia University formed the Chinese Student Alliance, while Harvard University was home to the first Chinese Greek society, the Flip Flap Fraternity (founded in 1908). Students at West Coast colleges and universities such as Stanford and the California State Normal School (later San Jose State College) formed small Filipino and Japanese clubs that offered members the opportunity to bond over discussions of news and events from their homelands. Other groups also attempted to establish outreach opportunities to fellow American classmates, hoping to use gatherings to expand their social circle beyond other Chinese, Filipino, or Japanese students. In essence, early student clubs and groups were primarily social survival strategies for foreign-born students.[2]

The cosmopolitan clubs presented another option for becoming acquainted with college life and fellow classmates but also signified an era of positive, if at times uneasy, American reactions to foreign students. "Cosmopolitanism" is a complex term, but I use it here in a specific way. Different strands of cosmopolitanism exist, including racial, national, class, and cultural cosmopolitanism, but at the core of this ideology is a belief that there is a connection among all humans that transcends national borders.[3] Although there are multiple and competing definitions and ideas of cosmopolitanism, I am referring to a movement in America during the early twentieth century that focused on identifying and appreciating other cultures and peoples, while using multicultural knowledge for the benefit of the United States. In this historical context, many Americans embraced cosmopolitanism as the belief that there was much to learn from foreign peoples, particularly from the educated and elite, and that cultural exchange was at the base of all friendly international relationships. While many reformers from the Progressive Movement emphasized American-ization of immigrants in the United States, Americans who identified with cosmopolitanism also saw benefits in learning from newcomers. The "immigrant gift movement" of the early twentieth century solidified the argument that foreigners had many cultural "gifts" to offer to Americans, an idea that helps to explain why cosmopolitan clubs became popular during the years leading up to and immediately after World War I.[4]

As "civilized" and educated migrants, foreign students played an important role in the rise of cosmopolitan clubs in the United States. The Institution of International Education (a New York–based organization that promoted student exchange and helped to establish special student visas following the 1921 Emergency Quota Act) found value in promoting friendly relations between foreign- and native-born students in order to create a worldlier American public. At the height of the cosmopolitan movement during the years immediately after World War I, universities were the key places to establish cultural connections. Institutions of higher learning provided an ideal environment for interaction and exchange: not only were there foreign students from a variety of countries on campus, but there was also an atmosphere of enlightenment that helped to create scholastic and cross-cultural relationships. White, African American, and foreign students formed cosmopolitan clubs across the United States, guided by the principle of the Association of Cosmopolitan Clubs that "above all nations is human-ity." Cosmopolitan clubs stressed "international goodwill by bringing into fellowship selected representatives of each nationality within a given university."[5] The emphasis on "selected representatives" in the goals of the Asso-ciation of Cosmopolitan Clubs is telling. The cosmopolitan clubs embraced particular groups of immigrants, specifically those who were interested in the more refined pursuits rather than those of working-class immigrants.

Many West Coast boosters, community organizers, and officials also attempted to fashion their communities as sophisticated, cosmopolitan enclaves. Cities in California and Washington became economic, cultural, and political "nodes" in a growing transpacific world during the early twentieth century.[6] San Francisco, for example, developed a reputation (even if reality proved otherwise) by the late 1800s as being a multicultural and open-minded urban area as a result of increased migration from Asia, Europe, and South America. The cities and the nation as a whole benefited from increased economic and trade activity between the United States and Asian countries, and many Asian immigrants and Asian Americans identified as transnational actors in these growing webs of exchange. In Seattle, Japanese immigrants and Nisei (second-generation Japanese Americans) used the cosmopolitan trend to create a political identity that rested on their power and agency in promoting an ideal image of Japan and their homes in the International District. In other West Coast cities, church groups, leisure clubs, and other social circles encouraged East-West interactions that provided opportunities for political and cultural bridge-building activities. Many immigrant leaders also identified the younger generation as particularly important for connecting cultures and building a "bridge of understanding" between Asia and America. Although cosmopolitanism did not lead to direct political influence and did not completely eradicate anti-Asian sentiments, it did create a form of minority agency that Japanese, Chinese, Filipino, and other Asian leaders and groups used to navigate the racial and ethnic landscape of the United States.[7]

Consequentially, Asian foreign students were active members of cosmopolitan clubs at San Jose State College, Stanford University, and the University of Washington, among others. If, as the historian Shelley Sang-Hee Lee explains, West Coast cities strived to become "international communities writ small," cosmopolitanism also influenced socialization among and between foreign students and their American classmates.[8] At the University of Arizona, Filipino students formed a cosmopolitan club in 1922 with the intention of "disseminat[ing] accurate information about the foreign countries represented," demonstrating that cross-ethnic interaction held the potential to create favorable reputations for the students' homelands.[9] The campus cosmopolitan trend offered educational activities that focused on cultural exchange and were primarily social in nature, and promoted a deeper understanding of transpacific engagement. While some clubs, such as the Stanford Crossroads group and Cosmos Club, were more focused on foreign affairs and invited scholars to lead discussions on foreign policy and diplomatic issues, most cosmopolitan activities included fairs, festivals, and other opportunities for fun and cultural enlightenment.[10]

The YMCA also joined foreign students in supporting the cosmopolitan spirit in America, with leaders of the organization identifying spaces for missionary efforts and fellowship on campus. Fearing that cosmopolitanism lacked a spiritual essence and that a majority of the students who joined the cosmopolitan clubs were not exposed to Christian ideas and principles, the YMCA encouraged foreign students to form their own Christian campus groups. In 1911, the YMCA founded the Committee on Friendly Relations among Foreign Students (CFR) to aid foreign students entering the United States. The CFR, headed by YMCA leader Charles Hurrey, strived to ensure that foreign students would benefit from a Christian atmosphere while on campus. Headquartered in New York City, the CFR worked with the Rockefeller Foundation to establish and maintain International Houses (places where foreign students could find lodging) across the United States, provide counseling to foreign students before they left their homelands, greet students at the docks when they arrived, and "acquaint students with industrial and institutional life in American cities."[11] Above all else, the aims of the committee were "to promote sympathetic and helpful relations between Americans and foreign students . . . to influence the character, spirit, and attitude of these future leaders . . . and to bring the educated young men and women of these different lands under the influence of Western Christian nations."[12] Despite its cosmopolitan sheen, the CFR was still a Christian and missionary-oriented organization devoted to evangelization as much as international cooperation and friendship.

Among the CFR's most important functions was providing administrative assistance to student-run Christian associations. The ideas of self-sufficiency and leadership stemmed from the YMCA's larger belief in encouraging racial and ethnic communities (such as Chinatown in San Francisco and Little Tokyo in Los Angeles) to establish their own branches. The YMCA utilized a similar strategy among African American branches of the organization in the South as well as in northern cities, specifically encouraging black "elites" from the educated and middle class of these areas to assume the roles of officials and leaders. While the YMCA had a hands-off policy when it came to supplying financial aid to African American branches, the CFR contributed modest funds to the student Christian associations for conference travel, events, and bulletins. Following the lead of the YMCA's belief that indigenous leadership was best in the overseas associations, the CFR advocated for student-led, ethnically based Christian campus groups to help foreign students adapt to American life.[13]

Although Chinese and Japanese branches of the YMCA already existed along the West Coast by the early twentieth century, the CFR argued that campus Christian associations were necessary for addressing the specific social and cultural needs of students.[14] Following World War I, the YMCA turned its efforts from providing support for the war effort back to spreading the influence of the organization domestically and abroad. To accomplish this goal, Hurrey recruited foreign students to work actively with the CFR in establishing branches of Christian groups on campus and across the country. Though the Chinese Students' Christian Association (CSCA—founded in 1909 with assistance from the YMCA) already existed, the CFR gained oversight control of the organization in the early 1920s and provided approximately $2,000 a year to the CSCA for the publication of its new bulletin and to hold conferences and other meetings or events the association desired to sponsor. At larger Christian conferences—such as the annual winter convention at Asilomar, California and the summer conferences at Silver Bay, Oregon; Lake Mohonk, New York; and Lake Geneva, Wisconsin—Hurrey and other CFR representatives spoke to groups of foreign students who might be interested in forming their own associations. Hurrey highlighted the importance of Christian fellowship, national brotherhood, and the promotion of cross-cultural exchange with Americans as reasons why student Christian associations were excellent opportunities for the foreign-born on campus.

Hurrey's descriptions of student-run Christian associations appealed to Filipino and Japanese students in attendance at a YMCA student convention in Indianapolis in 1923. During the meeting, groups of Japanese and Filipino students decided to form their own Christian groups, similar to the CSCA, resulting in the Filipino Students' Christian Movement and the Japanese Students' Christian Association (both formed in the same year and with the assistance of Hurrey). By the end of the 1920s, each nationwide association contained anywhere from 950 to approximately 2,500 official dues-paying members, with many other students across the country subscribing to the organizations' newspapers (the *Chinese Christian Student*, the *Japanese Student Bulletin*, and the *Filipino Student Bulletin*).[15]

In order to establish a wide base of support, the CSCA, JSCA, and FSCM maintained an "open membership" policy (meaning anyone could become a member of the associations) with various levels of participation. The associations all adopted the "active" (or "official") and "associate" member system: Christian Chinese, Filipino, and Japanese (foreign- or

American-born, though most early members were foreign-born) students were active members, while non-Christian or non-Asian students were accepted as associate members. The main distinction between the rights and privileges of the various types of membership was that only active members could run for office. Both active and associate members paid dues, while those who were not official members could still participate in functions sponsored by the groups and subscribe to their publications (although the FSCM eventually did away with dues by 1930 and relied on subscriptions to the *Filipino Student Bulletin* for revenue). Overall, the CFR approved of the membership requirements of the student associations as a way to ensure that the organizations appealed primarily to Christian foreign students, while remaining open and welcoming to non-Christians, Asian American students, and students from a variety of racial and ethnic backgrounds. Although males from more elite or wealthier families in China, Japan, and the Philippines dominated the student associations in their earliest days, the homogeneous make-up of the groups would later give way to greater numbers of female and American-born members as the influence of the organizations grew during the late 1920s and 1930s.[16]

The CSCA, JSCA, and FSCM were unique in scope and membership when compared with other Asian Christian associations and communities during the early twentieth century. Whereas Chinese and Japanese branches of the YMCA, along with churches, congregations, and temples, primarily served the needs of the local ethnic populations, the student associations were nationwide and joined foreign-born and, later, American-born Asian students together in an "imagined community" that bridged ethnic and nationalist identities.[17] Organizationally, the associations consisted of different "departments" in regions across the United States, with the Western departments (for West Coast schools) responsible for the largest number of members. Departments oversaw various functions of their assigned campuses and requested funds from the executive administration (headquartered in New York City at the CFR) for conferences and other activities. The aims and umbrella-like structure of the CSCA, JSCA, and FSCM created opportunities for members and those who subscribed to newspapers to connect with other Asian students. Unlike many church groups or organizations in ethnic communities, the student Christian associations were spaces for interethnic exchange, either through meetings or via student bulletins and publications. Although the goals and mission of the Christian student associations were somewhat vague and more cosmopolitan-oriented early on, their leaders and members paved the way for broader communication and discussion of Christian concerns and issues.

To facilitate interaction among and between association members, Asian Christian students often held meetings during larger YMCA conferences or sponsored their own conventions to strike up conversations about everything from their experiences in America to Christian theology to plans for the next social gathering. One of the most prominent topics students discussed at these larger gatherings was the problem of prejudice and lack of cultural understanding in America and in a global context. JSCA, CSCA, and FSCM members exchanged ideas on how to best conquer the world's ills while residing in the United States through creating interethnic networks. After attending the annual YWCA- and YMCA-sponsored student conference in Asilomar, California, in 1924, a CSCA member from Pomona College reported that the ideas she discussed with other CSCA students as well as those from the JSCA and FSCM were exhilarating and could give the student organizations a real Christian purpose in the world. She suggested that "a conference of this kind can accomplish much more than the League of Nations in establishing world peace," but she also acknowledged that there were "a good many . . . students who are dissatisfied with the way the Americans treat them," indicating that there were barriers to peace and fellowship that existed in the rocky relationships between Chinese and Americans. She urged her fellow students to distinguish between "the real Christians and the nominal Christians" in America and "go between them" to build better relations and erase prejudice. Although this CSCA member did not report any concrete solutions on how to use Christianity to shape foreign-American relations, she described the students' attempt to establish a dialogue that would assist them in growing socially and politically.[18]

Building the Cultural Bridge amid American Racism

Hurrey recommended that students take the first steps in initiating relationships with other foreign and American students in order to achieve their goal of creating Christian fellowship. "These students are ambassadors of friendship," Hurrey began in a 1923 article, "and they enable us to know their people and national aspirations, while, in turn, they reveal and interpret American life and ideals to thousands of influential friends in their homelands." He emphasized that the CFR "recognize[s] the need of friendly mediators between the foreign students and the people and institutions of America" and that "it is our desire that the student shall get what he came for and that in returning, he shall entertain feelings of affection for America."[19] While the students were formally in America to receive an education, they were also there to promote cultural understanding and create international friendships based on goodwill as Christians.

Members of the JSCA, CSCA, and FSCM described their task of creating lasting friendships as constructing a "cultural bridge" between themselves and their American classmates. They identified as the links between the "Orient and the Occident" and believed that educating Americans on Asia's cultural traditions went a long way in promoting transpacific understanding. As a result, many of the activities the students planned relied heavily on social events with a more cosmopolitan flair. An article from the University of Washington's student newspaper *The Portal* described an "Education Week" on campus that was jointly sponsored by the JSCA, FSCM, and the YWCA and offered an international tea for foreign and American female students. The student groups hosted the tea in rooms adorned with decorations from China, Japan, and the Philippines and "girls from all of these countries in their native dress to explain things . . . all meant to enlighten us concerning the ways of the rest of the world . . . and break down the barriers of race and prejudice."[20] Such activities presented opportunities for the students to mingle and meet their "unofficial ambassador" counterparts from other nations as well as American students. Members of the FSCM, JSCA, and CSCA all subscribed to and read one another's student bulletins and newspapers and learned of the various activities of each association, fostering a dialogue on ways to construct the cultural bridge while in America and build a network of Christian Asian students.[21]

But members soon discovered how difficult the task of building cultural bridges could be during rising racial discrimination along the West Coast. During the years immediately after World War I, anti-Asian sentiment and specifically anti-Japanese attitudes were on the rise in California, Oregon, and Washington amid anti-alien land laws and the exclusionary Immigration Act of 1924, which barred all Asian immigrants except for Filipinos. However, white West Coast inhabitants did not limit their racial attacks to the Japanese. While Japanese were the largest migrant group in parts of California, Oregon, and Washington, Chinese also experienced racial discrimination in Los Angeles, San Francisco, Seattle, and other urban and rural areas. Likewise, Filipino migrants, as part of a relatively new immigrant group during the post–World War I years, elicited racist and often violent responses from Americans not only for being a largely transient, male migrant group competing for labor but also for engaging in romantic and sexual relationships with white women. Chinese, Filipino, and Japanese migrants encountered a range of racially discriminatory acts and prejudice that forced a shared "yellow" and perpetually foreign identity onto these groups, resulting in continued marginalization, xenophobic outbursts, and racial discrimination.[22]

Some foreign students who traveled to the United States witnessed harsh treatment even before their ships docked at San Francisco's Angel Island. While the Asian exclusion acts allowed students to enter the country for temporary educational purposes, this did not prevent fellow white passengers and crewmembers from hurling racial slurs at the privileged group of young travelers. To the students' shock, many of the ships' crews did not discriminate between them and the working-class Chinese and Japanese who came before. Scholarly status often did little to insulate them from their new and harsh experiences as "Orientals" or "Chinks." Like other exceptional groups, such as merchants, many Chinese students also described incidents of harassment by immigration officials who challenged their travel papers and forced them into detainment while certain paperwork issues were being addressed. Although the unfavorable treatment the students received was a far cry from the more violent harassment that the laborers who traveled before them endured, it was certainly not the reception that students envisioned.[23]

Once settled, the rising tide of anti-Asian sentiment along the West Coast presented itself to students in a variety of ways. Despite appearing as bastions of cosmopolitanism and liberal understanding, universities and colleges were not immune to racism and prejudice on the part of other students and administrators. Many campus groups and organizations openly discriminated against minorities, including Jewish, African American, and Asian students. Takanaga Hirai, a Japanese student at the University of Washington as well as a JSCA member, wanted to broaden his education in America with as many extracurricular activities as possible. Along with a few other academic clubs, Hirai was excited to join a debating team at the University of Washington, but, to his dismay, quickly learned that the

rich/poor

men's debating society he wished to join "refus[ed] to admit Orientals."[24] While Hirai's disappointing experience was not as vehement as the forms of racism that other Asian students faced beyond the grassy quads of the university, the message that Asians were not on equal ground with their white classmates was clear.

More experiences with racial discrimination and segregation awaited those Asian students who ventured off campus and into larger communities. If colleges and universities provided Asian students with a more muted form of prejudice, experiences in Los Angeles, San Francisco, and Seattle showed Asian students the full strength of hatred for Asians. "There was a good deal of anti-Japanese agitation in San Francisco," former student Dr. F. T. Nakaya explained in an interview in 1924, "and when I went out on the street, people would say things to me and call me 'Skibbie' and 'Jap' and 'Charlie,' sometimes it made me so mad."[25] Another Chinese student explained that he received "all kinds of unpleasant and unchristian treatments" while traveling from Los Angeles to San Francisco. "The headwaiter in the dining car," he recounted, "refused to wait on me . . . and fellow passengers called me by the name of 'Chink.'" Once he arrived in San Francisco, his search for overnight lodgings was incredibly difficult, being "informed by many landladies that they did not take in yellow people."[26]

Students were often shocked by their face-to-face encounters with racism in the United States. Along with the surprise of finding such virulent prejudice in a supposedly Christian nation, the fact that the students' class and upbringing did little to mitigate the prejudice they faced was unsettling. While Filipino students were often self-supporting and came from more rural and less affluent backgrounds, many students from China and Japan were typically from wealthier or elite families and had joined the YMCA in their homelands. The experience of these students with discrimination ran counter to the social privileges they carried with them to the United States, adding a class-based element to their anger and humiliation. Their status as students and "cultural ambassadors" clashed with the treatment they often received off campus and created a challenge to their respectable responsibilities as Christian and cosmopolitan missionaries. Asian students were disappointed that their education and missions did little to distinguish them from others in Asian American communities, revealing an ugly and Orientalist component to bridge building. The students' reactions echoed the complaints of Chinese merchants who were still subject to scrutiny from immigration officials following the Exclusion

rich/poor

Act, Japanese elites whose attempts to leverage their business success to distinguish themselves from the working class failed, and Filipinos whose American national political identity did not afford social equality in the United States. While students did not openly argue for better treatment because of their Christian or socioeconomic status, feelings of class injustice undergirded their surprise at their often unwelcome receptions in the United States.[27]

Regardless of class background or social upbringing, however, once they arrived in America, many Asian students shared the difficulties in finding room and board in West Coast communities as "yellows" or Orientals. They were no longer "Chinese," "Japanese," or "Filipino," but grouped together as part of a larger racial menace in the United States. Although Asian students who received scholarships or came from wealthier families were eligible to stay in dorms, other students could often not afford on-campus housing and were forced to look elsewhere. The students' search for a place to live led them off campus and into the larger communities where their efforts to secure lodging in the face of anti-Asian sentiment were often futile and humiliating. Chotoku Toyama, a JSCA member studying at the University of California at Los Angeles, described his frustrations in finding a room: "For our students, it is not easy to rent a room from an American family or to lodge at a boarding house. Most of the boarding houses and rooms for rent are refused [to] the Japanese students."[28] Similar to the African American experience in West Coast cities such as Seattle or San Francisco, boarding houses, apartment complexes, and even hotels often refused to rent a room to Asian migrants, creating cloistered and isolated ethnic enclaves that often lacked access to basic services and resources.[29] Since the late nineteenth century, the West Coast had had problems with housing discrimination, and the students were not immune to de facto or de jure segregation. The problem with finding housing was often a surprise to foreign students who relied on the CFR to guide them in the right direction. Despite the CFR's efforts in suggesting that Asian students obscure their nationalities through use of "Christian" names when looking for homes or rely on word-of-mouth to lead them to more welcoming renters, a written reply to an ad might result in an interview but end with a denial of the rented space once the landlord learned that his or her possible tenant was not white.

Segregation in housing along the West Coast represented an especially thorny problem for the YMCA at the national level. Before World War I, the YMCA created the Colored Works Division, a committee to administratively, if not financially, support the establishment of separate African American branches in the South; by the postwar era, however, the South and its segregated form of Christianity troubled YMCA leaders. By maintaining the practice of segregated Christianity in the South, the YMCA (like many other Christian organizations and associations at the time) never directly challenged or questioned the discrimination present in its own operations. Still viewing separate African American branches of the YMCA as a chance for racial uplift and self-sufficiency, the organization embraced the "separate, but equal" doctrine of the Jim Crow South and did not support integrated YMCA branches. Although segregated branches of the YMCA appeared to run counter to the organization's Christian claims, the National YMCA Council did not release any policy statements or resolutions calling for white branches to open their doors to black members. In response, the National Council referred to its figurehead status, which assisted various branches in organizing, but had no direct legislative authority or power over local arms of the association. In other words, so long as the African American branches of the association were equal, the National Council of the YMCA had no reason to intervene. The YMCA was not alone in this practice as Social Gospel activists of the postwar era did little to challenge the racist policies of their own Christian organizations. The YMCA followed suit by generally deferring to local branches and practicing a form of "benign neglect" concerning the day-to-day business of its representatives and branches in the South and across the United States.[30]

The YMCA policy of supporting segregated facilities shaped the operations of its branches on the West Coast. The existence of Chinese or Japanese branches of the YMCA in larger cities in California and Seattle replicated the separate but equal practices of the local branches in the South as well as northern cities. Campus YMCAs and YWCAs did not typically shun or discriminate against Asian students, but whites-only community YMCAs that offered lodging did not admit Asian guests and even refused entrance to swimming pools and other facilities. Although YMCAs that catered primarily to Japanese and Chinese communities did exist in West Coast cities (such as San Francisco) during the early twentieth century, in many cases, they were not the closest facilities to campus and were not always easily accessible for students. Imagine many students' shock when, after being guided by the CFR and the YMCA to come to America, they were denied a place to stay by a supposedly Christian organization! The YMCA's refusal of rooms to Asians prompted many students to become wary of the organization. "A Japanese cannot belong to the YMCA," Dr. Nakaya explained. "I tried to get a room there and was told they did not rent rooms to Japanese and I have never been back."[31] The YMCA's rules of segregation puzzled students who believed the Christian organization to be accepting and inviting to all. The YMCA was, after all, the association that worked closely with Christians of all backgrounds and social standings in Asia. As a result, the students were unaware of the firm refusal of white branches to welcome Asians.

An explosive example of the how the YMCA's policies of segregation and benign neglect pushed students too far occurred in Pullman, Washington, in 1928. Filipino student and FSCM member Felipe Guarin came face to face with Christian hypocrisy in America when he began his first semester at Washington State University in 1927 and needed a place to live. Having scrimped and saved for his tuition for the first year of his studies, Guarin confidently crossed the Pacific, ready for his new journey as a college student in America. As a Christian and a student with little money, Guarin quickly became friends with members of the FSCM and found a room to share with another student at the Washington State branch of the YMCA. Housed in a small cottage not far from campus, the university YMCA was a popular gathering spot for Filipino students, Chinese, and Japanese students.

Unfortunately, by the winter of 1928, the local townspeople of Pullman who generously supported the campus YMCA grew suspicious of the large number of foreign students at the cottage, fearing that "the Filipinos were monopolizing all the games and [social activities]." In other words, locals feared that the Washington State YMCA had become little more than a "hang-out for foreign students" and had abandoned its "Christian principles" by "forcing American students to socialize with unsavory foreign students against their will." In retaliation, the Community Chest of Pullman met with the Washington State Board of Regents and threatened to withdraw its funding from the campus YMCA and other university organizations if the foreign students were not kicked out of the cottage. The YMCA agreed to try to convince the students to take up residency at the campus International House, but Guarin refused to move.[32]

Despite a personal invitation from the International House staff, the students were "tremendously hurt to think of being treated in such an un-Christian like manner and would not use the International House under any circumstances." In fact, Guarin, the other FSCM members, and the remaining foreign students "went so far as to suggest that their treatment on campus be made an international example" to expose the prejudice they faced as Asian students on American campuses. Eventually, the YMCA and the townspeople of Pullman won the battle for the cottage: the Washington State YMCA evicted all foreign students and were therefore able to keep their Community Chest funding. Despite forcing the students out of their temporary homes, Washington State YMCA council chairman Walter Robinson vowed to maintain a "friendly attitude more than ever toward the foreign students and try to make them feel that it was not the YMCA that was responsible for their situation." The incident at Pullman was not an isolated occurrence but indicative of a larger pattern of discrimination against Asian students along the West Coast in the 1920s.[33]

The YMCA's response to this basic contradiction in the Christian values that missionaries promoted abroad did little to remedy either the housing crisis among Asian students or the racist practices within the organization itself. Ironically, earlier in 1924, University of Washington YMCA member C. L. Maxfield, reported in *The Intercollegian* (the YMCA's national student periodical) that the University of Washington YMCA had "solved a problem" when it came to housing. Maxfield admitted that Japanese and Asian students at the University of Washington did face discrimination when they attempted to find off-campus housing, but claimed that the YMCA had addressed the issue and proposed a solution. In order to help Asian students find temporary homes, the YMCA suggested "enlisting individual Christian families" of good report and with no racial prejudice to "guarantee homes" to Asian students. By searching for good Christian families in the greater Seattle area, the YMCA proposed to eliminate much of the guesswork and trial-and-error processes that Asian students engaged in when searching for homes. Although Maxfield lauded the YMCA for its attempts to assist Asian students, both his article and the proposed plan of the association overlooked one glaring point: how would the YMCA change its policies in its *own* facilities to end discrimination against Asian students and Asian immigrants/Asian Americans? For the YMCA, the issue was relatively easy to dismiss because, as many argued, the problem was in the larger community rather than its own racist structures and organization.[34]

The experiences of the students with racism in the YMCA and among other Americans produced a devastating effect on their views of American Christians and Christianity in general. Like Dr. Nakaya, who neither returned to any YMCA nor attended any Y-sponsored function after being denied a room, Asian students decried the hypocrisy and shallowness they discovered in the United States. Many Asian students held America up to the highest standards, believing that, as a Christian nation, the United States should contain the most ardent and passionate of Christians. Their experiences with racism and discrimination made many students, such as JSCA member and Stanford student Hideo Oyama, doubt that there were any true Christians in the United States at all. "I respected Americans as truly Christian," Oyama explained, ". . . but it was most difficult to understand why anti-Japanese movements exist in such a Christian country like America."[35]

Other students expressed their profound disillusionment with Christianity more generally as a result of their experiences in America. Some students cited the "negative effect of life in the U.S." on those who had "lost their Christian faith" and were discouraged by "sham Christianity."[36] A CSCA member echoed these thoughts when he outlined his growing suspicion of Christianity while attending school in America:

I have always been a Christian and a very zealous one too, but my Christian faith is now very much unsteady on account of the experiences that I have received in this institution. . . . The fraternities refused to take me in because I am Chinese. My scholastic standing entitled me to receive one of the five fellowships annually awarded to the five highest standing men in college, but the college authorities refused to give me my due reward because I was a "Chinese." . . . I now feel quite uncertain as to whether there is true strength in this so-called Christianity.[37]

Asian students became increasingly dissatisfied, not only in their interactions with Americans, but also with their experiences with American churches and Christianity. Students offered their own analyses of the problems with American Christianity, explaining that the "Christian teachers are misinterpreting the meaning of Jesus' teachings" and that "the only way the race problem will ever be solved is for people to get the real spirit of Christianity and to love and understand each other."[38] As leaders of a Social Gospel movement in America, the YMCA did not respond to the problems of racism and discrimination, proving that the organization's policies of "benign neglect" and reliance on local chapters failed to apply Christian principles to race relations. The students held different views from white Protestants in the National Council and other YMCA leaders on the responsibilities of the organization in promoting a welcoming environment for all races and minorities.

The YMCA's nonchalant attitude toward discrimination also shattered students' expectations that America was equal and progressive. Students were disappointed at what they identified as a lack of real democracy and equality in the United States. Similar to preconceived notions of America as the true Christian nation in the world, students also left their home countries with visions of American democratic ideas and an excitement to travel to the land of Washington and Lincoln. Other students came with visions of America as a "rich, large, and good country built on the spirit of George Washington," "the land of democracy, rich resources, honesty, diligence, and great opportunities," and emancipation and freedom.[39] Discrimination and prejudice, however, quickly altered those perceptions and brought Asian students face-to-face with anti-Asian reactions and Christian hypocrisy. An anonymous FSCM member explained to a CFR representative in 1925 that his reason for coming to America was "a puzzle" and that "like all my countrymen who first came here, my heart was full of admiration for the United States, and I seem[ed] to see the opportunities lurking everywhere for our nationals," but "as one stays here longer, the reverse is true."[40]

The alien land laws, Immigration Act of 1924, and naturalization policies that prohibited Asians from becoming citizens also led to students denouncing America as a land of contradictions. Students explained in interviews and publications that the land laws of California and other states did "not have a good effect upon the true American spirit" and that one possible alternative to the discriminatory land measures would be to "make [Japanese] by Congressional Act . . . eligible to citizenship."[41] One Japanese student decried American prejudice against the Japanese in 1924:

> Are the Japanese of 70 or 80,000 a menace to America that has more than
> a hundred million people? No! Then why and by what reason do you dis-
> criminate us? Is it right to persecute so severely and so heavily the people who
> are willing to work and produce more for the welfare of American people?
> Didn't your fathers bring forth upon this continent a new nation conceived

in liberty and dedicated to the proposition that all men are created equal? Why don't you treat us impartially on the behalf of Humanity, Justice, and Equality? Americans! Treat us fairly, impartially, but not discriminately. Are you satisfied in discriminating us so harshly?[42]

Frustrated with the contradictions they faced while in the United States, Asian students warned Americans that the "realization of true democracy" was the only way to achieve the "abolition of biased race prejudice."[43]

For student association members, building a cultural bridge amid racial prejudice and discrimination in America was an increasingly daunting task by the mid-1920s. Experiencing American racism was disappointing and humiliating, and the larger Christian organizations provided little information or assistance in dealing with these issues. When the CFR did acknowledge the problems of the Asian foreign students with racism and discrimination, leaders rarely described the problems using those words. Instead, Hurrey often substituted "international misunderstandings" for racial discrimination, arguing that the problems the students experienced were based more on a general distaste for foreigners than any deep-seated racial hatred or prejudice. If the problem was one of misunderstanding or ignorance, then the issue could be solved by a continued focus on cultural bridge building and good behavior. Hurrey's understanding of the problems of the students reflected larger trends in the CFR and the YMCA. This was not a problem for the National Council but one that could best be solved by more understanding and patience form the students. Hurrey encouraged members of the Christian campus associations to identify their weaknesses in communicating with American students and devise ways to use their resources to solve their social and cultural shortcomings while promoting "friendly foreign relations."[44]

Hurrey stressed that Asian students continue to be mindful of their social and political opinions in the presence of Americans at all times. The CFR directed members of the JSCA, CSCA, and FSCM and other foreign students to remain on their best behavior while in the United States and to avoid seeming "aloof or noisy," reminding them that the cultural bridge could only be built with mutual cooperation and understanding. "It would seem best," Hurrey continued, "that students devote their energy to their studies and although ready to answer questions of a political nature, refrain from active propaganda in the political field."[45] Hurrey's message was a general discouragement to any foreign student wishing to speak out against any political issues, including racial discrimination. The YMCA's policy at the time of generally refraining from attempting to sway public opinion on controversial issues guided Hurrey's advice to the students but also reflected the politics of respectability that Asian students as well as the YMCA and CFR supported. As an organization originally designed to promote good values and morals among working-class men, the YMCA stressed the roles of respectable middle and upper class individuals in "civilizing" communities. In southern and northern cities, the black elite or the "talented tenth" typically ran the African American chapters of the organization and initially worked within the system of segregation to engage in "racial uplift."[46] By advising Asian students to remain polite and respectable in the face of hardships or social/racial conflicts, Hurrey applied the general theory of the YMCA'S purpose to the student associations: they were not political organizations for foreign students but outlets for unofficial ambassadors to benefit from and add to the Christian education experience in the United States.

In many ways, Hurrey's suggestion that the students focus on cultural exchange insulated Asian students from broader forms of racism and prejudice. In theory, cultural ambassadorship and Christian education would allow CSCA, JSCA, and FSCM members to engage in social activities without exposing them to the growing political and social tensions in the United States. And Hurrey was not alone in offering suggestions for remaining respectable—other leaders and organizations in Japanese, Filipino, and Chinese communities also sought to mold immigrants and Asian Americans into proper representations of their groups and homeland. The Chinese American Citizens Alliance and the Chinese Student Association (another student group, based in British Columbia but with ties to students and communities along the West Coast of the United States), along with the Filipino Federation of America and later the Japanese American Citizens League, worked tirelessly to "sell" Asians as well-behaved, hardworking, and eager cosmopolitans to white Americans (an early form, as historian Lisa Mar argues, of the model minority myth).[47] Selling the respectability and Christian values of the students reflected the desire of larger communities of Asian Americans to achieve a level of success and acceptance from Americans. In a situation where those on all sides appeared to encourage quiet, Christian acceptance of circumstances while developing patience in building a cultural bridge, the students had few places to turn for assistance.

From Cosmopolitans to Crusaders:
Constructing a New Type of Bridge

Hurrey's words of encouragement and the role of Asian students as model cultural ambassadors, however, did not hold sway over many members of the JSCA, CSCA, or FSCM. A prominent CSCA member named Y. T. Wu wrote a passionate reply to Hurrey in 1925 and eloquently criticized the CFR's recommendations for foreign students. In "The Boomerang of Criticism," published in the *Fellowship Notes of the CSCA*, Wu expressed doubt about the usefulness of Hurrey's warnings that students should remain apolitical while in the United States. He explained that his first reaction to reading Hurrey's original article was that "hereafter in talking to my American friends, I should close my mouth to anything that would be considered unpleasant and only talk about the weather or how great and wealthy America is and how much more so she will be." Wu also argued that through attempts to construct a cultural bridge while in America, foreign students became more familiar with many of the negative aspects of the American people, rather than the positives that Hurrey often trumpeted in articles and reports. Over time, "Chinese living and studying in America and the West have come to realize that the Western people are not all angels and their land not yet a paradise—that strong and wealthy as they may be, they have a great many dire needs which they are not yet able to meet." While Hurrey prompted foreign students to refrain from speaking out of turn, students such as Wu could not overlook that America had its fair share of problems with "prejudice and hate" underneath the appearance of "wealth and stability." By the mid-1920s, members of the Christian student associations saw that perhaps the CFR and YMCA embraced internationalism to a fault, using the concept of bridge building to disguise problems in American Christianity and race relations.[48]

The growing conflicts between Asian student association members and Hurrey were part of a gathering storm of racial problems for the YMCA during the 1920s. While attempting to embrace the idea of the interracial dialogue between whites and African Americans by forming subgroups such as the Race Relations Committee, the Student Work Committee, the Interracial Movement, and the Commission on Interracial Cooperation, the interaction was not always as interracial as the YMCA had hoped and barely resembled a dialogue. Few whites were willing to participate in such groups in southern areas, and many African Americans were suspicious of the intentions of those who did. Such moves did little to challenge the larger structure of segregation within the organization and the Social Gospel movement as a whole, with white progressive Christians paying scant attention to the racial fractures and denial within their own movement.[49]

Despite the potential for growth, even the YMCA recognized its own limits in what it could and could not do in terms of race relations in America. Creating interracial dialogue was hardly a permanent solution to the problem of racial tensions in the North and South, a failure that carried over to the Asian students and their problems with discrimination in the West. As Hurrey emphasized time and again, bridge building and international understanding were the cures for the Asian students' ills. The Commission on Interracial Cooperation explained in a *Chinese Christian Student* article that the "philosophy" of the interracial movement in the South was "not that of seeking to solve the race problem, but taking the next practicable step in the direction of interracial justice and goodwill." The article concluded by noting that "there are still vast areas of prejudice that have been scarcely touched, vast realms of injustice that so far have proved impregnable."[50] Meanwhile, Hurrey and the CFR did little to acknowledge the issues raised by Asian students or offer substantial ideas for fighting against racial prejudice and a West Coast form of "Jap" or "Charlie" Crow. Hurrey reflected the YMCA's vision of race as involving only blacks and whites and its view of racism as somehow being outside the realm of the Social Gospel and Christianity.

Without assistance from the CFR, Asian students turned their attention toward playing a more active role in addressing problems with racism. If the YMCA and the CFR were unwilling to help, where else could they turn except to each other as foreign students who shared a racial stigma while in the United States? Although some religious leaders and sociologists like the missionary Sidney Gulick argued for better Christian treatment of Japanese and opposed segregation and racism along the West Coast, they did not directly connect with the students or offer any real assistance.[51] Also, despite the presence of ethnic YMCAs in cities, students were still disappointed in the lack of integration in the main branches. Overall, there was a general distance between the reality of the students' concerns with racism and the suggestions that Protestant leaders offered.

During the early days of the Christian campus associations, CSCA, JSCA, and FSCM members were also willing to concede that their roles as

cultural ambassadors constituted a larger goal of building Christian brotherhood and creating a Kingdom of God on Earth. The students initially
embraced the respectability that Hurrey and the CFR offered as a path to
acceptance in America and a framework for greater intercultural relationships. Asian students also supported the YMCA in its mission of building
goodwill and faith, viewing racial tensions as forms of superficial prejudice
that would fade as Christian faith grew stronger. However, the students
challenged these ideals when Hurrey failed to respond to their grievances
regarding discrimination, and distrust came to characterize the relationship between the student associations and the CFR.

By the late 1920s, members of the student Christian associations discussed what they, as part of a minority group in America, could do to
help address racism. At the Oriental Student Conference at Oberlin
College in 1924, CSCA, FSCM, and JSCA representatives concluded
that among the most visible weaknesses of American Christianity were a
"lack of courage on the part of preachers and church members in opposing public opinion of racial issues . . . and superficiality and indifference
among American young people." The accusations of "lack of courage" and
"superficiality and indifference" revealed a growing displeasure among
Asian foreign students for the tepid response of the YMCA and the CFR
to racism. The students at the conference did not stop at describing what
the problems were in America, noting that "it was agreed that Oriental
students can make Christ more real in American student life by dealing
promptly and thoroughly with all cases of racial discrimination and dis-
courtesy, by enlisting the help of true Christian people . . . in overcoming
such practices."[52] The discourse at such meetings and conferences created
an emerging dialogue that would come to shape the associations' actions
in response to racism on and off college campuses. Not only did students
use their common identities as Christians to come together, but they also
realized that they shared a panethnic Asian identity in a racially unjust
society. Students at the Oberlin conference recognized that rather than
being mere "cultural ambassadors" or visitors, they were representatives of
minority groups and Christianity while in the United States.

When comparing the students' desires to deal "promptly and thoroughly with *all* cases of racial discrimination" against the YMCA's pas-
sivity, it is striking that members of the student-led Christian associations
were ahead of their parent organizations on the West Coast. Set on root-
ing out the "nominal members" of their organizations, student association

leaders such as President Carballo of the FSCM urged "fellow members and readers of *The Bulletin*" to "become active in their interest" and proclaimed in an article that he would "rather see one maintain an antagonistic attitude than an indifferent or passive attitude, for out of antagonism there shall come conflict and conflict means action."[53] The fight against discrimination required active members who were dedicated to bringing Christian equality and racial justice to America. And after facing prejudice and racism on and off campus, CSCA, FSCM, and JSCA members were more than willing to lend a hand, representing a shift in the students' self-identities and racial consciousness. A panethnic spirit was growing among members of the student associations.

Conclusions

Perhaps it was Lillian Kwai, a Chinese student who attended the University of California, Berkeley, and an active member of the CSCA, who best described the changing nature of the student associations in 1925. In her report to the rest of the CSCA on her days spent at an Indianapolis Student Christian Convention, Kwai explained that racism and racial discrimination were important topics of discussion among students. "For instance," Kwai recalled, "students from one college may emphasize lack of understanding as one of the causes of racial prejudices, while students from another college may bring up concrete causes probably unknown to other students in the first place."[54] Kwai summarized the basic changes in the student groups during the 1920s, moving from distinctly cosmopolitan bridge builders to students interested in actively making changes in the racial structure of the United States. When members of the CSCA, FSCM, and JSCA gathered to discuss their experiences as foreign students who happened to be members of the "yellow" race in America, it signified a growing multicultural and cross-ethnic connection among Chinese, Filipino, and Japanese Christian students. The early meetings of the members of the associations often resulted in little more than conversations and resolutions, but these results were the sparks that Asian students required to begin identifying larger problems as well as solutions. With the goals and the reputation of the organizations growing, the Christian student associations would become appealing to other students on campus, including Asian American classmates of the second generation.

2

A Problem by
Any Other Name

•••••••••••••••••••••

Christian Student
Associations, the "Second-
Generation Problem," and
West Coast Racism

In a 1925 edition of the *Japanese Student Bulletin*, Nisei JSCA member and University of California, Berkeley, student Walter Mihata explained to his American- and foreign-born readers that although both groups differed in citizenship status, their experiences in the United States were in fact similar. "Though Japanese by blood, we [Nisei] are Americans and have all the rights and privileges of Americans," Mihata began in his article "Americans of Japanese Ancestry," "but still, because we are Japanese we find ourselves placed under the same social and economic disadvantages as our parents who are NOT American citizens." Through his article, Mihata attempted to engage in a new type of bridge building based on a shared identity between Nisei and foreign-born students in America. Although Nisei students were Americans, Mihata argued that "the realities of minority discrimination have treated Nisei as though they were foreign students."[1]

Mihata's article reflects important changes in the JSCA and the other student associations following clashes with the YMCA over discrimination and prejudice. First, more Nisei and second-generation Chinese American students became members of the organizations. The changes in the composition of the student groups were a result of a demographic shift during the early twentieth century, particularly following the exclusionary immigration acts. A decline in immigration from Japan and China, coupled with a rise in the number of American-born Chinese and Japanese created a second-generation "bubble." By 1930, there were more Nisei than Issei in the United States and a growing number of second-generation Chinese Americans, creating what Eiichiro Azuma has described as a "transit from an immigrant era to Nisei era," a concept that also applied to Chinese communities in the United States.[2]

In order to accommodate the growing number of second-generation students on campus, the leaders of the associations turned their attention toward recruiting American-born members. As a result, second-generation students assumed leadership positions in the organizations, working alongside foreign students to solve problems of postgraduation employment, discrimination on campus, and prejudice in larger communities. While other ethnic groups such as the Japanese American Citizens League (JACL) and the Chinese American Citizens Alliance (CACA) also addressed the economic and social problems Asian Americans faced along the West Coast, the student associations strove for a wider-reaching and more inclusive platform. Association leaders and members used Christian conferences to connect with other foreign students and construct panethnic networks for discussing the needs of Chinese, Filipino, and Japanese students as a whole. By 1927, the foreign-born student leaders of the CSCA agreed that "since the number of American-born Chinese students is increasing, the CSCA should extend its services to them."[3]

By emphasizing the second-generation problem, the explicit discussions of "Christian citizenship" among the students became less common during the late 1920s. Christian conferences, meetings, and seminars served as a basis for communication among the association members regarding issues of racism and discrimination. In a significant departure from the earlier work of the associations, the students used Christianity as a means to unify their growing number of members rather than to promote an abstract idea of Christian brotherhood. The students did not abandon their Christian identity but rather applied the concept of a race-blind Christian world to discrimination against both foreign-born and second-generation Asian students.

Chinese and Japanese students were, however, not the only scholars interested in race relations in West Coast communities at the time. Sociologists were fascinated with what Robert Park deemed the "racial frontier" of the Pacific Coast, especially California.[4] Park and the sociologist William Smith focused on the specific concerns and problems of the second generation of Asian Americans who, by the 1920s, were coming of age on campuses and in communities along the West Coast. Smith and Park were particularly interested in the failure of Nisei to gain employment following graduation from top colleges and universities.[5] Sociologists approached what they identified as the "second-generation problem" as an interesting case study, but they rarely engaged in conversations that openly dealt with the racism of white inhabitants and failed to provide any solutions or suggestions for Asian American youths.

The leaders and members of the JSCA and the CSCA held different opinions on the causes and larger implications of the second-generation problem. As students, many association members attended classes and lectures in the growing field of sociology during the 1920s and learned the importance of the field's methods and concepts to understanding race relations. They recognized that the problems of the second generation of Asian Americans were directly related to the web of racism and discrimination on the West Coast and across the United States. Both leaders and members established committees of foreign and second-generation students to investigate racial discrimination on campus and within the larger communities as well as to survey association members on their reactions to prejudice and racism. Although Henry Yu and Lisa Mar provide useful insight into the role of Asian American students serving as research assistants for Park in projects such as the Survey of Race Relations, the JSCA and CSCA's own studies of the second-generation problem and racism (as well as their responses to what they uncovered) have yet to be fully explored by historians.[6] JSCA and CSCA members were eager to try their hand at conducting sociological studies and addressing discrimination during conferences and meetings and within their newspapers. Through such activities, the students mirrored other Progressive Era reformers in identifying problems, investigating the underlying causes, and offering potential solutions.

These activities, however, have been lost in the larger historical narrative of race relations during the early to mid-twentieth century. The CSCA and JSCA surveys represent a growing commitment among members to using their Christian networks and academic interests to analyze racism and navigate the racial terrain of West Coast communities, tasks the YMCA failed to accomplish. Although there was no "second generation" of Filipino students, the number of FSCM members also increased as more self-supporting students arrived in the United States and were drawn into discussions of racial discrimination. While economic class still created barriers between the students and the larger ethnic enclaves in their cities, the attention to the problems of the second generation brought foreign and American students together and produced a greater awareness of the need for panethnic cooperation.[7]

The "Second-Generation Problem"

In 1924, a research assistant for the Survey of Race Relations (a project planned by the Institution of Social and Religious Research and other liberal Protestants, financed largely by John D. Rockefeller, and conducted by Robert Park, Merle Davis, William Smith, and other sociologists to analyze relations between whites and minorities on the West Coast) interviewed Flora Belle Jan, a Chinese American member of the CSCA and a freshman at Fresno State College in California. Jan's interview was representative of the "life story" methodology of the Survey of Race Relations (SRR) that relied heavily on first-person accounts from minorities on their experiences in the United States. The interviewer described Jan as a "leader among the native born Chinese," and Jan eagerly described her life as a second-generation member, including her own take on white Americans and the sorority girls at her college. "It is very funny to watch the snobbishness of the girls at the state college," Jan candidly began, as "they judge people entirely by the clothes they wear and the money they spend and they get awfully stung this way sometimes." But it was not necessarily the "snobbishness" of her fellow American classmates that aggravated her. Jan matter-of-factly noted that despite the fact that "some of the girls are awfully good to me, of course, being a Chinese girl, I'm not eligible [for] membership in a sorority."[8]

Jan revealed a combination of racial and class prejudice at Fresno State that characterized many of the general relationships between Asian and white students. Jan's letters to friends reveal that while her experiences with both Chinese and white students were generally pleasant, there were times when, as she wrote to Park in 1925, "the more I learn about American men and boys and some girls, I think that friendly relations, at least in California, are for the most part, impossible."[9] Although this scenario may seem trivial when described in the context of sorority pledges, Jan's experiences were indicative of larger problems faced by members of the second generation along the West Coast. While Jan retaliated by writing a satirical sketch of American sorority girls called "Miss Flapper Vampire," she was constantly reminded of the racial distance between herself and her American classmates. Jan's life history provided the interviewer and organizers of the SRR with evidence of the overwhelming presence of racial prejudice. Her account and others like it were filed under the vague headings of "Americanization" and "Accommodation" in the larger collection of survey findings.[10] Jan herself would later become an assistant to Park at the University of Chicago, but her interviewer's classification of her experience as fodder for sociological accounts of "assimilation" and "acculturation" demonstrates the SRR's general lack of concern for the damaging effects of discrimination on Asian and Asian American students.

For Park and the other leaders of the SRR, Jan's reaction to the sorority girls was a prime example of the problem of the second generation of Asian Americans with assimilation and racial "hypersensitivity." Park's own race-relations cycle theory (stating that immigrants and other groups went through a series of steps before finally assimilating to American culture) shaped many sociological studies and projects during the 1920s, inspiring a generation of scholars to understand the immigrant's process with adapting to American culture.[11] As a result, most studies of Asian immigrants and their children focused on identity formation, arguing that, as a racially and culturally different group of migrants, their experiences with assimilating to American society were different from those of European immigrants. Sociologists paid close attention to Asian communities, theorizing that Asian American adolescents had a particularly difficult time reconciling the more traditional and "Asian" world of their parents with the "modern" world of their American friends. Consequentially, Asian American children and adolescents suffered an identity crisis: as children of Asian descent, they could never be white regardless of how American they became, but their largely successful cultural assimilation left them unable to relate to their parents. Asian American children and adolescents were, as Park explained, the perfect examples of the "marginal man," an individual caught between two worlds without a true identity.[12] Sociologists described this phenomenon as a case of heightened "racial consciousness," an extreme awareness of racial otherness that created a permanent state of depression and inferiority among second-generation Asian Americans. Scholars such as Park identified the second-generation problem as a unique identity crisis and a predicament with few solutions.

The SRR represented sociologists' unwillingness to fully address the effects of racism on the second generation of Asian Americans and the impact of this problem on all minorities along the West Coast. For Park, studying racism among Asian immigrants was one thing, but becoming involved in the problem itself was something that sociologists simply did not do. After all, scholars could not initiate policy, and providing an analysis of racism was more within the realm of academia. During a conference to discuss some of the findings of the SRR, Park stated that Americans "might solve the problem [of racism] . . . by establishing regions where the Negro could live and farm and where he could not live; or regions where the Oriental could live and where he could not . . . all these things need to be worked out." In other words, the findings of the SRR indicated that segregation was perhaps still the best policy in the West as in the South for dealing with the "Oriental" and second-generation problems. The historian Eckard V. Toy has argued that "the immigrants and their American-born children who were the focal point of the [SRR] played only limited roles as interviewers, researchers, and administrators" and, as a result, the problems of both immigrants and the second generation of Asian Americans with racism are buried beneath tables, charts, and other sociological data.[13] Sarah Griffith has also used the SRR in her own work on the interactions between white missionaries and Chinese and Japanese communities and has uncovered exciting sources within that speak to Jan's status as part of the second generation. However, the interviews in the survey are just the beginning: a large web of activism existed among the foreign- and American-born members of Christian associations that is evident well beyond the data of sociologists.[14]

Building a New Bridge: Connecting Foreign and Second-Generation Members

Jan and other members of the second generation found an avenue for expression in the CSCA and JSCA, organizations initially led by foreign-born Asian students. While Park and Smith discussed the problems of the second generation in terms of "racial hypersensitivity," JSCA and CSCA leaders and members spoke directly to American-born Asian students and addressed their concerns. As early as 1922, the CSCA established a special Western Department of the organization that consisted of a variety of branches from West Coast schools such as Stanford University; the University of California, Berkeley; the University of Southern California; and the University of Washington. Although members did not widely discuss the second generation at this time, they realized that "there were certain factors operating in the West" that made student life for Chinese and Chinese Americans different along the West Coast than in other regions in the United States. In a *Chinese Christian Student* article from the same year, CSCA member Y. Y. Tsu explained the need for a Western Department and cited "the preponderate number of students who are native-born" and "the racial prejudice which still remains in certain sections" as prime examples of why the CSCA should pay special attention to student experiences on the Pacific Coast.[15]

Similarly, during a JSCA conference at Asilomar, California, in December 1925, many members revealed their interest in the plight of the Nisei and their concern for the second generation of Asian Americans in general. Even though the majority of JSCA members at the Asilomar conference were students from Japan and not American citizens, they explained that an "effort to serve the cause of the younger generation of Japanese Americans on the Pacific Coast" would "contribute something toward the general welfare of the Japanese in America."[16] In reaction to the concerns of the second generation, JSCA leader and PhD student Roy Akagi appointed Ruby Hirose from the University of Washington, Francis Minoru Hayashi from Stanford University, George Kaneko from the California Institute of Technology, and Frank Iso Nakamura from Occidental College to form and lead a committee devoted to analyzing and investigating the problems of Japanese Americans along the West Coast.[17] All of the leaders of the committee were Nisei and represented Akagi's plan to make the JSCA an organization for the second generation as well as foreign-born Japanese.

Why did Akagi and other members of the JSCA and CSCA take a sudden interest in the second-generation problem during the mid-1920s? Apart from the rise in American-born members, another answer is both the foreign-born and the American-born Asian students' deep questioning of the racialized nature of US citizenship. The fact that even with citizenship, the second generation did not fare any better in many cases than their parents was a harsh realization for all Asian students. For a young Japanese or Chinese American, how useful was citizenship if you continually faced the same racism and discrimination as foreigners? As these children grew up and went on to college, they discovered that being an American of Chinese or Japanese descent prohibited entrance into dorms, fraternities, sororities, and off-campus housing. And later, upon graduation, they discovered that a degree from Stanford meant little to employers, who refused to hire Asians or saved the most lucrative jobs for whites. As the second generation came of age on the West Coast, they tried to express their dissatisfaction and anger over racism and prejudice in interviews with administrators of the SRR, but their growing disillusionment with the benefits of citizenship often escaped sociologists. The growing concern among sociologists post-1924 for the problems of the second generation translated into an equally growing concern among foreign-born members of the JSCA and the CSCA for the *racial* problems of their American-born classmates. JSCA member Tatsuji Suga perhaps best expressed the sentiment of fellow foreign-born students when he was interviewed for the Survey of Race Relations: "I think the Japanese born in America are not so fortunate as the Japanese born in Japan . . . for they cannot be proud of America when American white people are trying to deprive them of their right to citizenship."[18]

Interacting with foreign-born Asian students at colleges and universities who not only understood their frustration but also sought to address racism made the JSCA and CSCA attractive organizations for the second generation. While JSCA member Ruby Hirose explained in an interview for the SRR that although her "best friends have always been white people" and at the university she "prefer[red] to associate with white girls than to associate with Japanese girls and boys," in 1924 she became very active with the JSCA out of a need to "mingle with my own . . . who understood my problems and frustration." In the same interview with the SRR, Hirose described a rising anti-Japanese sentiment among even the teachers in her old schools as well as her frustration in having acres of "hilly, stumpy, poor land" in her name because her Issei father wanted land to cultivate but, per the California alien land laws, could not own property.[19] Hirose's negative experiences as a second-generation Japanese American with social and political forms of racial discrimination led her to consider befriending more foreign-born Japanese and Japanese American students in the University of Washington JSCA. Flora Belle Jan also began as a Chinese American girl who considered herself more American than Chinese, but her enrollment at Fresno State College and her interactions with racist sororities persuaded her to join the CSCA and mingle with more Chinese students. Scholars have always viewed Jan as a young woman who moved seamlessly between the planes of her Chinese parents and American peers, but her involvement with the CSCA reflects similar struggles with identity and racial belonging found among others like Hirose.

As more Japanese and Chinese American students of the second generation graduated high school and attended colleges and universities along the Pacific Coast, they learned that their friendships with white classmates at home did not always translate into similar experiences on campus. A Chinese American member of the CSCA who left his home in a small town in central California to attend college at the University of California, Berkeley, explained in a letter to the editor of the *Chinese Christian Student* that the fact that he had a lot of white friends in high school meant very little to him now that he was at college:

> The truth is I'm not so keen for this cosmopolitan or metropolitan life. I've learnt a bitter lessen these past few months. . . . I left with certain established connections, but now I have had them all smashed to pieces. Let me tell you, I was friends with every Tom, Dick, and Harry in high school and I got along with them first rate even though I was Chinese. You can imagine the disillusionment I experienced when I arrived in college. The first few weeks everyone was cold and some (most in fact) had that superiority complex. It hit me square on the chin.[20]

For this student and others like him who may have had good relationships with his white classmates in high school, venturing outside of their small communities and into the larger campus setting where they had to build interracial friendships from scratch could be frustrating and shocking. In cases such as this, the CSCA may have been one of the only organizations where a Chinese American student felt welcome, forcing him or her to interact more with foreign and American-born Chinese in college then they did in their hometowns. As more American-born Asian students joined the foreign-student-led JSCA and CSCA, the distinction between "foreign" and "American" Asians was blurred by shared experiences with racism and prejudice.

For other second-generation students, Christianity was always a guiding force in their lives, and they searched for opportunities to continue both their education and their involvement in Protestant organizations in college. Many American children of immigrant parents were either raised as Christians or became active in church and youth groups if their mothers and fathers joined Protestant institutions later on. Florence Chinn Kwan, a Chinese American daughter of Christian missionary parents who settled in San Francisco, credited God with her decision to go to college and become involved with the Berkeley chapter of the Chinese YWCA. Although Kwan did not speak for all Christian members of the second generation, her belief that "being Christian is a great privilege that God has bestowed upon every individual" informed her argument that "Christianity, then, gives us the privilege of using our intellect which is God-given."[21] Flora Belle Jan and Florence Chinn Kwan's desires to establish ties with other members of their generation or continue their activities with Christian organizations made the student Christian associations appealing.

In their high schools and in their home cities and towns, the participation of American-born children was usually confined to their community churches or groups, which were often ethnicity-based with limited opportunities for developing panethnic ties. There was also, as members of the JSCA described, a tendency of the Japanese churches that were "designed to meet primarily the needs of the first generation" to "take very little consideration of the . . . social and cultural divergences of the second generation."[22] Many West Coast ethnic churches run by established Issei leaders left Japanese-American youths "unprovided for religiously."[23] Language and cultural barriers between the second generation and their immigrant parents and leaders also existed in ethnic communities, often making it difficult for the American-born youth to feel included.[24] In a more practical sense, participation in Christian youth groups also provided Nisei with opportunities to escape the confines of home life, a tendency that carried over into a college setting and represented the role of Christianity in creating social as well as religious fellowship.[25] Only leaders among the second generation could help to bridge the gap between generations and the gap between foreign and American-born Japanese students. The Asian Christian groups provided a space for the second generation to branch out and discover the cross-racial and cross-ethnic possibilities of Christianity and also take control of their own religious experiences outside of their ethnic enclaves.

Through special conferences and committees, the CSCA and the JSCA invited more second-generation members to speak out on the problems of racism and discrimination, making these two topics important for the groups in moving forward. Members of the JSCA had much to say about the idea of a second-generation problem among Japanese Americans, as evidenced by editions of the *Japanese Student Bulletin*. One student delegate at a conference of Pacific Coast members of the JSCA reported that the entire second session of the conference was devoted to a discussion of the second-generation problem. The student explained that while some members were convinced that poor relationships with older Issei caused the second-generation problems, many other JSCA members were more concerned with the larger racial context of the West Coast, citing a "shared label as Oriental in America . . . as a cause of our current troubles with prejudice."[26]

With the feedback on the second-generation problem from members in mind, JSCA secretary Roy H. Akagi published an article titled "Interracial Goodwill" in a 1926 edition of the *Japanese Student Bulletin*. While prominent sociologists described the issues that American-born Chinese and Japanese faced as the second-generation problem, Akagi offered another explanation for his readers. "For one thing," Akagi continued, "let us at least be sure that we know the problem and the facts therein involved. As Japanese students studying in America, we, for better or worse, constitute ourselves as one raw material in the American racial relationship laboratory." He did not distinguish between visiting students from Japan and the second generation; both groups were "Japanese" as far as Americans viewed them, and they constituted a single racial minority group along the West Coast and across the United States. While Akagi was a Nisei (born in Oregon), he argued that he and his fellow second-generation students shared the experiences of foreign students in America, with their citizenship status effectively discarded and their ethnicity alchemized into "Oriental" or "yellow" in the racial laboratory.[27]

Later in 1926, Akagi continued his quest to transform the JSCA into a more active organization. The JSCA's early official stance on the problems that both Nisei and foreign students faced demonstrated a heightened awareness of the extent of discrimination in the United States. "The second-generation problem has been discussed long enough," Akagi began, ". . . featuring merely the pet theories of certain individuals," gesturing toward sociologists like Park and explaining that the second-generation problem was representative of a larger "American problem" with racism. The legal discrimination in the form of the California alien land laws of 1913 and 1920 and the restrictive 1924 immigration act reinforced waves of racism aimed toward all Japanese, regardless of citizenship status. Discrimination against Japanese immigrants created an atmosphere that condoned a culture of prejudice and racism that affected American-born Japanese as well. Japanese and other Asian aliens were perpetual foreigners in the United States, unable to naturalize and become American citizens and even unable to acquire access to basic freedoms such as the right to own land and make a living. Although Nisei students were "American in birth and training," Akagi cited the fact that "they are not taken as Americans in daily life and the constitutional possession of citizenship does not help them in the least" as his proof of the vicious cycle of racism along the West Coast. In short, "race prejudice, consciously or unconsciously, separates [the Nisei] from the bulk of Americans and almost always this action emanates from the latter group," barring them from American social life but also subjecting them to "discrimination and unequal treatment alike with their parents."[28]

Akagi also attacked the complacent attitude of many church groups toward racism. "Their problems and destinies," Akagi spoke of the second generation of Asian Americans, "do not ordinarily interest American organizations and clubs, even churches and other Christian bodies, which practically close doors in their face." He was certainly not exaggerating the less-than-welcoming response of Christian groups such as the YMCA to Asian students and immigrants. The solution to encouraging members of the second generation to become more engaged with larger discussions of the problems they faced was to make religious organizations like the JSCA "have more than local significance and . . . part of a larger movement, involving the entire Pacific Coast." If developing Nisei students into leaders on campus and in the community was the goal, then the "JSCA was the pioneer group in bringing together Christian members of the second generation in the institutions of higher learning all along the Coast and throughout the country." Other Japanese clubs and community organizations existed at this time, but the focus on Christian students and particularly assisting those of the second generation through larger discussions with other races and ethnicities were unique characteristics of the JSCA.[29]

Despite Akagi's call to arms, the JSCA also promoted the tactics of respectability and presenting a proper image in order to appeal to American society. The JSCA's emphasis on members' ability to reach out to Americans (particularly white students on campus) reflected a general trend among Asian immigrants and Asian Americans to, as Charlotte Brooks explains, "homogenize" native-born whites (regardless of class differences) and view them as one elite group. Many Asian immigrant and Asian American groups looked down upon "white" immigrants such as Italians, Hungarians, and Portuguese who settled along the West Coast, and considered them inferior. Efforts at appearing "respectable" were primarily aimed at the elite: upper-class whites and white students. In reaching to obtain respectability in America, Asians often associated most whites with the upper class, choosing to ignore the existence of the working class or poor. This desire for interaction with the best classes of white Americans seeped into the goals of the JSCA.[30]

Encouraging interracial cooperation was an important part of the Christian associations' missions, but here the burden was on Japanese students to project the proper image and correct any misunderstandings. JSCA leaders continued to approach their organization as an important bridge-building tool in some capacities, particularly for the Nisei, who had the potential to "Americanize" their immigrant families.[31] Shouldering most of the responsibility for creating interracial goodwill was an ambitious goal that added pressure on students already operating in a highly charged racial atmosphere. The JSCA encouraged Japanese students to go "ninety percent of the way if necessary" to meet American students and erase the inferior or "other" image of Japanese Americans.[32] The JSCA also set standards for hygiene and proper Christian morals in sexual relations among all Japanese students (foreign- and American-born) to ensure that Americans would receive them with respect. Not all of the organization's solutions for the second-generation problem were novel, radical, or fitting for destroying the larger system of racism at work. However, Akagi assured members that their organization would analyze the second-generation problem within the framework of racism.

By the late 1920s, members of the CSCA also discussed their interpretations of the second-generation problem during meetings and study groups along the West Coast. In May 1926, the CSCA sponsored a luncheon on the problems of Asian Americans at the University of California, Berkeley, and invited the JSCA and general members of the student YMCA to join. This meeting was part of a series of gatherings established by the JSCA and CSCA in hopes of creating cooperation in "bettering the condition of the Orientals in America" and featured a talk by Berkeley CSCA member and future secretary Chingwah Lee.[33] Lee's lecture, "The Cause of Unemployment among Oriental College Graduates in California," surveyed the "vocational possibilities" for both Chinese and Chinese Americans in California. He used his past experience as an assistant secretary in the Chinese YMCA employment department as well as his correspondence with fellow CSCA member Flora Belle Jan to highlight common difficulties of recent Asian graduates in finding employment. During his talk, Lee listed a "lack of progress among employers in . . . considering employment of Orientals" and "prejudice in cities and towns against peoples with great talents, but who are of different races" as the primary causes of unemployment among recent graduates and Asians in general. The fear alone of experiencing prejudice in the hiring process often discouraged Chinese students from seeking high-paying positions. At the luncheon, members of both the JSCA and the CSCA agreed that prejudice and discrimination had created an unhealthy environment for all Asian and Asian American students when it came to finding jobs after graduation, adding to "unchristian prejudice and waste of talents." Such discussions between JCSA and CSCA members paved the way for continued panethnic cooperation.[34]

Before Lee's lecture, many Asian students knew that unemployment after graduation was a problem in the United States. Despite having degrees from the best colleges and universities along the West Coast, American- and foreign-born (if they stayed for further graduate education or remained illegally when their student visas expired) Asian students found themselves in a similar situation: highly educated but without a job. These new graduates found that even with outstanding credentials and experience, employers consistently passed them over for white candidates. Also, when Asian graduates did secure jobs after graduation, these positions rarely allowed them the opportunity to utilize their specialized skills. It was far too easy for potential employers to argue that it would be "impossible" for them to hire Asian employees "for the feeling against [their] race [was] too great" among the majority white workers. As one Japanese American graduate with a degree in chemistry from Stanford University lamented in a letter to his university's Office of Employment and Appointment, his difficulty in finding a job was not his lack of ability, "but the barrier of human prejudice that I have to overcome before I can work among the American people."[35]

It became easier for employers to ignore the underlying racial causes of unemployment and underemployment as the economy suffered through the early years of the Depression. When employment opportunities were low across the nation, how could a group of minority students possibly blame white employers and accuse them of racism? While sociologists such as George Mears classified the discontent among Asian graduates as sour grapes in a lackluster job market, members of the CSCA and JSCA suffered from anxieties over their economic futures.[36] As the years progressed, CSCA members became more critical of the idea that Asian Americans possessed mental or character deficiencies because of their racial status. During an era when Chinatowns were becoming popular tourist attractions for whites to experience exotic Oriental lifestyles, many second-generation Chinese wanted Americans to view them as citizens and less as curiosities.[37] While some advocated for the cleanup and modernization of Chinatowns to achieve this goal, many CSCA members pushed for a greater awareness of the abilities of the second generation as well as their real struggles with racial prejudice.

With more American-born Chinese joining the CSCA, their criticisms of the "pet theories" of sociologists became more aggressive. "That so-called second-generation problem," Alice Fong, an assistant for the CSCA, began in a 1932 *Chinese Christian Student* article, "is NOT of our making, as we are victims of an environment forced upon us . . . and are NOT responsible for the plight in which we find ourselves." Fong vehemently argued, "If a changed economic outlook is necessary for our people, we will demand as well as make that change possible . . . if jobs are needed by our young people we will create them by operating big businesses and stimulating their growth by supporting them."[38] The way out of unemployment created by racism and economic downturn was to encourage young Chinese Americans to break free from a reliance on wage labor doled out by racist bosses and instead invest in businesses run *by* Chinese *for* the Chinese in all West Coast communities, not just Chinatowns.

Fong's suggestion was challenging, especially for a group of Asian minorities living on the Pacific Coast during the Depression. Her response to the employment problems of students was also indicative of disconnects between the solutions that the JSCA and CSCA offered and the realities for Asian immigrants and Asian Americans *without* college educations. While Fong's argument in theory offered a direct path to employment, upward mobility, and respectability (similar to arguments made by the African American middle class at the time), it was not representative of the problems of the working class or those who attempted and failed as minority business owners. Many second-generation members witnessed the discrimination and struggles that their own families faced in acquiring land and finding employment opportunities outside of manual labor. However, much like the shock that foreign members of the groups experienced when they arrived as students in America and were treated no differently from their fellow countrymen of lower station, second-generation students were frustrated that a college diploma did not guarantee a better life than that of their immigrant parents. While the discussions among CSCA and JSCA members concerning employment did create a foundation for discussion, these meetings were limited in terms of solutions and the reality of life beyond campus.[39]

Discussions on the problems of employment also revealed rifts between and among members of the associations. Not all CSCA members were as confident as their colleagues in the minority-student organization's abilities to effectively combat West Coast racism. In fact, some even questioned if such a task would benefit Chinese and Chinese American students. The *Chinese Christian Student* published editorials and articles that suggested other ways for students to overcome discrimination. In a 1931 *Chinese Christian Student* article titled "An American-Born Looks at Young Chinatown," Flora Belle Jan argued that "there can be no wholesale remedy" to the second generation's problems with finding employment or, more specifically, to racism anywhere in America:

> First of all, is the prize worth the struggle? With thousands of fair-haired, blue-eyed collegians at his elbows, looking for a job, with thousands of other similar tinted fellow employees working for a raise, ready to take his the moment he slips, is there a chance for a person with yellow skin? Is it worth a lifetime of hardship, with possible failure at the end—to prove the efficacy of the preamble of the Constitution of the United States? Let every American-born Chinese answer this question for himself.[40]

Jan echoed her previous letter to Park, in which she expressed devotion to improving relations but also a sense of hopelessness about being able to completely end prejudice. Despite varying reactions and opinions on how to move forward, the problems of employment were central to the operations and activities of the associations by the 1930s.

The racial discrimination that members experienced in the job market led the CSCA and the JSCA to think broadly about the problem of discrimination along the West Coast. Unemployment was a problem that affected both foreign and American students but did not garner serious attention from scholars, officials, or even the YMCA. What could two minority-student-run Christian organizations do to help members in their almost daily battles with prejudice? CSCA and JSCA leaders tackled these questions head-on and asked for guidance and suggestions from their fellow students. A key suggestion came from sociology major Francis Y. Chang, who proposed that Chinese Americans of the second generation engage in "making systematic surveys of the economic conditions of the Chinese in America" that were "critical, scientific, and constructive, with suggestions for improvement."[41] Like many other members of both the CSCA and the JSCA, Chang agreed that the next step after general discussions of the second-generation problem was to conduct thorough and extensive surveys of Asian American communities along the West Coast.

The CSCA and JSCA designed surveys that were different from those of Park, Smith, and other sociologists. Rather than focusing on topics of assimilation, identity formation, and intergenerational conflict, the associations' surveys included direct questions relating to the students' experiences with racism and discrimination. These questions were also more inclusive in that they did not restrict the surveys to only one ethnic group or only second-generation students. By making direct inquiries into occurrences of racism and prejudice, leaving room for discussions relating to discrimination, and seeking responses from both American- and foreign-born Chinese and Japanese students, the CSCA and the JSCA demonstrated how student responses to the second-generation problem presented opportunities for greater participation in social issues and pan-ethnic collaboration.

Whereas sociologists conducted the Survey of Race Relations, a group from the CSCA designed their own project in 1926 to uncover the different problems that Asian and Asian American students faced. In a 1928 *Chinese Christian Student* article, Chingwah Lee explained that when he agreed in 1926 to make a survey of the Chinese on the West Coast following the suggestion of then CSCA president Paul Meng that each CSCA unit should make a "social survey of each Chinese community" near its campus, he had "no idea of the difficulties" he would encounter.[42] The main challenges were the size and scope of the survey, which in the end, were far larger than what Lee expected.

Lee's original intent was to design a survey that would focus on the plight of all Chinese (students and nonstudents, immigrants and Chinese Americans) in the Central Valley of California (at the time, one of the most anti-Asian regions of the state).[43] The result, however, was that Lee's survey (distributed with the help other CSCA members) addressed the concerns of other Asian ethnic groups, including Filipino and Japanese students. In the article, Lee listed "interracial marriages, vocational difficulties, and racial prejudices" as the main concerns among all students after completing the survey and items for discussions at upcoming conferences. Although "racial prejudices" and "vocational difficulties" were broad categories, Lee observed that many of those interviewed seemed to have much to say in regard to interracial relations. The older Chinese explained that if "Americanization" and acceptance were the ultimate goal for themselves and their children, perhaps the best way to achieve this transformation would be interracial marriage, an idea that Issei and Nisei embraced as well. The younger Chinese, Chinese American, and Filipino students were more supportive of interracial relations for building cosmopolitan friendships but worried that, as minorities, they would have to intermix with the "less desirable stratum" of white society. Concerns over mingling with lower-class whites appeared to outrank hesitations in cross-ethnic relations or sexual encounters with other races. Both groups, however, also noted that racial discrimination seemed to play an important role in prohibiting interracial relationships between whites and Asians. From personal relationships to employment, Lee explained that "even a superficial reading" of the data he and his partners collected from the survey revealed problems that were of great importance for not only those who "cared about the general welfare of the Chinese" but also West Coast social workers, envisioning a use for his survey among charitable and welfare agencies.[44]

The CSCA's surveys are necessary for understanding the importance of Asian student involvement in investigating West Coast discrimination, particularly in that they addressed the concerns of a mixture of Asian ethnicities rather than just students or CSCA members. By venturing deep into California, Lee and his colleagues came into contact with the various Asian ethnic groups that called this region home. Although Lee did not provide specific suggestions for how to combat the problems of racial prejudice and employment discrimination, he made a powerful argument that all agencies (not just those that specialized in assisting Asians) should acknowledge and address such issues.

CSCA members also claimed that student-run surveys should go beyond the campus and engage Chinese inhabitants in the larger community. In the article "Chinese Students and Their Compatriots in America," a CSCA member explained that "there are about 2,000 Chinese students and 70,000 Chinese in various occupations in this country," and "as the former live around the universities and the latter largely in segregated sections, the two groups do not mingle freely." The student also called attention to "a mutual feeling that they should be nearer each other and show greater measure of mutual help" that was growing among Chinese students and the larger Chinese and Chinese-American communities. "Closer relationships between Chinese students and their compatriots in other walks of life," the student concluded, "is not only highly desirable, but also practicable."[45] Another CSCA member encouraged further investigation of the conditions of Chinese and Chinese Americans outside of the ivory tower and suggested that students conduct "a survey of the Chinese population in each college community and make it the topic of discussion at the various conferences next summer."[46]

Although another group, the earlier Chinese Students' Alliance, had been active in a general welfare program designed to assist Chinese laborers living in the United States, their focus on transforming the working class into respectable Chinese in order to improve China's image in America was different from the goals of the Christian associations.[47]

For the CSCA, the idea of assisting members of the Chinese working class created a Social Gospel–oriented plan that served as a reminder that a more oppressive life for ethnic and racial minorities existed off campus. As a result, CSCA members at Berkeley and in other areas of California and the West Coast assisted community churches with charity events and educational programs—activities that did not directly challenge racism or prejudice but helped the students to become more involved in the day-to-day lives of Chinese who lived and worked within the confines of racism. The addition of more Chinese American members to the CSCA also contributed to a concern for the wider community, possibly because these students came from working-class, laboring families who faced different experiences than foreign-born Chinese students. With these surveys, members of the CSCA attempted (not always successfully) to shed their identities as students or elites and become involved in wider problems of discrimination and racism.

JSCA members likewise developed questionnaires to be handed out to other students on campus as well as to the Japanese communities at large in order to "foster clearer thinking [on the problem] and gather data as well as various points of view." What was different in the JSCA's approach, however, was the initial desire to distribute the questionnaire as widely as possible in order "to coincide and evolve solutions to the problem not from a local and individual point of view, but from a broader, coast-wide or national and cooperative point of view." The JSCA (in similar fashion as the CSCA) discarded the hypotheses that scholars used to explain the second-generation problem and chose instead to use a broad surveying method to get answers.[48]

In 1931, the JSCA conducted a survey of Japanese students studying in America to gain a sense of how racism and prejudice affected their impressions of the United States. The results were overwhelmingly negative. The survey began with a general, open-ended question: "Do you consider, generally speaking, America to be as good as you thought she was while you were in your own country?" An overwhelming majority (70 percent) of the students answered that their impressions were "unfavorable" when compared with what they expected to find in America and cited "racial prejudice" against themselves and other minorities as the main reason for their answer. Another question asked students to describe specific instances of "not being treated right by American people." Answers included a number of experiences with discrimination (including being barred from YMCA facilities) as well as the "insulting immigration laws" that prevented Japanese and other Asian migrants from coming to America and gaining access to citizenship rights. One student even took the opportunity to explain how his experiences with racism in America had transformed his outlook on Christianity. He declared, "I have become a hater of Sham Christianity" because in America, even white Christians tended to "hate colored people," making Christianity "the religion of white supremacy."[49]

However, the JSCA and CSCA had trouble carrying through with their plans to apply their survey findings to city-, state-, and coast-wide racism. Although the JSCA and the other Christian associations were growing and gaining recognition on campuses and at larger YMCA-sponsored conferences, their dissociation with other established community groups contributed to their isolation. Organizations like the JACL, Filipino associations in Seattle, and Chinese business groups worked closely with those who were more immediate and active members of Asian American communities. Despite seeking to survey larger communities, and in some cases to reach out to those beyond campus, the students did not interact in a notable capacity with these groups or community leaders. Apart from participating in church events in local places of worship and engaging in the occasional lecture, JSCA, CSCA, and FSCM members were focused mainly on the problems that students faced and on developing opportunities for Christian, panethnic cooperation. While the community Japanese associations primarily represented the rights and needs of the older and established Issei, the student associations operated under leadership from both foreign- and American-born students, resulting in a more complex and at times abstract set of Christian brotherhood goals for achieving equality. Lacking connections to more prominent community leaders was in many ways detrimental to the students' attempts to involve others in their plans.

Although limited in their community connections, once the JSCA and CSCA analyzed the results of the questionnaires and surveys, the groups' members decided that a clear and definite plan was the best way to proceed. Both organizations began by focusing on secondary problems of racism that the students could tackle themselves and moved beyond discussions to assisting Asian students. Every year, association leaders received complaints from American-born members who faced difficulties securing room and board at their college or university, the same problems that foreign-born Asian students faced upon arrival. In response, the JSCA and CSCA created bureaus specifically to assist Asian and Asian American students find affordable housing off campus. These bureaus promoted tactics such as writing about landlords and YMCA officials who refused to rent to Asians and other minorities in campus newspapers and bulletins to raise awareness of the problem. The JSCA also developed a vocational bureau for the purpose of helping members and other Japanese students find employment during school and after graduation. Although these were commendable measures, JSCA and CSCA officials and fellow members knew that discrimination was too large a problem for any one organization to combat effectively.[50]

The Growth of Panethnic Cooperation

In order to address the panethnic problem of racism, members of the JSCA, CSCA, and FSCM advocated for interorganizational conferences and workshops. By the mid-1920s, Chinese, Japanese, and Filipino students were already convening mini-sessions to discuss their experiences as foreign students in the United States at larger YMCA and World Student Christian Federation–sponsored organizations. Following the turn toward understanding the racial problems of the second generation, however, many members called for more meetings and conferences that were specifically devoted to discrimination and prejudice. In a 1926 edition of the *Japanese Student Bulletin*, the JSCA outlined the next important steps in addressing the racial problems of Asian students, which included "encouragement of friendships between Japanese students and other foreign student groups . . . and joint meetings with the Chinese Students' Christian Association and other similar organizations."[51] CSCA members agreed with the sentiments of the JSCA and used the *Chinese Christian Student* to build support for increased interaction among Asian students of all backgrounds. In 1931, CSCA officials announced that there would be a meeting of West Coast Asian and Asian American students at Stanford University to "discuss the needs of American Born Orientals."[52] The conference brought together JSCA, CSCA, and FSCM members, along with Asian students from other religious and secular groups, on Stanford University's campus to establish an open dialogue concerning the "social and economic issues" prominent in the survey results. The meetings and conferences that the students attended and organized transformed the individual student associations into components of a large Christian network of Asian panethnicity.

As FSCM members attended more student conferences, they also used these meetings to call attention to the contributions of colonialism to racism. Rather than accepting that racial prejudice was simply another ugly aspect of life in the United States, Filipino students often viewed segregation and discrimination through the international lens of imperialism. Filipino students warned in editions of the *Filipino Student Bulletin* that racism was a byproduct of nationalism and imperialism. All imperial projects, including America's experiment with colonization in the Philippines, were "evidence of aggressive nationalism and a lack of respect for God's authority over humanity."[53] For Filipino students in America, prejudice and discrimination in Los Angeles, Stockton, or Seattle were results of ignorance and imperial pride on behalf of Americans. Filipino students explained that Americans treated them with contempt not only because of their racial status but also because colonization of the Philippines led Americans to believe that Filipinos were politically, socially, and culturally inferior. A group of Filipino students from Los Angeles suggested in a *Filipino Student Bulletin* article that one solution to this problem was to petition the US government for assistance in building a Filipino Club House in Washington, DC. This clubhouse would serve as a place where Americans could travel to learn about Filipino culture and develop a "worthy representation in the heart of the American nation of Filipino dignity, pride, and ideals."[54]

The response of FSCM members to their experiences with discrimination illustrates a continued reliance on the theory of cultural bridge building within the realm of racial rights activism. Rather than define racism in the United States as solely a product of racial prejudice, Filipino students approached the problem within an imperial framework, arguing that the deeds of Americans overseas fueled racist reactions (and vice versa). FSCM members identified a specific need for continued ambassadorship, not only for building bridges between the Orient and the Occident, but for attempting to move beyond the largely imperial relationship between Filipinos and Americans. As a result, these students worked to expose the connections between imperialism and racism in the United States and abroad, while highlighting the unchristian nature of these acts.

The desire of Filipino Christians to expose the connection between racism and imperialism for all to see resulted in the FSCM advocating for more Asian and Asian American conferences. In a *Filipino Student Bulletin* article titled "Filipino Students vs. Chinese and Japanese Students," FSCM president E. J. Carballo explained that Filipino, Chinese, and Japanese, despite whatever national tensions may exist among their homelands or their communities in America, should strive to read each other's student newspapers as "members of the human race and particularly of the Mongoloid race." As Christians and being of Asian descent, Filipino, Chinese, and Japanese students should bond together and share tactics for dealing with racism in the United States and with political, social, and economic problems abroad. While "Mongoloid" was a term bestowed on Filipinos and other Asians by anthropologists and US immigration officials, the FSCM used the term to argue for collaboration between the different

Asian student groups. Carballo argued, however, that the preoccupation with Filipino independence among many FSCM members prevented the strengthening of panethnic ties. While political independence is "the birthright of every one of God's peoples," Carballo explained that Filipino students in America should not let the project of independence from the United States overshadow all that could be accomplished through advocating for racial equality alongside Chinese and Japanese students. The article ends with a rallying cry for all Asian students in America to form a national organization to create a "powerful group for molding public opinion" and offer to the public a "terrific argument for the capacity of the people they represent" abroad and in the United States.[55] The powerful group that Carballo wished to establish represented a growing recognition among Christian association members that they shared an identity as Asians in America in addition to their identities as Chinese, Filipino, or Japanese. As early as the 1920s, the conferences and meetings of the students represented a form of "consciousness-raising" that would assist them in forming their networks and developing plans of action.[56]

As Carballo predicted, conferences became important settings for students to discuss racism in the United States as well as steps they could take in combating prejudice. At the 1926 conference in Asilomar, California, CSCA, FSCM, and JSCA delegates formed their own session, where they passed a number of resolutions concerning racial discrimination and prejudice. Such measures included drafting a petition to Congress in protest against the 1924 immigration law, which prevented the "spirit of true education and understanding from transcending racial boundaries," vowing to "unite in protesting against acts of racial discrimination on campuses . . . or in cities wherein [they] live," and assisting Japanese students at the University of California, Berkeley, with "rebuilding their recently burned Club House on the lot owned by them due to the discriminatory opposition of local property owners in Berkeley."[57] At other conferences held at Stanford University and Silver Lake, Oregon, students called for the development of specific Pacific Coast secretaries and bureaus to focus solely on the needs of students in California, Oregon, and Washington. For instance, during a joint 1927 Stanford meeting, Chinese, Filipino, and Japanese students devised a curriculum reform plan to add more Asian history and language courses in California colleges and universities and submitted the suggested revisions to the University of California system administrators.[58] While the administration did not adopt the students' suggestions, these were signs that the association members thought broadly of their impact on racial and ethnic relations on and off campus. These were not civil rights actions per se, but they were important markers of a growing racial consciousness among the students that helped them to challenge the status quo.

Along with education, the JSCA also advocated interracial cooperation on a variety of levels. "Interracial group contacts" were necessary for achieving the JSCA's goals of both creating partnerships with Americans and ending racism and discrimination. The YMCA/YWCA and World Student Christian Federation relied on sponsoring large coast-wide, national, and international conferences in order to establish networks among Christian students, and Asian students embraced this strategy as well. The JSCA also valued conferences as a means to promote interracial and multiethnic communication among Asian, Asian American, African American, and other minority and foreign students. Whether in the form of conferences, discussion groups, forums, or retreats, "more occasions must be created where the Japanese and the American younger generations can get together and think together and come to know each other's problems intimately." The JSCA officials reminded members that if they were to encounter resistance to interracial cooperation, "they must go sixty or seventy percent, ninety percent, if necessary, of the way first" to develop mutual action.[59]

Asian and Asian American students discussed the results of their surveys and their own ideas with African American, Latino, and other foreign students. During an annual YMCA/YWCA-sponsored conference in Evanston, Illinois, in 1929, CSCA, JSCA, and FSCM members had the opportunity to collaborate with church leaders and other Christian students to discuss issues of race as well as listen to guest speakers. By the end of the conference, Asian, African American, and white students concluded that "present relationships between the races [were] inconsistent with the mind and teaching of Jesus" and resolved that they "give [themselves] to an unbiased study of the races in an effort to find a solid basis for relationships of equality and mutuality, work to remove discrimination against Negroes . . . and endorse the Dyer anti-lynching bill and inform Congress to that effect."[60]

Both the students' attendance at this conference and their contributions to the conversations were important steps for the associations. Not only did building interethnic networks require work and dedication from both foreign- and American-born Chinese, Filipino, and Japanese students, but creating interracial ties was also a daunting task. The racial hierarchy of the United States often prompted Asian immigrants as well as Asian Americans to strive to remain closer to the white and therefore respectable side of the black/white divide for socioeconomic advancement. As Weili Ye explains, Chinese foreign students in particular tended not to challenge the racial caste system in the "modern world," but rather "sought to improve China's position in it."[61] Race based on skin color was in many ways a new concept for foreign students, although more tangible for members of the second generation. Even among Asian American students, however, there was a perceived disconnect between their struggles and those of other minority groups in the history of the United States. The interracial and panethnic exchanges at Evanston and other Christian youth conferences provided Asian students with a framework for approaching racial equality that could not be achieved through ethnic or racial isolation.

As students, the association members focused much of their attention on the role that education could play in overcoming prejudice and discrimination while continuing to build panethnic networks. The importance of education as a preventative measure against racism was reminiscent of the associations' earlier cultural-bridge-building approach to encouraging better relations between foreign and American students. This time around, however, the use of education was directed toward increasing interracial understanding rather than cross-cultural exchange. Over Thanksgiving break in 1927, sixty American- and foreign-born students of West Coast colleges and universities met at a conference sponsored by the Northern Institute of Pacific Relations and the YMCA at the Montezuma Mountain School near Los Gatos, California, to discuss a variety of foreign and national issues. Although the topics of the conference were wide-ranging, a CSCA student who attended the conference reported in the *Christian World Education Scrap Book* (a WSCF publication) that "perhaps the most concrete suggestions by students were made with references to race prejudice by the group discussing Pacific Coast problems." As students, the attendees "suggested that university departments preparing students for the teaching profession incorporate within the regular curriculum a course designed for the specific purpose of considering how to remove racial prejudice." At this meeting, students argued for addressing racism on campus at the root level by raising awareness of discrimination among all students.[62]

The resolutions passed by the students at the conferences and meetings were indications of the Christian student associations' potential as well as the limits in their strategies. Holding discussions, reaching a panethnic and interracial consensus on the causes of discrimination, and developing plans for action were the primary goals and tactics of the groups, rather than attacking the oppressive legal systems in place. Although individual pieces of legislation, such as the Immigration Act of 1924 and the alien land laws, were popular topics at large-scale meetings and in student publications, discussions rarely went beyond acknowledging these problems and connecting them to larger issues of Christian hypocrisy and un-American behavior. This can partly be explained by the hesitation of foreign students to place themselves in precarious positions as visitors, but the students' focus on campus issues and their experiences were also factors in their conceptions of what prejudice, racism, and discrimination were and how to fight them. Despite surveying their larger communities and interacting with local churches, the students (as educated Christians) assumed leadership of a campus movement for equality without developing relationships with other Chinese, Filipino, and Japanese groups that were also striving for an end to prejudice. However, the act of building networks and collaborating in a panethnic and multiracial manner set the students apart from other groups like the JACL or the CACA, making the student associations an important component of Asian American activism during the interwar years. Creating specific bureaus and departments within the associations was also no small feat and contributed to a larger history of bottom-up social action for addressing problems of discrimination.

The discussions, resolutions, and plans for future action that characterized Asian student meetings highlight the evolution of the Christian student associations. While the students originally viewed their purpose in the United States as serving as unofficial ambassadors, this changed by the late 1920s and through the 1930s. In tackling the issue of the second generation, members of the CSCA, JSCA, and FSCM not only strengthened their ties with one another but also connected with other minorities on campus and at larger conferences, moving toward more politically oriented activism. As a result, students transformed their organizations from cosmopolitan-minded cultural groups into budding activist associations with a Christian base.

The actions of the association members also coincided with changes in the attitudes of the YMCA, WSCF, and the CFR toward racism. By the 1930s, the YMCA was becoming more interested in issues of race, reacting to increased pressure from student groups around the country. The growth of interracial, multicultural, and radical organizations associated with leftist groups and organizations during the Popular Front period of the New Deal era also created a greater sense of activism and community involvement in Christian associations like the YMCA. These movements prompted the YMCA to reach out to other racial groups and construct a more inclusive racial framework for their goals and missions. During a 1938 Asilomar conference, Miriam Matthews, the head of the Race Commission of the Pacific Southwest division of the YWCA, reported that "we feel it necessary to extend our work to other minority groups than the Negro" and that the commission required "help in getting information about other minority groups which are particularly large in our region such as Chinese and Japanese."[63] Fortunately for Matthews and the YWCA/YMCA, the CSCA and JSCA already pursued such changes and offered to assist with achieving these interracial goals. Similarly, the WSCF acknowledged the influence of the student Christian associations in helping the organization to "become such a powerful factor in promoting right race relations" in 1937.[64]

Even Charles Hurrey, leader of the CFR, admitted by the 1930s that the CSCA and JSCA had become influential organizations for the promotion of civil rights, an increasingly important topic for Christian organizations. In 1934, Hurrey explained in his article "Oriental Students in America" that "prevailing racial and color prejudices on our part often humiliate [Asian students] in their social relationships in this country," and in order to "improve cooperative relationships with Oriental students, we must practice Christianity which our missionaries preach . . . which will mean speedy recognition of racial equality, repeal of discriminatory legislation, and the early granting of citizenship rights annually to Orientals."[65] And where could the Committee on Friendly Relations and other Christian groups turn for examples of how to address these problems? The answer was relatively straightforward: the committee should "seek to enlist the help of the Japanese and other student Christian associations" to assist with dismantling "prejudice and the problems of the second generation of Asian Americans with hatred."[66] By the late 1930s, the Asian student Christian associations in America had established a reputation for creating spaces for the discussion of race relations along the West Coast that would propel members into further activism.

Conclusions

In 1924, JSCA cabinet member and University of California, Los Angeles, graduate student Kazuo Kawai wrote a letter to Robert Park, asking for assistance in addressing the second-generation problem. "We have some wild, vague, ambitious plans," Kawai explained in his letter, "but we are so inexperienced and limited in our ability that we shall need many practical suggestions from people like you."[67] This letter illustrates how much the JSCA grew during the 1920s and 1930s in terms of understanding and attacking discrimination on the West Coast. While Kawai and other JSCA and CSCA leaders were initially overwhelmed and puzzled by the depth of racial problems, they eventually led their organizations in openly discussing racism and discrimination. It is not clear if Park ever replied to Kawai's early letter; however, the JSCA leaders and members decided to take matters into their own hands when so few outside of their organizations were willing to help.

The concern of CSCA and JSCA foreign members over the second-generation problem created a lasting impact on the organizations as well as on members' understanding of racism along the West Coast. The deep questioning of the limitations of American citizenship also brought CSCA and JSCA members into contact with other minorities on campus. As Akagi suggested, Asian students were able to see that they were, indeed, a raw element in the racial laboratory of America and that their experiences were similar to those of other oppressed groups. A broader understanding of the extent of racism as well as Christian networks allowed the CSCA and JSCA to build their reputations as interracial and panethnic forces.

Despite the CSCA, JSCA, and FSCM's heightened involvement in racial issues during the interwar years, their approaches in the form of discussions, resolutions, and surveys did not address all of the race-related problems of their members. The limits of the solutions that campus groups offered for daily struggles such as discrimination in employment became painfully clear for working-class FSCM members who toiled in less-than-ideal jobs, but their principles of racial equality extended beyond campus.

3

"We Ask Not for Mercy, but for Justice"

• • • • • • • • • • • • • • • • • • • •

Filipino Students and
the Battle for Labor
and Civil Rights

One day after rising early in the morning before the crack of dawn and consuming a daily breakfast of "salmon and blubber," FSCM Vice-President Trinidad A. Rojo reflected on his grueling experience of working in an Alaskan fish cannery in the form of a poem, questioning, "Why, oh why did I come to the Land of the Midnight Sun—I used to dress and eat well in my beloved Philippines."[1] Although Rojo may have lacked the literary flourish of his celebrated fellow Filipino and laborer Carlos Bulosan (author of the classic *America Is in the Heart*), his poem described the experiences of many Filipino student-workers.[2] Beginning in the late 1920s, however, stories describing the inherent racism and discrimination in the canning industry alarmed Filipino students more than boredom or the relentless morning bugle. And if any group could attest to the harsh conditions in canning and other forms of migrant labor, it was Filipino students.

FSCM members often worked in the Alaskan salmon canneries as well as the vegetable fields and fruit groves of Washington and California during the summer to pay for tuition in the fall, providing firsthand descriptions of the racism they encountered.

Antonio Hamay, an FSCM member from the University of Nebraska, wrote a 1936 *Filipino Student Bulletin* article on his experiences and decried the misery and isolation of agricultural work, focusing on American perceptions of Filipinos as "trash." He asserted, "Americans want [a Filipino] only because he works for them and because he patronizes their business."[3] As scholars, Christians, and also American nationals living under the complicated colonial relationship between the Philippines and the United States that granted them migration privileges, the students were also shocked that their education and religious affiliation meant little to Americans. Filipinos were part of the "yellow peril" and, as a result, were often at the receiving end of hostile and discriminatory treatment. Hamay was so outraged by his experiences that he encouraged other Filipino workers to return to the Philippines. However, FSCM members such as Rojo, D. H. Ambrosio, and Sebastian Abella chose a different path: they became members and leaders of the Seattle-based Cannery Workers' and Farm Laborers' Union (CWFLU) and fought for racial equality and labor rights. Although the CWFLU holds an important place in Filipino American history, historians have not fully explored the important roles FSCM members played in the organization and their contributions to labor activism.

Understanding the influence of FSCM members in the development of the CWFLU highlights the ideological and civil rights activism that students brought to labor organizing. Founded in 1933 by Filipino cannery laborers known as *Alaskeros,* the union was an opportunity for Filipinos to demand better working conditions and pay. Long hours, low wages, and corrupt labor contractors characterized seasonal work and presented Filipino laborers with obstacles to achieving financial stability and the dreams that many Filipino migrants brought with them to America. Dorothy Fujita-Rony and Rick Baldoz have both described the crucial role of the CWFLU in forging a Filipino American identity out of competing regional affiliations among Filipino immigrants, while Chris Friday has called for understanding the union's influence on later Asian labor movements.[4] As Fujita-Rony argues, the CWFLU reminds us of the connections between American empire, the demand for labor along the West Coast, and the early stages of Filipino migration to the

West Coast. However, FSCM members also contributed to the evolution of the union into an interracial and interethnic organization that supported civil rights movements before World War II.

Filipino students who helped to shape the CWFLU represented a unique cross between student and worker that explains the union's focus on racial equality and liberties as well as labor rights for its members. From its beginning, the CWFLU was staffed by Filipino student-workers, but some of the organizations' key leaders also participated in the student Christian associations. Irineo Cabatit and Rojo, both active FSCM members, became two of the CWFLU's most important administrators and transformed the CWFLU into a civil rights organization. As I argue in this chapter, the experiences of students in leading the FSCM also assisted them in leading a Filipino labor and civil rights movement off campus. Coming from an organization devoted to building fellowship, ending prejudice, and promoting panethnic and interracial cooperation, FSCM members viewed obtaining racial equality in the workplace as the first step toward achieving labor rights and expanding the influence of the Christian associations.

Imperialism, race relations, and labor are themes that come together in the telling of the FSCM's involvement with the CWFLU and create a richer story of the relationship between labor and civil rights. Against the backdrop of the Depression, a rising labor movement, and the questionable status of Filipinos as "Americans," FSCM members and the CWFLU are important for understanding changing racial landscapes. It was not a coincidence that many influential members of the union were also participants in the FSCM. The records of the CWFLU as well as the writings of the FSCM student laborers reveal an unexplored connection between the two organizations. While the concept of "civil rights unionism" is certainly not new, this chapter adds complexity to our understanding of this theme by exploring the role of Filipino students and nationals who challenged the limitations of their noncitizen and racial status. Like the CSCA and JSCA members who analyzed the second-generation problem within the context of West Coast racism, FSCM members used the CWFLU to expose and fight racial discrimination in the workplace and in other settings. While the growing panethnic solidarity of the students failed to adequately address the problems of laboring scholars like the Filipinos, individual members applied concepts and ideas developed through their experiences with the associations to situations beyond campus.[5]

Cannery Life: Racism on the Job

"O what thrills are coming with the advent of June!" University of Washington student Victorio Velasco penned in a 1934 *Filipino Student Bulletin* article describing life as a cannery employee in Alaska. Velasco, who was the editor of the *Bulletin* and a veteran in the seasonal cannery industry, spoke favorably of life in "the land of the midnight sun," painting vivid pictures of canoeing, romances with Native American girls, friendships with other students eager to earn money, and, of course, the "manly labor" that characterized the work. For Velasco and the hundreds of other Filipino students along the West Coast who signed up to labor in Alaska from June to August, cannery life was part of the experience of living in the United States as a self-supporting student striving to make the most of the American educational system. Although Filipino laborers began to arrive in Hawaii during the early 1900s to work in the pineapple and sugar cane fields, by the 1920s, thousands had moved to the mainland to pursue work in agriculture when Asian exclusion laws increased the demand for workers. Hundreds of Filipino students were part of this migration, straddling the line between scholar and laborer. Year after year, students such as Velasco returned to Alaska, letting the "punk smell of the fish bin," old friendships and loves, and the promise of a decent wage lure them back to their "overalls [and] heavy working shoes."[6] (See figure 1.)

To characterize Velasco's account of his summer in Alaska as sugar-coated, however, would be an understatement. Although Velasco would later became a leader of the CWFLU and an ardent opponent of labor exploitation, as editor of the *Filipino Student Bulletin*, he was uncomfortable speaking out against his employers in print. For many students and other employees, the canning industry gained a negative reputation through the 1920s. In 1922, the San Francisco *Daily Observer* journalist Max Stern traveled to the canneries from the West Coast with a group of Alaskeros and wrote an exposé of the industry. Stern told the story of a "crowd of college boys from the University of California" who, "thinking the voyage would be a lark," did not make it much farther than the China Basin section of San Francisco before two of them "jumped over the side of the vessel . . . and [swam] ashore." The cramped, crowded, and unsanitary conditions aboard cemented the transporting boats' reputations as "Hell Ships." Stern reported the "neglect, distress, danger, privation, and exploitation" that characterized life in the Alaskan canneries, turning an opportunity

Victorio A. Velasco
FOR TREASURER
Cannery Workers & Farm Laborers' Union,
Local 7, UCAPAWA, C. I. O.

Union Activities:
Plant Committee, Koggiung, 1940, 1941.

Chairman, Election Committee, 1940, 1941.

Plant Committee, Excursion Inlet, 1942, 1943.

Trustee, since 1942.

Chief Clerk, since 1942.

Editor of the 1944 Annual Report of Local 7.

Assets:
Training, Character, Honesty, Leadership, Industry, Independence of Judgment, and Courage of Conviction.

Endorsed by:
| C. N. Briones | C. L. Camarillo |
| P. P. Mori | A. Aurora |

FIGURE 1. Campaign flier promoting the candidacy of Victorio A. Velasco for the position of treasurer of the Cannery Workers' and Farm Laborers' Union, Local 7, undated. University of Washington Libraries, Special Collections, UW23241Z.

for summer employment into an often dangerous and demeaning under-taking. While other forms of labor in the agricultural industry were more back-breaking and intensive, cannery work and the journey did not appear to fit into Velasco's descriptions of fun and adventure.[7]

With stories circulating of the less-than-ideal working conditions in the canneries, why would students like Velasco commit themselves to two to three months of exploitative labor and return year after year? While his readers may have wanted to believe that the summer romances, canoe trips, and friendships were what drove him back to the canneries every summer, there were two explanations as to why he and other students continued with the hard work: education and money. Unlike the early wave of Fili-pino students, who came to the United States during the early twentieth century from elite families and on government scholarships, the majority of students in the 1920s and 1930s were from lower-class families in the Philippines who could barely afford to pay for their children's steerage, let alone their college educations.[8]

Filipinos who entered American colleges and universities dreamed of becoming educated professionals and returning home with riches, gifts, and, more importantly, a new level of respect. "I was in grade school," an Alaskero and former student Ponce Torres explained, "when I thought of coming [to America]." As the son of a farmer and part-time carpenter who had fallen upon hard times in the Philippines, Torres found hope in the belief that "coming to America [would] help a student to be able to get an education through his own efforts." For Torres and other students, the plan was simple: apply to an American college, find your own way across the Pacific, and at the end would be a bona fide degree from the United States. Torres's father borrowed money from friends and family and mort-gaged off some of his farmland to help his son purchase a $75 one-way ticket to Seattle on the S.S. *President McKinley*. In 1925, at the young age of seventeen and armed with little more than a steerage ticket, a high school diploma, a few bucks, and big dreams, Torres arrived in Seattle to begin his studies at the University of Washington.[9]

Eutiquio "Vic" Bacho also traveled to America during the 1920s, stat-ing that his "real purpose in coming to this country was to obtain a col-lege education." Unlike Torres, who came to the United States fresh from high school, Bacho had already attended Cebu Junior College in the Phil-ippines before arriving at the University of Washington. Although Bacho was well on his way to receiving a degree in secondary education from a college in the Philippines that was technically part of the American educational system, he wanted more. "The desire to travel abroad, to work my way through school prompted me to leave Cebu and come to America," he later explained in an interview.[10] As with Torres, there was something that drew other young Filipino men (and later women) to America for an education. Although, as the historian Catherine Ceniza Choy describes, there were postsecondary opportunities available in the Philippines, spots in these colleges and universities were often reserved for students from the elite, colonial classes who could afford the steep tuition.[11] While Cebu Junior College and other similar institutions were always options for the less affluent, Filipinos such as Bacho did not want to settle for less than the best. The faith in a Protestant work ethic that American teachers praised in classrooms in the Philippines inspired young Filipinos. Many longed for the chance to travel to America, to see the land that they learned so much about during their school days in the Philippines, and to return home with an American diploma, the symbol of respectability and success.[12]

By continuing their education in colleges and universities in the United States, Bacho and Torres were following the path of any American student longing for advancement. Filipino students identified college education as the avenue to intellectual and economic fulfillment. The American-style education system in the Philippines did much to condition Filipinos to the idea that there were educational opportunities for any American, regardless of their economic or class backgrounds. Fred Cordova, a Filipino student migrant, argued that "the American educational system was already implanted by 1910 so that these men, who could have come in [to America] as young as seventeen and eighteen, were already part of that American school system where Abe Lincoln was the emancipator and George Washington was the father of the country."[13] Historic tales of patriotic glory, self-reliance, and determination filled the lectures, lessons, and textbooks that teachers provided to students in the Philippines, helping to create what Benedict Anderson has described as an "imagined community" that connected young Filipinos to their American counterparts.[14] For many Filipino students, "all of their heroes . . . were *puti* (white) . . . they felt *puti.*" Filipino students felt "very, very American" and genuinely believed that they were entitled to the same opportunities as Americans, including access to colleges and universities in the United States.[15] A college education in the United States was more than a chance for economic and class advancement for Filipinos; it was a way for them to work hard and prove that they too could follow in the footsteps of Lincoln by fulfilling the American dream of self-sufficiency. To succeed through hard work was the essence of what it meant to be an American for many young Filipinos, and this definition of "American" drew them to the United States in search of an education.

In order to pay for their dreams, male Filipino students often acquired summer jobs in the canneries to help cover tuition, room, and board for the following school year. Typically, a summer work season would begin in early June and end in late August, just in time for the workers to strip off their overalls and don their scholarly attire once more. They would receive approximately $150 in pay for three months' work, as well as transportation to and from the work site, meals, and lodging. Lured by the promise of a decent wage and an all-expenses-paid trip to Alaska, students would sign up in groups with the local labor contractor, attempting to make the journey and work environment more hospitable by surrounding themselves with college buddies. Velasco often traveled to Alaska with a group of University of Washington and Washington State University journalism students committed to sharpening their skills by writing informal reports for each other on the labor conditions in the canneries. Despite the terrible stories of life in the canneries, many students did not have many choices when it came to earning their keep while far from their families. They could tolerate three short summer months as well as cramped boats and run-down bunks, so long as they came one year closer to a college degree.

But the summer days proved to be anything but short, with many Filipino students pushing on through work conditions that proved all of the rumors of life in the canneries to be true. One of the major problems that Filipinos and all cannery employees faced was corruption among labor contractors hired by the cannery owners to drum up workers along the West Coast. Reports from individual cannery employees as well as investigations into labor conditions in the canneries by unions and the National Recovery Administration (NRA) in 1934 and 1935 revealed a tacit form of indentured servitude in Alaska. Although Filipinos composed a large portion of the work force in the canneries after the Asian Exclusion Acts, many labor contractors were Chinese, Japanese, Filipino, or white and gained a reputation for corruption and exploitation.[16]

Ponce Torres explained that by the end of May, labor contractors would begin to gather around local hangouts, looking for students and particularly recent Filipino migrants to sign up for cannery work and promising "a chance to go [to Alaska] so long as we went along with their techniques."[17]

Such "techniques" consisted of packing ships headed to Alaska full with employees (often 500 to a ship that had a maximum capacity of 250, leaving the contractors to split the extra money for steerage with the ship captain) and forcing laborers to buy food tickets that would increase their transportation debts. One cannery worker later explained that the Filipino workers were "packed like sardines . . . [with] no space to move around" on the *North Sea* ship.[18] The contractors also provided cigarettes, alcohol, and gambling opportunities to employees in exchange for extended contracts or additional debt. Contractors also used sexual exploitation and prostitution of workers in exchange for back payments and garnished wages. In many instances, contractors would make "wives" of some of their workers, taking the laborer's pay for sexual services as well as debts.[19] Torres described the ways in which Filipino and other Asian employees suffered the most on the trips to Alaska, crammed and squeezed into steerage and given the white employees' and contractors' leftover scraps (or, in one instance, only bones). Not only were the labor contractors cruel and predatory, they often showed favoritism to employees from their own ethnic group and bestowed discriminatory treatment on others.[20]

Racism in the workplace and in larger communities was also a fact of life for migrant laborers. Filipinos who worked in the canneries often migrated throughout the West Coast during the off months, searching for other forms of employment in areas of central California, Oregon, and the Yakima Valley of Washington State. Discrimination against Filipinos existed in both legal and social forms in communities such as Watsonville and Stockton, California (two of the areas in California with the largest Filipino populations) and was a shock for Filipinos who were "all of a sudden . . . slammed into the wall called American racism." Similar to the surprise that Chinese and Japanese students experienced when arriving in the United States, Bacho was also shocked at the less-than-warm welcome he and other Filipinos received from Americans along the West Coast. He lamented that "it was hard to make contact with the Americans because they seemed to feel that we were a different kind of people and they could not deal with us . . . unless [we] were working for them." Torres also found himself in cannery work before he had the opportunity to graduate, having realized that Filipinos "were not given a chance to deal with American society." Signs stating "Positively No Filipinos Allowed" were indicative of the blatant racism, discrimination, and segregation common in West

Coast communities and forced Filipinos to learn the hard way "that [white Americans] hated us, especially when they harmed us physically."[21]

White inhabitants of Alaska expressed discontent with the large number of Filipino and other Asian cannery workers entering their territory during the 1920s and 1930s. S. O. Calder, deputy marshal for the Bristol Bay region of Alaska, told a reporter in 1922 that "seventy percent of all the insane that Alaska is supporting come out of the salmon canneries and practically all of that seventy percent comes from the Chinese gangs." About a "dozen insane" were left up in Alaska every year from the cannery crews, and while Calder believed that most of the insane were "Mexicans and other Latins [*sic*] who go crazy from the marihuana weed, or booze, or venereal disease," he insisted that "we want Alaska made safe for white cannery hands, not a dumping ground for all the cheap labor from the states." Similarly, a former commissioner for Dillingham, Alaska, W. S. Craig, credited the Chinese labor contractors and Asian crews with "selling booze to our natives and taking their last dollar," while resident Dan Sutherland insisted that "we want white men sent up here to help colonize Alaska instead of Asian and minority workers." Later in 1938, after the majority of Chinese and Japanese cannery workers were replaced with Filipinos, Republican Party member Frank Foster submitted an article to the *Alaskan Fishing News* in which he vowed to fight for an "Alaska for Alaskans" and prevent the "Filipino union" (CWFLU) from stealing jobs by passing a law to prohibit the employment of nonresidents in Alaska. From the early days of the canning industry in Alaska, Asian and minority workers often received unfriendly receptions from white inhabitants of the territory.[22]

Filipino laborers also routinely faced scorn from other Asian groups. In the central valleys of California, Filipinos worked in the lettuce and asparagus fields, helping with the annual harvests and migrating through the state to follow the different crop seasons. As more Filipinos arrived in the United States and congregated in Little Manilas after the 1924 immigration act, Japanese immigrants who practiced truck farming and also worked as migrant laborers in the same fields to supplement their incomes viewed the newcomers suspiciously. Japanese who had lived in the region for decades before the Filipino influx feared unwanted competition for land and wages and also viewed Filipinos as ranking beneath them on a racialized hierarchy (with whites at the top and Filipino laborers at the bottom). As the Japanese workers set out to distance themselves from the transitory, suspect, and supposedly inferior Filipinos, the interethnic conflict culminated in a Filipino boycott of Japanese businesses in Stockton, California, in 1930 after a Japanese father became furious upon hearing of his daughter's relationship with a Filipino laborer. The strike by the Filipino Agricultural Laborers' Association (a union formed in 1937 as part of the Congress of Industrial Organization–backed United Cannery, Agricultural, Packing, and Allied Workers of America) during the lettuce harvest of 1939 in the Sacramento–San Joaquin delta further exacerbated class and ethnic tensions between Japanese and Filipinos. Although the examples of Filipino/Japanese conflict above occurred in one region of California, they were symptomatic of the class and racial discrimination that characterized Filipino life along the West Coast.[23]

Physical violence against Filipino male laborers in communities in central California and parts of Oregon, Washington, and Alaska was the most horrific example of racial discrimination. As Paul Kramer explains, mob violence, including the burning of Filipino quarters and beatings from white males, was primarily the result of perceived competition for agricultural jobs. More pervasive was a belief among local men that Filipinos had voracious sexual appetites that could only be satiated by seducing local white women. Considering that relatively few Filipinas migrated along with Filipino men and that Filipinos believed that they were, in fact, Americans, Filipino men had one of the highest rates of interracial relations with white women of all Asian immigrant groups along the West Coast. Whites in West Coast communities, however, believed that Filipinos cold-heartedly took advantage of white women, often forcing them into prostitution or taxi dancing. Of course, Torres had a different explanation for why young Filipino men ended up in the taxi dance halls with white women, asking, "What could we do? There was nothing there [on the West Coast]. . . . [P]eople would go to town after work and when they were there they would amuse themselves playing pool, dancing, going around with cheap women . . . whores. . . . [T]hat was about the only entertainment they could get."[24]

These suspicions would come to an explosive head in 1930. Violence ignited when a group of local white men attacked a Filipino-run dance hall in Watsonville where white women worked. Although the women enjoyed frequenting the halls either for employment or entertainment, the locals believed that no respectable lady would willingly choose to come within ten feet of a Filipino. After hearing rumors that the Filipino men in charge of the dance establishment prostituted white women, a white mob retaliated by brutally attacking Filipinos in the dead of the night and setting fire to their homes and businesses. Whether motivated by perceived competition for jobs or by competition for white women, the Watsonville scene played out in different communities up and down the West Coast during the 1930s when economic hardships intensified long-simmering racial tensions. This is the world that Filipino students and FSCM members entered when they left the relative security of their campuses and Christian associations.[25]

The horrifying experiences of the Filipino students who worked during the summer did not always elicit sympathy from other FSCM members. Some were concerned that the rumors of student-workers' gambling, drinking, flagrant sexual exploits, and other unchristian behavior harmed the overall reputation of Filipinos in the United States and, ultimately, persuaded Americans that Filipinos were far from respectable or civilized. Living with a form of "triple consciousness" (to borrow from W.E.B. Du Bois and authors such as Juan Flores and Miriam Jimenez Roman), FSCM members who promoted respectability as well as equality were acutely aware of their three identities while in America: Filipino, student, and colonial other.[26] Balancing these three identities could be complicated, and many Filipino students expected their fellow countrymen to assist them in putting their best image forward. FSCM member Luis Quisano argued that Filipinos who misbehaved had "gotten themselves into a great deal of a mess" and now constituted a "real social problem" for other Filipinos in America.[27] Similarly, an editorial from an anonymous student in a 1936 edition of the *Filipino Student Bulletin* encouraged other members to "admit that, by and large, we have been poor ambassadors" while in the United States, prompting Americans to judge the Philippines based on the disgraceful actions of a few rogue student-workers.[28]

The FSCM's emphasis on proper behavior resulted in members blaming student-workers for the prejudice and discrimination that whites directed toward Filipinos. Unemployed FSCM members wrote articles in the *Filipino Student Bulletin* that accused their laboring compatriots of losing focus on their studies and jeopardizing Filipino respectability. These pieces also highlighted the class tensions between the remnants of the elite pensionado class and self-supporting students. In 1925, FSCM President E. J. Carballo, concerned with the negative image of Filipino student-laborers, pleaded for fellow members to "realize more and more the part they must play in the promotion of goodwill between men and nations" and recognize that they "have to deal with those institutions [in America] that endeavor to portray the heart and soul of the Filipino people."[29] *Filipino Student Bulletin* assistant editor Manuel Escarrilla supported Carballo's call to fellow Filipino students but focused on the "failure students" who had "become a burden and a problem to whichever Filipino community they happen to fall into." "A good number of the irresponsible class," Escarrilla continued, "have already raised such serious social and industrial problems, that there have been rumors already in the Congress of the United States of a measure to exclude us from immigration like the rest of the Asiatics . . . cannot our government help the situation by at least paying a little more attention to those who shall henceforth leave our shores?"[30] The working Filipino students were also such troublemakers and failures that they could make it difficult for "more worthy students" to come to the United States to study. Other FSCM members recommended that academically underperforming student-laborers be expelled because "they give the country [the Philippines] a black eye in the University where they enroll," making acceptance among American peers more challenging for successful Filipino students.[31]

Even Charles Hurrey, the director of the CFR, doubted the continuing potential for Filipino students in the United States. In 1929, Hurrey reported in an article for the YMCA's *Intercollegian* that although Filipino migration to the United States had rapidly increased, "far too many unprepared young men have attempted to carry on their education here" and blamed the "full 80% of Filipino students who are self-supporting" for this unfavorable reality. After discussing at length the dangerous and unsavory activities Filipino student-workers engaged in when not on campus, Hurrey concluded "we are not meeting, in four-fifths of the Filipino students in America, a representative class who can hold their own scholastically, socially, or economically with students of other nationalities." The Filipino students' problems, he noted, resulted from their lack of ambition and weak will in the face of temptation rather than any larger economic or racial issues.[32]

Other FSCM members, however, understood the plight of the student-worker and his struggles. Articles from students such as Hamay elicited responses from subscribers of the *Filipino Student Bulletin* who denounced judgmental attitudes and snobbery in the organization. Dominador B. Ambrosio, an assistant editor for the *Bulletin*, conceded that "a good number of Filipino students have undoubtedly failed, in the scholastic sense of the word, to complete an academic course," but insisted that "this should not carry a stigma, nor should it be made the butt for sneer or ridicule."[33] Another FSCM member suggested that the Filipino student-worker served as an opportunity to analyze the current socioeconomic relationship between "the student and the non-student" in Filipino communities in America, explaining that the more pretentious FSCM members "think that just because a man cannot express himself in good English or just because he is not identified with any one college or university he is not fit to be associated with."[34] In this sense, the student-workers represented a unique opportunity to examine structural racism along the West Coast, similar to the surveys conducted by the JSCA and CSCA.

FSCM member and Berkeley student A. Almonte was perhaps one of the strongest advocates for student-workers in his organization. In his 1924 *Bulletin* article "The Filipinos in San Francisco," Almonte set out to dispel the "cruel accusations" levied against Filipino workers by other students. He used the tensions between working-class and wealthier Filipinos to promote what he believed to be the true message of the FSCM and Christians in general: friendship and understanding across class and other boundaries. Almonte noted that many of these Filipinos came to America with "high and noble purposes in life" and unfortunately fell upon hard times by no fault of their own. Along with suggesting that Filipino students "study carefully and intelligently the supposedly unclean life of his countrymen in San Francisco and befriend them first of all," he also scolded other FSCM members for forgetting an important verse from the book of Matthew in the Bible: "Judge not, that ye not be judged." Intent on reaching out to working-class Filipinos, he encouraged other FSCM members to become mentors to the laborers "so they might become better citizens possessed of Christian spirit and character." "Christianizing" the Filipino student-worker resembled few of the more activist-oriented resolutions and suggestions passed by the JSCA and CSCA, but Almonte's piece highlights class tensions between members of the FSCM that did not always appear in the *Bulletin* or in other organizational writings.[35]

Emerging Student Activists

The student-worker FSCM member represented a cross-class position and a connection with the larger Filipino working-class community that other members did not always experience or appreciate. While the FSCM existed to protect the interests of students, this same protection did not always extend to those who spent two to three months of the year away from campus living in a more hostile environment. Although student-workers were able to find some support among fellow FSCM members, their (wrongfully or rightfully) negative reputations forced them to search for acceptance and understanding elsewhere. Student-laborers in the FSCM embraced the Christian ideas of their student organizations but also understood that labor rights were crucial to the promotion and protection of Filipinos and other minority workers. Many working-class FSCM members carried the ideas of fellowship and interethnic/interracial cooperation with them to the worksite but developed ways to achieve their goals of racial equality and labor rights outside of the *Bulletin* or other FSCM venues.

Creating company newspapers and distributing information on problems and issues among the different canneries became a way for FSCM members to build labor-specific networks. Filipino students who worked during the summer were some of the first to report on the racist working conditions that characterized life in Alaska. In fact, journalism students such as Victorio Velasco created company newsletters, an activity that allowed them to share experiences with other student-workers, gain journalistic experience, and call attention to discrimination. Although reports of social activities, events, and gossip were staples of these periodicals, special articles describing the racism among cannery employers and supervisors were often front-page news.

The student editors of the *Chomly* [*sic*] *Spectator*, for example, devoted the first page of their July 13, 1929, edition to denouncing a segregationist policy developed by the employers at the Chomley cannery in Alaska. After white employees blamed Filipinos for spreading meningitis in the camp, Filipinos were quarantined and placed under strict supervision without any health checks or clear evidence that they carried the disease. "In Chomley, where Filipinos stationed for work are declared and found free of the disease by the Seattle Health Officers before they come," editor Emeterio Cruz explained, "our white workers still fear our contact." Cruz lamented that, despite the fact that "impure air and unsuitable food given to steerage passengers" were the primary causes of the disease among any employee regardless of color, the employers blamed the "natural unsanitariness" of the Filipino workers for the outbreak and issued a "prohibitive order" that called for immediate discharge of any white employee found among the "Oriental quarters" of the cannery.[36] Although the policy of the cannery employers appeared to punish whites more than the Asian employees, the Filipinos found the order discriminatory and insulting. A July 28 edition of the *Spectator* followed up on the incident and was more direct in its criticism of the superintendent's decision:

> If there is any real importance in the publication of this paper, it is to attain friendship between the White and Brown[37] populace of Chomley.... To this, *The Spectator* is religiously devoted and is champion of it without fear of contradiction of any kind. We recommend that freedom and rights of contact be given to both the Whites and the Browns. We abhor the idea of social seclusion as a breeder of personal, if not national, hatred. This is the cardinal point of importance for both peoples.[38]

While Cruz protested against this specific instance of discrimination, he also touched on the larger subject of racism in the canneries. Cruz identified the segregation policies as a breeding ground of hatred at the cannery and on the national level. (See figure 2.)

The student-workers' response consisted of a call for the protection of civil rights and an attack on what the historian Natalia Molina has described as "medicalized nativism."[39] During the early twentieth century in port cities such as Seattle and Los Angeles, whites often accused Asian and Latino immigrants of carrying germs and diseases to America, endangering all inhabitants upon their arrival. In 1928, the city government of Seattle attempted to limit Filipino immigration to the city when 339 Filipinos were exposed to meningitis, touching off a wave of anti-Filipino sentiment.[40] As Cruz explained in his article, whites overlooked the structural issues such as a lack of public sanitation services and contaminated water that often contributed to outbreaks of tuberculosis and typhoid fever. Instead, many blamed the immigrants' so-called "uncivilized," "backward," and "unhygienic" practices for spreading disease throughout the cities, leaving Asians and Latinos open to racial attacks and discriminatory legislation designed to protect the general public.[41] Cruz and the other Filipino employees also attacked the belief that they were less than American and somehow dirtier and more prone to diseases. Since the *Filipino Student Bulletin* served as the primary source of communication and network building for FSCM members, the student editors of the cannery papers applied the same strategies in Alaska. Students such as Cruz used their journalistic experience as well as their

FIGURE 2. *The Chomly Spectator* 1 (1), July 13–29, 1929. University of Washington Libraries, Special Collections, UW36377.

vision of themselves as Americans who deserved respect to challenge the supervisors' denial of their rights in Chomley.

Almost immediately after the supervisors at Chomley prohibited contact between whites and Filipinos, another incident involving a group of missing local girls created more unrest among the employees. Once again, the *Spectator* and Filipino students covered the developments of the story and described their growing displeasure with the racism in the canning industry. An "Extra! Extra!" edition of the *Spectator* on Monday, July 29, featured a front-page story with the headline "Natural Rights in Danger." As the article described, supervisors placed Filipino workers on lockdown after locals from Chomley reported a group of young Native American women missing. Those who reported the incident to the local law officials and the cannery supervisors recalled that they had last seen the women with a group of "brown" men who appeared to be cannery workers. Eventually, officials found the "missing" women (who failed to report home by curfew), but the cannery supervisors still punished the Filipino workers with another restrictive policy. As the article explained, the new order prohibited contact between Filipinos and local women as well as ensured that "no walking with the girls or going to their places" would be allowed. The weekly or monthly dances that were held at the cannery and attended by employees of all races and ethnicities as well as local Native American women were also now considered punishable offenses (either through denial of employment for the following season or a fine).[42]

Although the Filipino employees were vexed by the discontinuance of one of their main forms of entertainment, students expressed a deeper concern for basic rights. In the "Natural Rights" editorial, Cruz and assistant editor Jose Blando argued that "as [part] of a group identified with this affair, we are more concerned with the matter . . . and consider the order as the most daring and restrictive attempt to ever lay on the way of man's enjoyment of his natural rights." As the "mouthpiece and spokesmen for the whole Oriental group" at the Chomley cannery, Cruz and Blando declared that "it will be both a mistake and a failure on our part if we let this order go unnoticed and stay unanswered," urging others to join in protesting the prohibition of Filipino and Native American mixing.[43]

Not only did the editors denounce the segregationist polices of the Chomley cannery, but they also insisted that rights guaranteed by the US Constitution were basically natural rights guaranteed to all men, regardless of race or nationality. While the cannery employers only restricted the rights of the Filipino workers to date Native American women, Cruz and Blando read this policy in context with the racist reaction to the meningitis outbreak and found a pattern of denial of the human right to speak and interact freely. The "right to happiness" was indeed a broadly defined form of a civil/natural right and reflected the youthful idealism of many of the student-workers. However, the discussion of natural rights would further galvanize the students in labor and civil rights movements. More importantly, the editors concluded that the only way to combat the discrimination and rights violations was to unite all workers together to form an interracial bond, which would include white, Filipino, and other workers such as the Japanese and the small number of African Americans. As the largest group of minority employees at Chomley, the Filipino students used the meningitis and Native American women incidents as well as the *Spectator* to call attention to the racism that plagued the canneries.

For Cruz, Blando, and other FSCM members who worked in Alaska, solidarity and organizing were not always choices but rather the only options for improving their lives as student-laborers. Unfortunately, many Filipino students who labored in the canneries found themselves with little money for room, board, and tuition in the fall. Without sufficient finances after exploitation and poor pay, remaining in the United States as a college student was impossible for financial and personal reasons. For Ponce Torres, returning to the Philippines was simply unthinkable. Not only was he "completely broke" and "had no way of going home," but Torres also explained that he was "ashamed to go home without going through school" and that he knew he was going to stay in the United States because "he had no face to go back." "You see," Torres continued, "if you go home without any change at all—without money or an education—it would be *nakababain* [shameful]." A variety of social, economic, and personal factors forced former students who had left universities and colleges to remain in the United States, making labor organization an important avenue to labor and civil rights when their Christian associations failed in achieving these goals.[44]

Between the racial discrimination, the unfair working conditions, the brutal violence, and the indentured servitude, Filipino employees in the cannery industry decided that they had reached their breaking point by the early 1930s. This was not the first time that employees attempted to unionize the cannery industry. Other ethnic groups previously turned their frustrations with working conditions into a semblance of labor solidarity with limited effect. In 1867 and again in 1877, Chinese employees in Alaskan canneries had attempted to organize and strike for better wages and job stability, but their efforts resulted in a piece-rate system of pay that benefited the labor contractors more than the employees.[45] By the time of the Depression, the unsuccessful history of cannery organization created an atmosphere of doubt in the ability of a multiethnic and multiracial group of workers to join together. Fortunately, students who originally publicized the climate of racial humiliation in Chomley along with other employees recognized that civil rights were directly connected to the promotion of labor rights, producing a shift in the goals and purpose of organizing. As labor leader Ponce Torres explained, "Our last resort was to fight back . . . we learned to fight back, organized ourselves into unions . . . we wanted to organize to combat against white people who were beating us up and to raise the wages of our people and to get the public to sympathize with us."[46]

However, developing an effective labor group that would represent all members of the industry was a challenge, particularly for idealistic student-laborers who desired to apply their ideas of Christian fellowship and solidarity in the workplace. Early talks of forming a new cannery union reflected the difficulties in organizing as well as the lofty goals of the students. A group of Filipino students originally met in 1932 to form a labor organization that would "FIGHT RACE DISCRIMINATION ANYWHERE . . . and to seek through proper legislation in the State legislatures and Congress the general betterment of Filipino laborers in the U.S. . . . as well as improvements in their social, economic, and political status," but it failed to gain enough support from non-Filipino employees.[47] The vague mission of ending race discrimination wherever it may be found reflected the broad and often abstract ideas of the FSCM members. The students' still-born attempts at connecting broad ideas of natural rights to labor rights reflected the classic miscommunications between the student Christian associations and the more working-class members of larger communities. Even though Filipino student-workers were closer to manual laborers than other members of the Christian associations, they faced initial difficulties in applying their desire to end prejudice to labor situations.

In contrast, the CWFLU began as a series of conversations among a group of Alaskeros and student-laborers who temporarily settled in Seattle at the end of the season in October 1933. In pool halls and cafes, dormitories and flophouses, Trinidad Rojo, Tony Rodrigo, Aurelio Simon, Joe Mislang, Frank Alonzo, and Virgil Duyungan (all but Duyungan and Rodrigo were University of Washington students and members or former members of the FSCM) met to discuss what they could do as laborers to address the wretched working conditions and blatant racism of the canning industry. With the help of other members (including Victorio Velasco) who spent many cold days during the winter of 1932 drumming up support for the organization on the streets of Seattle, the American Federation of Labor (AFL) officially granted a charter to the CWFLU in June 1933 at the beginning of the season. The 120 mostly Filipino union members voted Duyungan and Simon as their leaders and attacked their first major problem: the corrupt and dangerous labor contractors.[48]

But the fight against contractors proved to be difficult starting point for the CWFLU. The Filipino contractors were a powerful group and held sway over the Filipino workers they exploited. One of the most prominent Filipino labor contractors in the canneries was Pio De Cano, a Seattleite and prominent member of the Filipino community who donated hundreds of dollars to charities, Filipino benevolent associations, Filipino community newspapers, and scholarships. Some CWFLU members who were ardently anti-contractor when it came to dealing with Chinese, Japanese, or white contractors held a more favorable view of the Filipino contractors who supported their education. Victorio Velasco was a follower of De Cano and even worked on his newspapers along with fellow CWFLU and FSCM member Trinidad Rojo. Also, the Filipino contractors showed favoritism to workers who migrated from their own hometowns or regions from the Philippines, creating regional conflicts within the Filipino ranks. As a result, early elections for various positions within the union were often volatile. The disorganization of the CWFLU also resulted in rival Filipino "unions" such as the Filipino Labor Association (a group that resembled more of a fraternal or benevolent order than a labor organization) that competed for members. While the CWFLU struggled to undermine the contractor system (which was formally ended by the NRA's Code of Competition for the salmon industry in 1934, but continued to operate informally in the canneries), it ultimately failed early on to forge solidarity among all Filipino laborers, let alone create interethnic or interracial connections.[49]

Amid a struggle against the powerful contractors and the failure to create solidarity, the CWFLU faced an unthinkable tragedy in 1936, just three short years after its beginning. On December 1, the nephew of a noted labor contractor invited Duyungan and Simon to dinner at a Japanese café in Seattle, claiming he wanted to discuss the CWFLU's plans for abolishing the contracting system. As soon as Duyungan and Simon arrived, the nephew shot and killed both men, leaving the CWFLU leaderless and its members stunned and deeply saddened. Those two fatal shots could have destroyed whatever existed of a labor-based Filipino rights movement, but the CWFLU members picked themselves up after the funeral for the slain leaders and installed former University of Washington student and FSCM member Irineo Cabatit as president.[50] Instead of dwelling solely on the issue of demolishing the contractor system, Cabatit and Conrad Espe (a white member of the union) encouraged members to focus on broader goals, including promoting interracial cooperation and ending discrimination on the shop floor and in communities.[51]

Despite the trauma of losing important leaders, the CWFLU benefited from the implementation of the 1935 National Labor Relations (or Wagner) Act. Under Section 7, the National Labor Relations Board (NLRB) recognized and guaranteed the rights of laborers to form unions and engage in collective bargaining with their employers. The impact of this New Deal provision reverberated throughout the world of labor relations, creating new opportunities for workers as well as new tensions between organizers and employers. With Section 7 in place, the Pacific Northwest and Alaska became active and often volatile sites of union activism, particularly by the CIO-supported International Longshoremen's and Warehousemen's Union in the Seattle shipping industry. Although the AFL initially backed the CWFLU, by 1937, the association joined ranks with the CIO. Section 7 provided a framework for organizing for better wages and working conditions in the salmon industry that did not exist before the Depression. Of greatest importance for the burgeoning CWFLU, the NLRB targeted the contractor system as well as reports from employees of the poor working and living conditions that characterized life in the canneries for employees. As with other unions, the Wagner Act bolstered both the new CWFLU leaders in implementing strategies for change and action among cannery employees.[52]

However, federal labor policies and the Wagner Act alone did not solve all of the problems in the canneries, particularly the issue of ethnic tensions. Cabatit and the other members of the CWFLU realized that while ending the labor contracting system was an important step, building solidarity with other cannery employees was necessary for fighting racial discrimination. Cabatit was the first CWFLU president to make uniting the various ethnicities in the canneries a priority. Building a unified organization out of a multiracial and multiethnic workforce was a traditionally challenging goal since the earliest days of the industry, but also a goal that FSCM members and former students embraced. The Filipino members of the CWFLU set out to convince the Chinese and Japanese employees that the discriminatory actions of the employers against the Filipinos were proof of a larger racist system in the canneries. While Filipinos formed the largest minority group in the Alaskan cannery industry, the Japanese were also a significant component of the workforce, but relations between the Japanese and Filipinos were often strained.[53] Japanese employees often benefited from associating with a foreman or labor contractor who was also Japanese and did not necessarily see the need for the Filipinos' push to end the system. Also, antagonisms between Japanese and Filipino cannery workers often spilled over into everyday interactions between Filipino laborers and Japanese cannery foremen.

Ethnic tensions between the two groups of employees heightened when either a Japanese or Filipino obtained a position of power in the canneries. In 1937, a group of CWFLU- affiliated Filipino workers from the Astoria and Puget Sound Canning Company, located at Excursion Inlet, Alaska, wrote a letter to Cabatit and the other leaders of the CWFLU expressing their concern over the anti-Filipino and anti-union attitudes of two Japanese foremen at the plant. The workers charged the Japanese foremen with "favoritism" and creating "poor working conditions," but they were most appalled when these two foremen called the CWFLU a "f—k union" and snarled that "union or no union, we will always get our jobs as foremen anyhow."[54] The workers urged the executive board of the CWFLU to take "immediate action" but did not specify what form the action should take. While there is the possibility that the workers exaggerated their claims against the Japanese foremen, the petition reflected the animosity between Japanese and Filipino workers.

The greatest struggle for the CWFLU in overcoming ethnic tensions was the competition from a Japanese union. Clarence Arai was a Japanese former student from the University of Washington and JSCA member who labored in the canneries during the summers and later became a powerful lawyer for many of the Japanese contractors. Arai was a respected leader in Seattle who advocated for the rights of the Japanese community, but he assumed a different role in the canning industry. He inflamed ethnic antagonisms between the Japanese and Filipinos by advocating for a rival, all-Japanese labor union to compete with the CWFLU (naturally, Arai insisted on serving as the leader for the proposed union).[55] Arai also claimed that the CWFLU was infiltrated with communists and other radicals in hopes of luring potential Japanese members away from a "red" union. The charges of radicalism as well as Arai's accusations that Rojo discriminated against African American and Japanese employees and mishandled union funds placed the CWFLU in a difficult position. Arai's claims that there may have been Filipino CWFLU members who instigated fights with the Japanese or former Filipino contractors and foremen who were guilty of favoring their own ethnic group over others were not completely unfounded, considering the sour relations between both groups. Also, the mishandling of funds and discrimination were difficult for the CWFLU to deny. In the early days of the union, CWFLU members who ran for elected positions would often levy charges (sometimes true, other times not) of corrupt money handling against competing candidates, while a 1937 incident involving two white CWFLU workers who refused to travel or live with "Orientals" or African Americans in the cannery was fodder for Arai's cries of discrimination.[56] In general, Arai took advantage of the rocky relationship between Japanese and Filipino workers in order to undermine the influence of the CWFLU.

Espe, Cabatit, and CWFLU leaders Sebastian Abella (an FSCM member) and A. B. Bigornia responded to Arai's threats by bolstering the organization's potential for interracial and interethnic solidarity. On February 11, 1937, Abella, Bigornia, and Espe hosted a special meeting to stress the benefits of joining and supporting the CWFLU to Japanese workers. While Espe set out to "clarify and enlighten" the Japanese employees on the "erroneous" message that Arai had spread, Abella and Bigornia emphasized that the union "was not only for Filipinos, but for all races regardless of religious creeds or political affiliations." Any attempt from Arai or the cannery employers to "split the organization by separate charter based on race prejudice [was] futile and wrong."[57] All three union leaders also called attention to the new CWFLU charter, which explicitly stated that the organization welcomed all members and did not discriminate based on "color, creed, or religion."[58]

The emphasis of the CWFLU leaders on interethnic solidarity in the industry was also representative of the larger goals of the student associations. While FSCM members who remained on campus were often uninterested in the plight of the student-worker or more concerned with Christian fellowship and respectability, Rojo, Abella, and others connected with their fellow workers. Such opportunities were not widely available to those students who did not venture forth into the working-class world, demonstrating the limits of the tactics and goals of the student associations. The labor activism of the FSCM members was not characterized by the same emphasis on Christian principles and ideas, but the emphasis on publicizing violations of rights, advocating for broad cooperation, and building action on discussion was similar to some of the strategies of the JSCA, CSCA, and FSCM. These would continue to become important principles for the CWFLU as more students obtained leadership positions.

Later in February, Bigornia held a successful meeting to resist Arai and lay to rest the tensions between Japanese and Filipino workers. The "express attempt" of the meeting was to "enlighten the minds of our Japanese brothers that our UNION bars racial discrimination . . . and to cast away the confusion created by Mr. Arai in propagandizing and stigmatizing our Japanese group to make them an isolated race." According to Bigornia, the "main issue of the evening, however, was to give Mr. Arai a chance to appear and express his viewpoints regarding the cannery labor situation for the next coming Alaska season." Espe and Bigornia extended an invitation to Arai as well as Japanese employees to come to the CWFLU-sponsored meeting and explain their positions to the whole union with "the assurance that he be given a democratic hearing." Arai failed to respond to the invitation and did not appear at the meeting that evening, leaving Bigornia and the group to identify him as "a man devoid of principle." In addition to exposing Arai's rejection of large-scale and interethnic activism in the industry, the CWFLU succeeded in drawing a "great number of Japanese brothers" to the meeting. Espe and Bigornia fielded questions from potential Japanese members "regarding doubts and confusions pertaining to the stand and purpose of the union" and highlighted the broad appeal of the organization to all workers. Although the letter did not state how successful the union was in persuading all Japanese at the meeting to become members, Bigornia explained that "everything seemed to have been ironed out," and the CWFLU appeared to have made a strong inroad with the Japanese employees.[59]

The formal discussions with Japanese workers were an opportunity for the CWFLU to bolster its image as an all-inclusive organization rather than solely a Filipino labor/civil rights group. By meeting with the Japanese, the leaders of the CWFLU initiated the first steps in correcting the longstanding problem of ethnic distance that plagued previous unionization attempts. As a follow-up to the meeting, Cabatit issued an official statement in April 1937 to all employees and the general public clarifying that the CWFLU was a "democratic union open to all cannery workers, irrespective of race, color or creed," where "Japanese, Chinese, Filipinos,

Negroes, and whites [were] all welcome to be members of [the] union" so long as they were employed in either the canneries or another form of agricultural labor.[60] Cabatit was firm in his declaration that "Japanese, as well as other racial groups, have equal standing in our union ... THERE IS NO RACE DISCRIMINATION IN OUR UNION." To demonstrate the potential of the CWFLU as an interracial organization and possibly to play on Arai's rumors that the CWFLU was infiltrated by communists, the letter concluded with a rousing call for "WORKERS OF ALL RACES STAND UNITED!"[61] Cabatit's letter rallied workers and also reflected an application of FSCM and Christian association goals to labor problems and race relations beyond campus.

In addition to building activist networks among the various ethnicities and races in the canneries, Cabatit and the other leaders also recognized the passion of other Filipino student-laborers for various causes. Of primary concern for CWFLU members was House Bill 301, initially proposed by the Washington state legislature in 1936 to prohibit interracial marriage. The most offensive language in the bill was found in Section 2, which stated that "all marriages of white persons hereafter performed or solemnized in the state of Washington with negroes, Mongolians, or Oceanics as herein defined [would be deemed] illegal and void."[62] The proposed law was similar to other anti-miscegenation bills along the West Coast that targeted marriages between white women and Japanese, Chinese, and Filipino men. The CWFLU rallied the union members to send delegations, write letters, and draft petitions to defeat the discriminatory piece of legislation, but student-workers (including Cruz, Blando, and other FSCM members and former members) did not forget the incident involving prohibitions on interactions with local females in Chomley or their protests against violations of natural rights. Interracial relationships were already pertinent topics for students in the canneries; the CWFLU's job by 1937 was to turn that youthful clamor for protection against discriminatory treatment into organized action against the racism inherent in HB 301.[63]

In February 1937, Cabatit and fellow CWFLU/FSCM member Antonio Rodrigo, formed a special "Youth Section" of the union to help rally college students and cannery workers in protesting the HB 301. During the regular membership meeting in February, Rodrigo (who was chairman of the committee) reported that the youth committee was "busy fighting the intermarriage bill now pending in the state legislature" by raising funds to support a "youth caravan to go to Olympia on March 2nd" to protest the bill. At the meeting, Rodrigo encouraged "everyone who can afford to come to lobby the said Bill which, as planned, discriminates colored people to marry white women in the State."[64] By forming the special youth committee, Cabatit and Rodrigo organized approximately one hundred student cannery workers to help the CWFLU tackle HB 301. Since many of the student-workers were also active in other organizations on campus and in their larger communities (such as the FSCM and other Filipino associations based in Seattle and other cities), they were important in spreading the message about the looming piece of legislation among the canneries as well as on college campuses. Cabatit and Rodrigo's plans for involving the students in the struggle not only supported the role of the students in the union's civil rights efforts but also ultimately helped to kill HB 301: Washington legislators never passed the bill, thanks to the joint efforts of the CWFLU and other civil rights organizations in the state. Cabatit, Rodrigo, and other members of the CWFLU understood the power of student activists both within and outside of the union and succeeded in applying the often abstract goals of the FSCM to broader political and social rights campaigns.

The Yakima Incident and the CWFLU

The real test of the CWFLU's commitment to civil as well as labor rights and the students' ability to tackle these issues, however, came in 1937 in Washington's Yakima Valley. After a decade of simmering tensions, Yakima whites launched discriminatory campaigns against Filipino agricultural workers in the region to drive them out of the area. Two instances occurred during the tense winter of that year which resulted in the CWFLU taking a prominent stand against such action. The first involved the Yakima law officials' confiscation of property that Filipino members of the CWFLU who owned or tenant-farmed portions of land on the Toppenish Indian Reservation in 1927. Similar to California's 1913 Act that attempted to end competition with Japanese farmers, Washington's Alien Land Law of 1919 also prohibited aliens ineligible for naturalization from purchasing and owning land. While Washington's 1919 anti-alien law targeted Japanese, Filipinos, who were American subjects at the time, did not technically fall under the category of immigrants. The United States recognized Filipinos as American nationals in the 1920s, and with this title, Filipinos successfully purchased land before and after the implementation of the various alien land laws. Filipinos also became sharecroppers on Japanese-owned portions of the Yakima Indian Reservation (since this was not technically US property), allowing them to form cooperatives.[65]

The national status and purchasing power of the CWFLU members remained intact until 1934 when the US enacted the Tydings-McDuffie Act. This measure was largely a response to growing white-Filipino violence along the West Coast and reclassified the Philippines as a commonwealth, making Filipinos aliens ineligible for citizenship and subject to the 1924 quotas. Congress followed the Tydings-McDuffie Act by passing the Filipino Repatriation Act of 1935, which reinforced the Filipinos' new alien status by encouraging and providing financial assistance to those wishing to return to the Philippines. The Immigration and Naturalization Service publicized repatriation in Filipino communities in cities like San Francisco, Seattle, Stockton, and Los Angeles, emphasizing that those who chose to return to the Philippines would not be able to reenter the United States "except as a quota immigrant." The repatriation experience was largely a failure in the sense that only around two thousand Filipinos (mostly men from California who were not destitute) returned between 1936 and 1941, but the message was clear: Filipinos were not and never would be welcome in the United States. Filipino laborers had always garnered negative attention from many white Americans who regarded them as unsavory influences on their communities; however, the legislation of 1934 and 1935 codified these anti-Filipino attitudes and supported racism under the guise of foreign affairs and imperial politics.[66]

The Yakima Filipinos' new identity as aliens made it more difficult for them to maneuver around the Washington Alien Land Law. When Filipinos lost both the ability to migrate freely between the Philippines and the United States and their "national" status after 1934, white residents were able to use legal means to justify their long-held hatred of Filipinos. Following the Tydings-McDuffie Act, the State of Washington amended the previous land law in 1937 to prohibit "all non-citizens ineligible for citizenship" from owning property, targeting all Asian migrants including Filipinos. While Pio De Cano would ultimately lead a successful fight in overturning the 1937 amendment to the land law (which was declared unconstitutional by the Washington Supreme Court in 1941), the immediate effects of the provision on the Yakima Filipinos were devastating. After a new Washington State bill passed later in 1937 outlawed cropping contracts for those "ineligible to citizenship by naturalization," Yakima officials seized the property of the Filipino CWFLU members soon after and auctioned off the land to the highest bidder.[67] Yakima County then charged six of the Filipinos with perjury (for lying under oath by claiming they were Americans), two with violation of the alien land law, and one with assault after resisting arrest.

Later that year, conflicts between laborers and employers in Yakima created similar problems. A group of fifty CWFLU members employed on William Beauchane's hop farm asked for a raise to compensate for the $.65 that Beauchane deducted from their wages for room and board. After the deductions, employees were left $1.00 for a twelve- to fourteen-hour day (depending on the workload). Having grown weary of Beauchane's exploitative practices, the Filipino workers applied the principles of the CWFLU to their situation and demanded fair compensation for their work as well as a release from the credit/debit style of pay that Beauchane utilized. The CWFLU members on Beauchane's farm rose up to challenge a corrupt labor relationship and demand justice. In response, Beauchane, a group of white employees, members of the Hops Growers' Association in Yakima County, and the Yakima County Highway Patrol forced the Filipino employees to flee the county on foot, chasing them down the road in cars and trucks and warning them to never again show their faces in Yakima.[68]

Cabatit wasted no time responding to the events and calling on all union members and West Coast communities to recognize the assault on civil rights in Yakima. The CWFLU partnered with the Filipino Defense Committee (a special interest group formed in direct response to the Yakima incidents) in issuing a joint resolution on behalf of the Yakima Filipinos, claiming that they were "subjects owing allegiance to the United States Government, and therefore, [were] not aliens and entitled to these lands." The CWFLU described the officials' confiscation of the Filipinos' property as "flagrant proof that these brothers [were] being abused and being robbed of their civil rights to life, liberty, and happiness." The Yakima officials had engaged in a "vicious violation of civil liberties . . . [that] constitutes a serious threat not only to foreign-born workers, but all workers as well" that reflected the fact that "civil authorities in Yakima have systematically discriminated against Filipino workers in particular" for years.[69] The working conditions of agricultural workers often led to violent clashes between workers, employees, and, in the case of the Yakima Valley, police and community vigilantes. As a result, the CWFLU became more focused on the needs of agricultural workers and saw that the problems these laborers dealt with reflected on a larger loss of civil rights for all minorities. Attaining rights for CWFLU members and all employees merged into one goal for the union during the late 1930s, reflecting the organization's new outlook on its role in labor, politics, and society.

The CWFLU leaders and members also used the Yakima incident to accentuate the failure of New Deal policies to ensure civil rights for minorities in the West. Despite the Wagner Act and the changing landscape of labor activism during the 1930s, many outside (as well as within) the unions did not equate labor rights with civil rights. It was largely left to the laborers to illuminate these connections and fight for equality and justice on both fronts. The CWFLU exposed the contrast between the reality of the Yakima incidents and the rhetoric of economic renewal and social equality that many New Deal supporters supported. In a special "Statement on Yakima Vigilantism," Cabatit and Rojo described Beauchane as a "feudal baron under the present intolerable set-up in Yakima County" who, along with the Hops Growers' Association, "make their own Fascist laws and call upon the tax-supported state highway patrol and private thugs to enforce them." The workers "who were subjected to this vigilante terrorism asked nothing unreasonable nor un-American," but Yakima County and the United States in general had failed to recognize their plight as minorities and exploited laborers in the land of the free.[70] The CWFLU leaders concluded their statement with pointed questions:

> We ask the civil authorities of Yakima County: Where is the New Deal in the state of Washington? Did 26,000,000 people vote for vigilantism and coolie wages when they went to the polls last November? The People of Washington demand that the New Deal be imported to Yakima and that the civil authorities there . . . enforce at least the bare minimum of civil rights to which every workingman in the United States is entitled to under the construction of the New Deal.[71]

In their statements regarding the tragedies of the workers from Yakima, Cabatit and fellow CWFLU member and FSCM leader Trinidad Rojo made it clear that they believed in access to basic American liberties for all laborers, regardless of racial and ethnic identity or citizenship status. This reflects, as Devra Weber describes, the complex relationship between workers and the "economic, social, and political conditions they lived and

labored within."[72] The structure of the New Deal and its labor rights policies did not always succeed, but CWFLU members (as did other workers at the time) used the concepts of economic rights to argue for a broad
consideration of human and civil rights. The rights to a decent wage, racial
equality, and protection from discrimination and violence were all inter-
twined, and if anyone or any group violated one, they violated them all.
The CWFLU criticized New Deal policies for neglecting racial minorities and turning a blind eye toward all agricultural and cannery workers in
Washington and along the West Coast. Anyone who labored in America
had earned basic protections and natural rights, an idea that reflected the
earlier cries for justice found in the write-ups featured in student newspapers and cannery newsletters.

The protests and actions of the CWFLU led to a small, yet memo-
rable victory for the union as well as for Filipinos along the West Coast.
On November 16, 1937, the Filipino workers who were arrested in Yakima
County for perjury, conspiracy, and assault met with prosecutors along
with CWFLU leaders to plead their innocence. Not only did the prosecutors agree to drop the charges, the court also released warrants for the
arrest of more than a dozen white men accused of inflicting mob violence
on the Filipinos.[73] After ten years of persecution of Filipino laborers in
central Washington, the CWFLU had succeeded in helping to provide
justice for its members. Through such actions, the organization made its
mission clear: Filipinos and all workers of various races, ethnicities, and
immigrant status who labored, lived, and contributed to American society were entitled to racial equality and equal protection. The former students and FSCM members worked to promote and protect both labor and
civil rights for racial minorities in a variety of labor settings and helped the
union to mature into an activist organization. These passionate student-
workers also expanded the reach of the Christian associations by venturing
into the larger world and addressing racial discrimination among working-
class minorities.

Conclusions

As current and former students became more active in leadership roles in
the CWFLU, the union continued to take the shape of a civil rights organization during the later 1930s. Fujita-Rony has argued that the late 1930s was

a period when the student "literati" among the union members came into conflict with those cannery workers who did not share in their ideological pursuits or goals.[74] The election of Trinidad Rojo (national vice president of the FSCM when he first became active with the CWFLU) as president of the union in 1939 is often viewed as a turning point for the CWFLU, or the "beginning of the end." The union fell on difficult times during World War II, followed by accusations of communism and red-baiting.[75] Through the 1940s and 1950s, general suspicion of radical and communist infiltration in unions (particularly those whose membership included a large number of immigrants or ethnic and racial minorities) during the height of McCarthyism prompted legislators to respond with laws such as the Immigration and Nationality Act of 1952, which provided for the detainment and deportation of migrants who posed a threat to national security. Like other unions supported by the CIO (before it merged with the American Federation of Labor in 1955), the members and leaders of the CWFLU found themselves defending their ideas and principles against accusations of radicalism and subversion. Such challenges, however, cannot be attributed to Rojo alone but are representative of the larger struggles for unions and labor/civil rights activists at the time.

Rather than a downturn, the elevation of Rojo to the presidency was a culmination of important civil rights initiatives established by Cabatit and other student members of CWFLU. While Rojo gained respect from the workers for leading a strike at a cannery in Kiawak, Alaska, in 1929 (years before the formation of the CWFLU and while Rojo was still a student at the University of Washington), he also quickly earned a reputation for commitment to issues of racial justice. Rojo's position as vice president of the FSCM also challenged that organization's previous stance on student-workers. With a laborer as a leader, the FSCM became less focused on the concerns of the thinning pensionado group and more focused on issues of discrimination against Filipino workers and the problems of Filipino communities in America in general. Rojo's presidency, much like Cabatit's, placed the CWFLU within a growing movement for racial equality along the West Coast, not just for Filipinos, but for all ethnic and racial minorities. Under Rojo's leadership, the CWFLU plunged further into the larger struggle against inequality and discrimination. His work with national civil rights organizations (such as the National Association for the Advancement of Colored People and later the Congress of Racial Equality) characterized much of the activism of the CWFLU during World War II and the

For PRESIDENT
C. W. & F. L. U., Local 7, U. C. A. P. A. W. A., C I O.

T. A. ROJO
A New Dealer and Square Dealer

Summary of Activities:

1. Knows the problems of Cannery Workers. Worked eleven summers in Alaskan canneries.
2. Led a successful strike in Klawak, Alaska, 1929.
3. Technical Adviser to Hon. Francisco Varona, Labor Envoy of President Quezon to U. S., 1938.
4. Helped frame the constitution of C. W. F. L. U., Local 7, U. C. A. P. A. W. A., CIO.
5. Private consultant to V. O. Navea, Business Agent of the Local.
6. Quieted the rebellious spirit of 1500 members of the Union who booed the officials at a meeting May 20, 1939.
7. Forceful speaker, able writer, honest leader.

FIGURE 3. Campaign pamphlet for the election of Trinidad A. Rojo to the position of president of the Cannery Workers' and Farm Laborers' Union, Local 7, undated. University of Washington Libraries, Special Collections, UW36375.

following years. Rojo's commitment to causes as varied as racial justice, the protection of workers around the world, and independence for the Philippines continued the pattern of activism that Cabatit and other members of the FSCM established during the mid- to late 1930s. Although the CWFLU became more fragmented over the years as a result of disagreements on a variety of topics including worker benefits and positions of leadership, Rojo represented the lingering legacy of the idealistic and ambitious goals of the students. As the times and the issues changed, so did the causes that the CWFLU supported. However, the student-workers' recognition of labor rights as civil rights and vice versa ensured the union's continued involvement in interethnic and interracial issues. (See figure 3.)

The contributions of FSCM student-laborers both to the development and guidance of the CWFLU and to West Coast labor and civil rights struggles created a framework for further interracial, interethnic, panethnic, and cross-class movements. The few historians who have noted the role of Filipino students in the organization of the CWFLU have been quick to point to the class tensions that the "college men" brought to the union but have not discussed the ideological contributions that helped to place the organization in the center of social movements during the 1930s. Treated as outsiders within the FSCM, those members who worked to support their educations found brotherhood and purpose in the canneries or agricultural fields and formed relationships with other laborers when they could not find them on campus. These relationships later developed into social and political organizations fueled by the experiences of the students with racism in the canneries as well as the solidarity-building skills and knowledge they gained at school. While the FSCM was not preoccupied with the struggles and problems of the student workers, individual members sought alternative ways to engage in political action outside of YMCA-sponsored conferences and workshops.

The activism of FSCM members such as Rojo and Cabatit demonstrate the potential as well as the limits of the Christian student associations. While the JSCA, CSCA, and FSCM supported noble goals of racial integration and equality, leaders and members focused their energy and Christian ideas on challenging institutional forms of racism on campus and within organizations such as the YMCA. FSCM members who also belonged to the working class stepped beyond these limits and the cherished notions of respectability that often restrained other Christian Filipino students. Student-workers used their education, ideas of Christian and human rights, and desire for change to influence other social movements. The FSCM members who toiled during the summers and later went on to lead the CWFLU juggled multiple identities and straddled class, ethnic, and racial lines—difficult positions for any students to find themselves in, but also opportunities for pushing the boundaries of the Christian associations' influence. Although the FSCM members succeeded in expanding their reach into the realm of labor, the Christian ties of the students would soon be tried as the world plunged into terrifying violence during the late 1930s and 1940s.

4

"A Sweet-and-Sour World"

· ·

The Second Sino-Japanese
War, Christian Citizenship,
and Equality

Heightened international tensions challenged students to balance their
devotion to worldwide equality and Christian fellowship with their transnational ties to their homelands. During the 1930s, Chinese, Filipino, and
Japanese students (both foreign- and American-born) paid rapt attention
to global political and social unrest as a result of new and growing nationalist movements. As dictators gained power in Europe, political and military troubles in Asia also caused increasing concern. Japanese encroach-
ment on Chinese territory in Manchuria would give way to the Second
Sino-Japanese War in 1937, while Filipinos and Americans came to question the imperial relationship between the Philippines and the United
States. These conflicts did not escape the members of the CSCA, FSCM,
or JSCA, who anxiously read the reports on incidents in Asia from across
the Pacific and offered opinions on what one FSCM member described as
the complex "sweet-and-sour world" in which they lived.[1] As these students
were attempting to combat racial inequality while earning their degrees,

transpacific ties potentially threatened their panethnic and interracial movement for racial equality in the United States, given the escalating international tensions. The students, however, did not allow their progress to disintegrate during diplomatic problems. CSCA, FSCM, and JSCA members attempted to look past ethnic conflicts raging in both Asia and the United States by focusing on the sins of imperialism and nationalism. Students argued that these two unchristian "isms" fostered prejudice on a global scale. In turn, many students identified imperialism and voracious nationalism as threats to equality in America and around the world.[2]

However, the Second Sino-Japanese War and the growing threat of Japanese military power during the 1930s led to ethnic clashes among Asian immigrants and Asian Americans. For foreign-born Christian Chinese and Japanese students, rising Chinese and Japanese nationalism during the late 1920s and early 1930s placed them in a difficult position: should they support their homeland or should they hold fast to their Christian beliefs of pacifism, equality, and humility? The topics of nationalism and expansion were also controversial. While some argued that national pride and growth were necessities for economic and political independence, others claimed that Christianity, by its very nature, rejected the notion of dominance of one land or group of people over another (the end product of nationalism). As a result, the military and political conflicts in Asia complicated the principles of brotherhood and cooperation that the students embraced. Although the idea of owing allegiance to a worldwide Kingdom of God appeared plausible during times of peace, this Christian concept of cooperation was more complex and abstract in times of war. What was the place of the students' goals of ending prejudice and ending discrimination within the context of international chaos? Such concerns and questions created conflicts that forced the students to further define their roles as Christians and activists and encouraged association members to return to the idea of cultural and ethnic bridge-building.

This chapter follows the student organizations through the turbulent decade of the 1930s and argues that members used imperialism, nationalism, and inequality to relate racial struggles in America to unchristian events on a global scale. Opinions differed within the organizations on the exact level of incompatibility between the concept of "Christian citizenship" (or allegiance to a worldwide federation of peace rather than any nationalist movement) and nationalism. However, students generally agreed that once humans learned to respect one another and embrace a Christian life, the desire for conquest and oppression would fade. Foreign- and American-born CSCA, FSCM, and JSCA leaders and members organized multiple Oriental student conferences along the West Coast and across the United States and used student bulletins to discuss how political unrest in the Pacific affected their lives in America. In many cases, students maneuvered around the heady topics of ethnic tensions and specific nationalist movements by attacking the larger systems of aggressive nationalism and imperialism. This tactic served as a way to preserve their ties to Asia and their panethnic organizations without forsaking their commitment to Christian principles. A focus on the connections between worldwide political oppression and prejudice also allowed both foreign- and American-born members of the student associations to continue to challenge racism and preserve their interethnic networks. While the students' attempts to reconcile their ideals and the reality of the increasingly violent world they lived in were not always successful (especially with the onset of an all-consuming world war), association members used their Christian goals to make order and sense of the tragedies surrounding them, from a world of warfare to the racial inequality in the United States.

The students combined Christian principles of citizenship to promote human rights abroad and civil rights in the United States. Although historians Mary L. Dudziak and Thomas Borstelmann have argued that a transnational American civil rights movement emerged after World War II, the actions of the students in the 1930s and early 1940s demonstrate an earlier wave of civil rights discussions that adds to our understanding of W.E.B. Du Bois's international "color line."[3] Whereas both Glenda Gilmore and Nico Slate use radical international groups like the Communist Party and cosmopolitan connections between immigrants from India and African Americans (respectively) to highlight a global movement for rights and protections, there remain understudied layers of ideas in the social movements of the interwar years.[4] This chapter builds on this theme of international cooperation by arguing that the students' Christian concepts of nationalism and citizenship also contributed to a growing movement for racial equality and rights along the West Coast. Meetings, discussion groups, and conferences served as opportunities for students to explain how Christianity could offer solutions for Pacific tensions as well as racial inequality. Impending global conflict created new avenues for discourses surrounding old topics (imperialism, colonialism, and racism) among the students but also challenged their ideas and exposed the limits of their interethnic and interracial Christian fellowship.

Christian Citizenship and the Threat of Nationalism

Both the CSCA and JSCA faced challenges in attempting to interpret the actions of their homelands through the lenses of nationalism and Christianity during the 1930s. At times, students expressed a need to proceed carefully so as not to destroy their sense of Christian citizenship. In other instances, the duty of the students to their nations overrode their duties in promoting pacifism. As the students discovered, the path of pure pacifism was difficult to walk when violence put Christian citizenship to the test. While the student Christian associations had clear plans and strategies for building panethnic and interethnic networks and tackling racism in the United States, international politics presented difficult obstacles in achieving such goals. The pan-Asian identity that brought the students together showed signs of fragmentation during the Second Sino-Japanese War.

Christian citizenship was a concept that characterized the world outlook of the students since the earliest days of their organizations. The members of the CSCA, for example, had long held the belief that just as they were citizens of their home countries, they were also citizens of the Kingdom of God. As early as 1913, the CSCA explained that the political duty of a Christian citizen was "fearlessly us[ing] one's political influences for social betterment of the people."[5] Social betterment was a goal for students in improving human relations, be they in China, in the United States, or in the world. Regardless of their nationality, students had a duty as Christians to overlook their national allegiance if it meant serving the greater good. The ideas of Christian citizenship resounded with foreign-born members of the student associations and assisted them in integrating the political and diplomatic goals of Christianity with their work on racial equality in the United States. Peace and goodwill would lead to a godly world as well as an end to political and military strife between nations.

A Christian citizen was also expected to support pacifism, another tenet adhered to by many members of the CSCA. When Wellington Liu attended the annual YMCA Indianapolis Convention in 1924, he was surprised by how many Christian students from various campus organizations were open to the idea of war in order to solve global problems. Liu reported back to his group that whereas he and the other representatives of the CSCA stressed peaceful resolutions to conflicts, the YMCA's student volunteer representatives "are professed Christians, but they are not professed pacifists, although from a Christian point of view, the two terms should be coterminous." Many of the other students in attendance argued, "In certain dire events, particularly those which result in one nation losing influence over its own affairs, war is necessary to maintain a balance in diplomacy." Liu was shocked that Christian students would support war for any reason, especially for maintaining power or control. "So if we acknowledge that war is unchristian and yet hold that in some circumstances we are obliged to take on an unchristian way," Liu pondered, "then either the church is using religion to exploit nationalistic and class ends or the church has only a weak religion upon which, in a crisis, it does not dare to depend. . . . It is high time for us to discontinue our hypocrisy." For Liu, not only were the other students' opinions on the use of war disturbing, but they spoke to a greater need for Christian students to fully understand pacifism as a necessity.[6]

Other Asian students also shared Liu's concerns over the readiness of many Christians to advocate for war. The *Japanese Student Bulletin* often featured articles from JSCA members arguing that a peace movement would override warfare and global oppression. In an anonymous article from 1924, a member reported on the sixth anniversary of the Mobilization Day for World Peace (held on Armistice Day) in the United States and used the peace movement to argue that the "Prince of Peace is coming to the world, slowly but steadily."[7] The author's views were similar to those of the World Student Christian Federation, which, as an organization devoted to creating a federation of Christian students around the globe, emphasized peace and the construction of a "community which transcends nationalism."[8] As organizations connected to the WSCF, members of the JSCA and CSCA shared similar goals of working toward "a total allegiance to a brotherhood which the one Father of us all has created."[9] The devastating results of World War I led many JSCA and CSCA members to view Christian principles of equality as the best foreign policy solution for China, Japan, the United States, and other nations.[10] In situations of political and social unrest around the world, Christian citizenship should trump national citizenship, with nationalism being little more than "an emotional pattern" and "a burning desire to exalt one's own nationality at all costs and by a truculent attitude toward other nations."[11]

But by the late 1920s, rising political and military unrest in Asia strained the relationship between nationalism and Christian citizenship. In Japan, the government turned toward emphasizing military prowess and expansion in all aspects of society, creating a strong and growing nationalist

movement. At the end of World War I, Japan protested the disappointing reception of their ideas for worldwide rights and equality during the
Treaty of Versailles and argued for a pan-Asia front that would remove
Western domination from the Pacific once and for all. Many members of
the JSCA attempted to distance themselves from militarization, explaining that the militarists did not represent all Japanese and certainly did not
reflect the values of Japanese Christians. Ryozo Okumura warned in his
article "The Plight of the Christian Students in Japan" that "the nationalistic tendency of nations after the World War, especially the anti-Japanese
movements and the exclusion legislation of the United States of America,
has strongly affected the Japanese youth and they are saying today that
the Christian brotherhood of yesterday was merely a kind of cheap optimism and that they must now build upon the foundation of true Japanese
spirit—Japanism."[12] The questioning of the practicality and logic of Christianity in an age of nationalist movements was disturbing for Okumura
and signified a new threat to Protestant order and social reform in Japan.
However, Okumura assured his readers that despite the rise in virulent
Japanism, many Christian students still attempted to steer clear of mili-
tant nationalism and strived "to believe that the more practical movement
of 'Love' will rise from within Christianity."[13] As foreign students studying
in the United States, Okumura and other JSCA members used their pens
to challenge Japanese policy from across the Pacific.

Okumura's writings signify an important shift in the relationship of
Protestant Japanese students to the changing political and military atmosphere in their homelands. Prior to these developments, Japanese students
(as noted in chapter 1) often used Christianity to criticize racism in the
United States and the ways in which institutionalized prejudice created
discriminatory American policies. From a Japanese Christian's standpoint,
America's faith in the superiority of the white race not only devalued Asians
immigrants but also promoted imperialistic programs abroad (if not officially as in the Philippines, then in unofficial ways through attempts at
economic and cultural manipulation of other Asian countries). Christian
students were not so much pro-Japanism as they were "anti-American imperialism." However, once a new nationalist society emerged in Japan that was
different from the spirit of internationalism during the early 1920s, many
JSCA members worried that their own nation would travel down the same
path as other land-hungry Western countries.[14] Nationalism supported by
militarism (and vice versa) was not part of the students' plan for peaceful

coexistence around the world. Those who shared Okumura's views challenged others to see that Japanism was not an attempt to overthrow white domination in Asia, as so many supporters of the regime argued, but rather a growing threat to Christian freedoms and rights. Okumura (as well as other Christian Japanese students both in the United States and in Japan) chose his words carefully, voicing concern over the changes he saw in his homeland, but doing so in a way that also chided Americans and other nations for their own participation in corrupt imperial projects. Placing Japan's nationalist actions within the context of historical, unchristian patterns allowed Japanese students to express their religiously grounded concerns over "Japanism" while also building a discourse of protest among other students over the abandonment of Christian goals.

Like JSCA members, Chinese students in America viewed developments in their home country during the late 1920s with an anxious eye. Growing tensions between the Communist Party of China and Chiang Kai-shek's nationalist party (Kuomintang, or KMT) came to a violent head in 1927, sparking a civil war between labor activists and supporters of the communists and the urban strongholds of the KMT. Many CSCA members, studying safely across the Pacific on college campuses but concerned about the safety and welfare of friends and family at home, expressed conflicted views on the state of China. The appropriateness of nationalism in a Christian world in relation to the civil war was a particularly vexing topic that appeared in discussions and student publications. Communism, no less dangerous an "ism" than nationalism for the students, threatened the inroads made by Chinese Christians. In contrast, Chiang and the KMT's emphasis on social reform, hygiene, and education were similar to the goals of the Social Gospel movement. While Chiang did not officially mention Christianity in his New Life Movement, his desire to combine the traditional principles of moral obligations to the self, family, and community of Confucianism with progressive goals for the nation also appealed to Chinese Christians. Chiang promoted his vision of a new China built on modernity and advancement as a way for the Chinese to receive equal treatment with other nations around the world. Chiang's plan was a form of nationalism, but one that appeared more Christian-minded than Japanism. Still, the relationship between nationalism and Christian citizenship was a puzzle for students: was pride in one's national culture, political structure, or economic progress anathema to Christianity, or was there room for nationalist projects in the Kingdom of God if they did not spawn oppression or greed? Some students argued that nationalism need not violate Christian principles. "To a Chinese mind," one CSCA member wrote in a Council of Christian Associations bulletin, "nationalism and internationalism have not been considered as two opposing or mutually exclusive principles."[15] For this student and others who shared similar opinions, nationalism did have a place in the Christian world, provided that a nation used its strengths to help its own citizens as well as others in building Christian internationalism.[16]

At the same time, other CSCA members wondered how (or if) this new nationalism would mesh with their larger worldviews on Christianity and peace. The New Life Movement's focus on modernizing and reforming China would appear to fall in line with the students' goals, but members were concerned that the movement would lead to national pride that might hinder international relationships. CSCA member H. S. Lang admitted in a 1927 *Chinese Christian Student* article that "since Chinese nationalism is, at the present at least, of a purely defensive nature . . . a force used solely in the interest of liberating China from the political domination and economic exploitation of foreign powers," there was no clear violation of Christian citizenship.[17] Those students who viewed the New Life Movement as a reaction to Western imperialism argued that this form of nationalism was well within the realm of a Christian worldwide fellowship that advocated for an end to aggressive expansion and oppression. However, Lang asked readers "will Chinese nationalism always remain a defensive force as it is today?" and "what assurance is there that Chinese nationalism will not someday too be used to exploit and plunder the weaker countries and races," drawing comparisons with French, British, German, Spanish, and American nationalism.[18] In these instances, nationalism had led to brutal imperialism and colonization, a fate that could very well become China's if nationalism broke from Christian principles (which, according to Lang, it was often prone to do). Even in its most innocuous form and characterized by social progress and uplift, there was still the fear that nationalism could present an overwhelming challenge to Chinese Christians as well as to Christianity on a global scale.

Other students, however, were more supportive of the Chinese nationalist movement. Although Japanism was suspect, Chinese defensive nationalism was a reasonable, if not necessary, response to the history of Western imperialism. Both JSCA members and CSCA members often spoke highly of China's struggle for national pride and modernity. JSCA member Suichi

Harada presented a Japanese student's view of the New Life Movement in his 1927 *Japanese Student Bulletin* article "Japanese Students See Chinese Affairs." Rather than focusing on the conflict between the CCP and the KMT, Harada placed the political development in the larger context of Western plans to economically control the trade resources of China. "Japanese students are whole-heartedly in sympathy with Chinese aspiration for seeking equality and justice in her relationship with the nations of the world," Harada began. Students "may pray for 'Thy Kingdom come, Thy will be done on earth . . .' but as long as there [exist] nations oppressed and exploited by other powers, there will be no international peace and no basis of co-operation can be found." Harada accused Japanese, Chinese, and Filipinos of being too submissive in the face of Western imperialism and passively accepting "racial, color, and national boundaries," "intoxication by the glorious name of patriotism," and the "exploitation of the weaker by the stronger." Harada's arguments also spoke to a growing pan-Asian or "Asia for Asians" movement in Japan and other Pacific nations at the time. Those who embraced Japanese militarism often used the concept of pan-Asianism to argue for the necessity of nationalist, anti-imperial movements. The idea that people of various Asian nations could join together to overthrow imperialist influences reflected the student's work in creating panethnic networks in the United States.[19]

However, open critiques and discussions of nationalism became more challenging for Christian association members after Japan invaded Manchuria.[20] On September 18, 1931, Lieutenant Kawamoto Suemori and other Japanese military personnel secretly detonated a small amount of dynamite by Japan's South Manchuria Railway and subsequently blamed Chinese radicals for the act (which became known as the Mukden Incident). The Japanese Kwantung Army under the command of Shigero Honjo then defied Tokyo's orders to avoid a full-out invasion and effectively gained control of Liaoning and Kirin provinces along the railway.[21] Despite continued resistance from the Chinese armies, the Japanese secured Northern as well as Southern Manchuria by the fall of 1931. In 1932, the Japanese created Manchukuo from Manchuria, a puppet state governed by Puyi, the last Qing emperor of China. When the rest of the world learned that the Mukden Incident was a sham attack designed by the Japanese military and that Manchukuo existed to isolate Manchuria from the rest of China, many leaders (including Herbert Hoover and later Franklin Delano Roosevelt) denounced the Japanese actions. The

League of Nations also refused to recognize Manchukuo, resulting in Japan's leaving the international organization.

The immediate responses from JSCA and CSCA members to the growing unrest in the Pacific represented their dilemma as Christians but also as citizens of their own countries. Whereas general criticisms of Western expansion were the focus of ire before the events in Manchuria, now students were forced to confront the issues of nationalism and militarism within the context of their nations' acts. While attempting to maintain their support for Christian pacifism, both Japanese and Chinese students nevertheless rose to defend their respective homes, with each claiming that any military action stemmed from purely defensive motives. Roy Akagi, former general secretary and president of the JSCA, defended Japan's detonation in the Mukden Incident (before the world knew of Japan's provocation), arguing that "China's armed infringement of Japan's treaty rights in Manchuria . . . was a challenging climax to China's deliberate policy of violating or disregarding Japan's treaty rights in Manchuria."[22] Other JSCA members recounted tales of brave Japanese who sacrificed their lives to fight against the Chinese.[23] Initially, leaders and members of the JSCA framed the Mukden Incident as a necessary reaction to challenges from the Chinese rather than a violation of Christian principles.

As the Manchurian crisis continued, there were varied statements from JSCA members that either defended the Japanese or embraced neutrality. Transnational ties to China and Japan challenged the idealism of the students in building a pacifist Kingdom of God and denouncing military aggression in any capacity. Furthermore, the growing conflict between Japan and China was the first test of the student associations' commitment to peace and Christian fellowship. Interethnic cooperation might be possible in the United States, but how realistic was such an idea in a global arena? During the upheaval, however, the JSCA continued to promote peaceful interactions among the student associations in America. JSCA members reminded readers of the *Student Bulletin* in editorials from 1933 and 1934 that the organ was a "Christian student publication" and was "not to be used for any other purpose of propaganda." Purposes of propaganda included actions such as reporting "unworthy news items and sensational 'eye witness' accounts" and other attempts at using the paper to sway opinions on the growing conflict. Similarly, the JSCA urged its members and friends to maintain "sober thinking" in regard to the "unfortunate situation in the Far East" and hoped that "readers would see the whole thing with [a] warm heart and cool head." Objectivity and the use of Christian principles to temper student reactions, however, were not always effective.[24]

Responses from Christian Chinese students in the United States to the Manchurian conflict were also as complex and reactionary as those from the JSCA. CSCA members initially defended the retaliation of the Chinese armies against Japanese occupation. Despite previous calls to Christian youths to avoid warfare in the face of a crisis, the *Chinese Christian Student* often published articles from students who demanded otherwise. In 1931, an anonymous CSCA member questioned the reality of attempting to create a Kingdom of God and a peace movement when so few nations wanted to adhere to the basic principles of Christianity. "What is the use of preaching fatherhood of God and brotherhood of man when the country which we call Christian takes no action in defense of the peace pact which she solemnly signed and guaranteed?"[25] "Let us not be hypocritical," the author continued, "Let us face facts. It is not God that will save China. It is not Jesus Christ, our savior, who will deliver us from our enemies, but a strong army and navy that can command the respect of this civilize[d] world is what we need."

Such a statement was telling: Japan's aggression transformed some CSCA members from global promoters of peace into victims demanding military action. Violent retaliation in the name of protection and self-defense was a justifiable action for Chinese students, regardless of such a measure's antipacifist characteristics. The calls for pacifism from Wellington Liu, the CSCA member who spoke out against war during an earlier convention, were now sounds in the distant past among members who feared for China's wellbeing. As the tensions between Japan and China grew, CSCA members juggled their identities as representatives of the Kingdom of God with their connections (direct or indirect) to transpacific tensions.

The CSCA also reported the increasing number of Chinese students who were eager to abandon their studies in order to return to help their fellow countrymen in China.[26] Flora Belle Jan married a Chinese national in the late 1920s and, by the time of the Mukden Incident, was living in China and reflecting on her experiences as a Chinese American in her ancestral home during the crisis. Like other CSCA students, Jan expressed a growing discontent with the aggression of the Japanese as well as the unchristian behavior of both nations. However, Jan also became fervently devoted to the Chinese cause and moved away from the ideas of panethnicity when she wrote letters to friends in America.

As a result of tensions in the Pacific, the CSCA members initially placed their roles as coordinators of pro-Chinese forces in the United States and China above developing programs for equality, rights, and assistance to the second generation of Chinese Americans.[27]

Reconciliation in a Time of Conflict

Despite the early defensive and passive-aggressive stance of the JSCA and CSCA, many students became more open to reconciliation and discussion as the conflict grew. This shift in how the students approached their role in the Manchurian conflict reflected larger changes in the Japanese and Chinese communities in the United States. In ethnic enclaves along the West Coast and across America, the conflict between China and Japan was certainly a divisive and raw topic. Since many community leaders were immigrants from China and Japan, the older, foreign-born members were often passionately supportive of their homeland's actions and reactions. Arguments for necessary defense or a strong emphasis on the importance of national pride shaped responses to the Mukden Incident. The Issei adopted a defensive stance against Americans' support of China that exacerbated existing ethnic tensions between Japanese communities and Chinatowns. As Brian Hayashi explains, Japanese Protestants in California generally became more nationalistic as Americans became more critical of Japan.[28] Although an atmosphere of suspicion pervaded the early to mid-1930s, immigrant parents turned to their American-born children to build bridges between China or Japan and the United States. Immigrant leaders and parents argued that Nisei or Chinese Americans who were more versed in American culture as well as fluent in English could serve as ambassadors for the respective nations. At times, this notion of constructing a cosmopolitan bridge assumed tangible actions, resulting, for example, in Issei sending their children to Japan for their educations to gain an appreciation of their heritage as well as their dual-citizenship. On other occasions, Chinese leaders encouraged Chinese Americans to reprise a cultural ambassador role by speaking to American audiences or writing essays on the importance of China and its need for support.[29]

Chinese American, Nisei, and foreign-born members of the JSCA and CSCA, however, held different views of the type of bridge building they should engage in during this time of unrest. While the Issei and older

members of the ethnic communities urged members of the second generation to strengthen political ties between China or Japan and the United
States, Christian students did not often agree. This is not to say that all
American- or foreign-born students were not defensive or nationalistic
about the growing conflict (they too had family in China and Japan and
were just as frightened for them as their parents), but a more conciliatory
atmosphere existed on college campuses, especially among the Christian
associations. As the Manchurian conflict waged on, many CSCA and
JSCA members supported greater understanding of one another's viewpoints as Christians rather than as Chinese or Japanese nationalists. Furthermore, there was a growing concern among students that Christians in
Japan who spoke out against Japanism or the Japanese occupation would
face violations of their rights and freedoms. Rather than focus on US-
Asian political and diplomatic relations, the students emphasized their
status as educated and enlightened Christians who viewed the Mukden
Incident from a global and Christian point of view. The Chinese American
sociological researcher Pardee Lowe observed that in San Francisco's Chinatown and surrounding communities, "Chinese and Japanese college students are able to converse intelligently and without anger over the question
of the Japanese invasion of Manchuria."[30] Like the students mentioned in
Lowe's observations, members of the CSCA and JSCA encouraged their
organizations to meet and discuss the problems across the Pacific. Overall,
members in the associations during the 1930s discussed the Manchurian
crisis in a larger, more Christian and international context than many others in their communities. As a result, the student Christian associations
attempted to serve as bridge builders, combining political goals for peace
with the continued desire to promote equality and interracial and interethnic fellowship. As the violence mounted between China and Japan, the
Christian students in America identified as agents of reconciliation rather
than extensions of China or Japan.

Articles outlining the differences between Christian Japanese students
in America and Japanese militarists across the Pacific were a popular way
to encourage discussion. In 1932, CSCA member P. C. Hsu from Stanford
University recalled that when he initially came to the United States, he
arrived with "the same nationalistic feelings towards the Japanese, thinking
that all Japanese were in one way or another connected with the imperialistic designs of their government." After increased interaction with students
from Japan, however, Hsu "completely altered his view" on the Japanese

and "found them to be almost without exception peace-loving and fine Christians." Because of his new friendships, he decided to dedicate himself to "the cause of international cooperation between the liberal elements of these two nations."[31] The leaders of the CSCA also issued an official stance on the Sino-Japanese conflict in March 1932, recognizing that Japanese students were often just as dismayed by Japan's imperialistic projects as the Chinese. The CSCA stated, "We deplore the muzzling of Japanese liberals and Christians" by the Japanese government and vowed to cooperate with all Japanese students (Christian and non-Christian) who desired to "reach across national boundaries" and engage in open discussions.[32] Here were statements that again attempted to shift the focus away from the wrongs of each nation and toward broader violations of Christian principles.

Japanese Christian students responded by further distancing themselves and their organization from the militarism of Japan. Findings outlined in the Lytton Report (the product of a League of Nations investigation into the Mukden Incident) of 1932 that identified the Japanese as the aggressors in the bombing and subsequent invasion also contributed to the JSCA's more conciliatory stance toward the CSCA. JSCA members sought to relay their eagerness as Christians to reach out to Chinese students and continue panethnic cooperation. Some of the Japanese students' articles became nationwide and even worldwide testimonies to the Christian devotion to forgiveness and fellowship above national pride. JSCA member Masahiko Takahashi's 1932 "Letter to the Republic of China" was published by the *Japanese Student Bulletin* as well as the WSCF's *The Student World* and reached a wide audience. Takahashi passionately admitted to his nation's wrongdoings, lamenting that "if we do not reflect and repent, we shall receive God's punishment!" Japanese Christians were "deeply ashamed" of their nation's actions, and despite "whatever the militarists and so-called men of intelligence say, their will is not our will, their action is not ours. . . . we pacifists are weak yet, but we are fighting against militarism and imperialism." Takahashi assured Chinese students that "we [Japanese students] hold out our hands to your country; heartily do we long for the completion of the revolution and for the union of Asia."[33] Expressions of shame and guilt by students were powerful and moving statements of faith in the possibility for Christian friendship between Chinese and Japanese, if not between their two nations. While the article was published only in a student bulletin, Takahashi's piece represented a sincere interest on behalf of other

Japanese students in setting aside differences while in America and working with Chinese students to create a less oppressive world. Members of the associations were not statesmen and could not alter the course of military interventions in Asia, but they could draw on their experience in building networks for social change to ease tensions between students. In many ways, the written word was the students' best Christian weapon against prejudice and interethnic conflict.

With a growing trend toward mending rifts, Masatane Mitani, president of the JSCA and editor of the *Japanese Student Bulletin*, used the Mukden Incident to build stronger relations between his organization and the CSCA. In 1936, Mitani admitted to readers of the *Student Bulletin* that "the gesture of the Japanese army in North China is creating a furious sentiment against Japan on the part of the Chinese people," but he also encouraged CSCA members to look beyond warfare as the solution to the problem. "What is wrong with us Christians," Mitani asked, "if we say follow the way of the cross, why should we be too anxious to compromise with a political trend which fosters hatred and bitterness against others?"[34] Defining Japanese militarism as a mere trend was a bold move to help readers understand the JSCA's position on the conflict. Similarly, Mitani urged both foreign- and American-born Chinese and Japanese students in the United States to "keep a level head" and "pour their energy into the noble cause for building up the kingdom of God."[35] The Manchurian conflict signaled a need for students to return to bridge-building ideologies in order to promote friendly international relations.

To meet the goal of bridge building for interethnic and interracial friendships, the JSCA and CSCA brought members and leaders of their organizations together to address the situation in Asia and its global effects on equality and oppression. These conferences, however, did not reflect the old, cosmopolitan ideas of cultural interaction but rather a way to reinforce the solidarity among Christian students in America that grew prior to the Sino-Japanese aggression. In response to the conflict, the CSCA and JSCA formed and sponsored a number of Sino-Japanese workshops, discussion groups, and conferences on the West Coast and across the United States.[36] The most successful and well attended of these meetings was the "Keep Our Ocean Pacific" conference at Mills College in Oakland, California, during the summer of 1936. The Oakland conference also attracted Christian students from a variety of ethnic and racial backgrounds. Here JSCA and CSCA members joined with Filipino, Korean, African American, and Indian students from along the West Coast to discuss questions such as "What are the underlying reasons for conflict [in the Pacific]?" and "What part are students taking in movements for social reconstruction in Asian and America?" The problems of "social reconstruction" in America in terms of "shelter, employment, and racial relations" were just as important as those related to reconstructing Asia following the military conflict in Manchuria. The fact that so many students from different backgrounds participated in the discussions demonstrated that the Manchurian conflict represented worldwide problems of inequality and oppression, rather than simply an Asian or even a Pacific problem. During this conference, the JSCA and the CSCA joined together to gather donations for the recently formed Far Eastern Student Emergency Fund. This was an opportunity for JSCA and CSCA members to raise money for both Chinese and Japanese students and to set themselves apart from the charitable organizations in America that focused on providing assistance to only Chinese students affected by violence in Asia.[37]

The Keep Our Ocean Pacific conference reflected the success of similar gatherings across the country. In April 1934, representatives from the student Christian associations joined together for the three-day Oriental Students Conference at New York's Riverside Church to discuss the Mukden Incident in the context of larger world problems. Although this conference was not held on a West Coast campus, it was a sign that the influence and impact of the associations were growing. Chinese, Filipino, Japanese, and Indian students joined together and discussed variants of the conference's theme: "the place of the Christian student in world reconstruction." A student author for the *Filipino Student Bulletin* reported that many conversations focused on issues of "nationalism and its rightful place in Christianity." Interestingly, several students in attendance at the conference (it is not clear from which associations) expressed their opinions to the other attendees that "there is a place for nationalism," considering that "nature created national states" and that "these states are on stage [*sic*] in human evolution." The Christian students' justifications for nationalism in terms of "natural creation" and "human evolution" are both interesting and puzzling when placed in the context of a Christian conference. However, these students qualified their statements by explaining that the promotion of national pride could help certain countries in developing and "setting their own houses in order before they ... contribute towards an international society."[38]

Most students agreed that individual nations did have a right to tend to their own (pointing toward the United States and its own issues with race relations and discrimination), but many were not convinced that a strong sense of nationalistic pride was necessary for such reform. Several students challenged the viewpoints of their colleagues, arguing that "a truly Christian outlook leads to recognition of human values among peoples of other races and nations as well as in one's own group; and Christianity involves a higher loyalty which rises above national consciousness." Despite the many different opinions, all students concluded that nationalism was the primary cause of the conflict in Asia, but it also presented a larger problem beyond the Pacific. Their solution (as potential future leaders) was to "pursue a more active application of Christian principles to diplomatic and international affairs," reversing what they believed to be a tendency for Christians "to do much talking, but little acting in accord with their ideas."[39]

The Oriental Student Conference reflected similar opportunities and limitations in the students' international strategies as in their plans for ending prejudice in the United States. Once again, the students primarily interacted with other students and used concepts of Christian citizenship to approach the problems in Asia, actions that restricted their interactions with other ethnic communities. Also, as neither foreign-born and nor American-born students were diplomats or politicians, they of course could not create treaties or engage in diplomatic actions to promote peace, with foreign-born Japanese students being particularly hesitant about speaking out beyond the association bulletins. However, discussions and conferences were the tried-and-true methods the students used in creating panethnic, interethnic, and interracial networks, and they applied similar tactics to larger political and foreign affairs. These meetings were innovative and unique at the time, with students seeking to use Christianity to reach across ethnic lines to continue to build panethnic groups for ending prejudice and promoting peace. Student discourse crossed ethnic boundaries, planted ideas, and facilitated the growth of large networks. The student conferences and meetings prove that activism in its most basic form is the product of groups first recognizing that they have shared experiences and then coming together to discuss steps for moving forward. The fact that the students were able to accomplish this level of interaction in an atmosphere of suspicion and unease in America was impressive.

The growing cooperation of the Christian student associations encouraged other Americans to carefully study the Manchurian conflict and analyze larger issues of imperialism and nationalism. The editors of the *Chinese Christian Student* published editorials, letters, and articles from Americans who argued for international understanding rather than pointing fingers at the Japanese. In December 1931, Jerome Davis, a professor at Yale University, wrote a letter to the CSCA describing his view of the Sino-Japanese conflict as well as those of his colleagues at the university. "It must be remembered," Davis began, "that Japan in her policy has done no more than Christian nations in the past have done before her" and reminded readers that "we in America must blush with shame when we think of how our policy in Nicaragua and other Latin American countries has had even less justification than that of Japan in Manchuria" and that "two wrongs do not make a right."[40] Similar to the students' overall rejection of imperialism, other Americans also compared the actions of the Japanese to their nation's own history of oppression and colonialism. Although many denounced Japan for its actions in China, the student newspapers offered intellectuals an opportunity to participate in Christian and international debates on foreign crises. The CSCA became a valid source of information on the affair, and as a result, members were often invited to deliver talks and lectures at clubs, meetings, and universities across the country. A positive outcome of the violence in Asia was the growth of a national reputation of the CSCA and JSCA as inspirational internationalist associations that welcomed various and inclusive opinions that were not necessarily pro-Chinese or anti-Japanese.

However, the student associations' ability to attract intellectuals to their activities did not often carry over into their interactions with other members of their own ethnic groups beyond campus. Similar to the distance that most Chinese, Japanese, and Filipino students kept between their groups and the more working-class members of larger ethnic enclaves, the Christian students allowed their religious focus to consume all conversations that had the potential for reaching a wider audience. The goals of world peace and Christian citizenship were abstract and did not reflect many of the views of other Asian Americans on the Mukden Incident. Maintaining panethnic connections among Asian student groups during the Manchurian conflict was no easy feat and required planning and organizational skills. Unfortunately, the students were limited in what they could do outside of the academic realm and often did not challenge the unchristian views on warfare among other groups in the United States. Many Japanese and Chinese had more practical concerns regarding the violence in the Pacific and sought aid and support for friends and family back home. Other Americans were also more concerned with aiding the Chinese than with waxing intellectual about the perils of nationalism. The meetings and discussions highlighted the difficulties in transporting lofty, Christian goals to the political realm, a problem that many activist groups faced.[41]

The student associations faced more difficulties in building panethnic ties as Japanese aggression in Manchuria reached new heights by late 1937. Although China had signed the He-Umezu Agreement with Japan in 1935, effectively turning all control of the province of Hebei in northern China over to the Japanese, Chinese volunteer forces continued to resist Japanese rule. On July 7, 1937, a skirmish between Chinese and Japanese forces at the Marco Polo Bridge near Beijing turned into a full battle between the opposing troops, with Japan eventually taking control of Beijing and the port of Tianjin. Historians credit the Marco Polo Bridge Incident as the formal beginning of the Second Sino-Japanese War, with attacks from both the Chinese and Japanese continuing through the late 1930s. As various nations joined forces with either the Chinese (assisted by the Soviet Union and, later, the volunteer forces of the United States) or the Japanese (contentiously aligned with Germany after 1938), people around the world watched anxiously as the Manchurian crisis turned into a full-scale war.[42]

In the United States, public opinion continued to favor the Chinese, with Americans generally viewing the Japanese as the ultimate nationalistic and imperially driven aggressors. Many in the United States decried the actions of the Japanese and expressed sympathy for the plight of China. National groups such the American Committee for Non-Participation in Japanese Aggression (headed by the former secretary of state and opponent of Japanese expansion Henry Stimson) and United China Relief organized events such as "Bowl of Rice" parties to raise funds for the suffering Chinese and developed publicity campaigns for donations under the motto "To Them—A Little Means a Lot."[43] Newspapers such as the *New York Daily News* encouraged full American support of the Chinese, stating "if we must fight for pacifism, let us put everything we have got into the fight—and get back to peace as soon as possible."[44] Even the International Department of the YMCA, an organization that typically attempted to avoid a firm stance on controversial or political issues, supported an embargo against Japan, arguing that "in our capacity as citizens, we should bring pressure on the American government to carry out the will of the

American people as indicated in the Gallup poll and bring about the cessation of the flow of war materials from this country to Japan."[45] By the close of the decade, 74 percent of Americans polled supported a boycott of Japanese goods and expressed pro-Chinese sympathies.[46]

The Committee on Friendly Relations (CFR) also worried about the impact of the Second Sino-Japanese War on relations between the JSCA and the CSCA. Specifically, Charles Hurrey questioned whether the existence of two Christian associations organized along national/ethnic identities were appropriate or even necessary amid the conflict in Manchuria. "For many years," Hurrey wrote in a report to the Intercollegiate Christian Council of America (a nationwide student organization), "nationality groups were fundamental units in the work of the Committee," but he wondered, "is a racially or nationally separate group now a sound basis for the work of the CFR?"[47] If the purpose of Christian citizenship was to promote international fellowship beyond national ties, then why should the CFR (which existed generally to support foreign students in the United States, not play into national conflicts) continue to support ethnic student associations that represented two nations embroiled in war? What Hurrey failed to take into account, however, was how much the associations had grown within the past decade, encompassing the interests of both foreign- and American-born members. Without considering the representative power of the student associations, Hurrey and other members of the YMCA failed to see that Christian students approached the war in the Pacific a global issue rather than one between nationalities.

The members of the CSCA and JSCA argued that, contrary to Hurrey's beliefs, the Sino-Japanese War made their associations more crucial. Students viewed their organizations not as ethnic groups but rather as forces that promoted cooperation and action that transcended political strife. Students often revealed that their own transitions from Chinese or Japanese to Christian citizens were not always easy, but they credited the student associations with assisting them in their transformation. In 1939, George Kao, a CSCA member from the University of Washington, wrote in a *Chinese Christian Student* article that at first he was suspicious of Japanese and Japanese Americans and their views on the Manchurian conflict but explained that he knew "better than to knife the first Japanese I see, even if Japanese airplanes are bombing my hometown [of] Nanking." Although Kao was Chinese, he was also "a fellow member in an international friendship organization" that deemed "it a lack of courage as well as wisdom on the part of those who—with all the facts of the world staring him in the face—deny my Japanese colleague and I the opportunity to exercise boldly our embryonic world citizenship."[48]

Toru Matsumoto, then the president of the JSCA and editor of the *Japanese Student Bulletin*, agreed with Kao that the student associations set much-needed examples in the United States for internationalism and Christian citizenship rather than interethnic strife. "The longer the conflict with China continues," Matsumoto began in a 1939 editorial, "the greater the suffering of the peoples involved would be," emphasizing that "nothing would be better than peace in which two peoples share the opportunities and responsibilities of life together." Members of all Asian Christian associations should work together "for a serious realization of their duty to restore the lost and losing faith of themselves and others in the real Master of mankind" and to recognize that "man's struggle for domination among nations, classes, or individuals cannot be accepted within the creed of the Universal Church." Like Kao, Matsumoto encouraged other students in the United States to realize that the Second Sino-Japanese War was representative of a global struggle with nations adhering to imperialism, expansion, and the oppression of other nations, races, and classes. These were indeed large problems, but Christian association leaders and members had faith in their ability to address these issues as best as they could. The above writings suggest that the students viewed their groups and fellow CSCA/ JSCA members as succeeding where others had failed in stepping back and viewing the Manchurian crisis from a positively dissociated Christian standpoint. Although Matsumoto admitted that the students were limited in their means of creating peace between China and Japan, they could continue to work within their realm of interethnic solidarity and use discussions and conferences as "motives for [their] thinking and actions during the 1939–40 academic year."[49]

While members and leaders of the CSCA and JSCA looked to bridge the potential ethnic faults between their two organizations, the Filipino Christian students used the Second Sino-Japanese War to speak out against imperialism. The opportunity to assess the negative long-term impact of colonial relationships on Christian values brought FSCM members into the fold of CSCA and JSCA conversations. The Philippines also faced political uncertainty during this time after undergoing a transformation from US colony to commonwealth. After the Tydings-McDuffie Act was enacted in 1934, large questions loomed for Filipinos about the practical definition of a commonwealth, the political place of Filipino migrants in the United States as a result of the change, and the future of an independent Philippines. FSCM members were no less aware of the challenges they and those in the Philippines faced as a result of changes in political relationships in the Pacific. After decades of generally avoiding public denunciation of American control of the Philippines, many Filipino students became more open in larger conversations about the unchristian effects of colonialism and nationalism as a result of the Second Sino-Japanese War. As more Filipino students contributed to the interethnic collaboration in conferences, publications, and discussion groups, the influence of the Christian associations continued to grow and incorporate more nuanced approaches to the concepts of oppression, nationalism, and prejudice.

FSCM members were quick to state where they stood on the topic of the Second Sino-Japanese War and often spoke on behalf of the Philippines as well. In his 1936 article "Moderation Beckons Us," FSCM member Juan Dahilig attempted to set the record straight concerning which "side" the Filipinos favored in the conflict and also to demonstrate that Filipino students were just as committed as the CSCA and JSCA to reaching beyond national and ethnic boundaries. "To favor an alliance with Japan simply because of the similarity of color between the two nationalities and because of being prejudiced by the white people is deplorable," Dahilig explained, but he continued by stating that "to oppose a diplomatic act with Japan because of an alleged difference between Japanese and Filipino ideas is to be short of the genuine sense of fairness and Christian intelligence." Like Mitani and other members and leaders of both the CSCA and JSCA, Dahilig approached the war as a grenade that could possibly explode and destroy the level of panethnic cooperation the students achieved. FSCM members would "show the world that Filipinos can be bigger than prejudice and arrogance" and that Filipinos and all Christian students "owe[d] it to humanity, to God, and no less to our own people" to be open and objective when dealing with international conflicts. Here was an opportunity for JSCA, FSCM, and CSCA members to be "Christian statesmen in the sincere and honest sense of the word" when many other ethnic groups in Japanese communities or Chinatowns had failed to do so.[50]

Although there were still Filipino students who feared being viewed as independence "propagandists" by Americans, others felt more comfortable providing analyses of America's involvement in the Philippines. Filipino students denounced the hypocrisy in Americans' attacks on the Japanese for their desire for expansion while at the same time upholding their own imperial projects in Philippines, Puerto Rico, and Nicaragua as forms of "national uplift."[51] FSCM member D. H. Ambrosio passionately attacked American revulsion toward the Japanese and encouraged other Filipino students to speak out against the United States' history of oppression in his *Filipino Student Bulletin* article "Kicking Against the Pricks":

> It is necessary and imperative that we kick against things hateful, abominable, and hypocritical; we should and we must kick against race prejudice born out of the superiority complex of the Nordic myth; against the hypocritical and sanctimonious declarations for peace by imperialistic nations armed to the teeth; against those who with one hand hold . . . the Declaration of Independence . . . and with the other hand hold on tightly to the treasures of Porto Rico, the wealth of Haiti, and the sugar-centrals and rubber plantation possibilities of the Philippines.[52]

Pieces like Ambrosio's were not isolated rants but rather meaningful contributions to Christian associations' critique of the Second Sino-Japanese War and larger systems of government control that ran counter to Christianity. The student publications circulated widely among CSCA, FSCM, and JSCA members, creating what Albert Park and David Yoo describe as a public space for Christian students to examine the multiple impacts of the war.[53]

Written denouncements of imperialism resulted in more face-to-face interactions among CSCA, FSCM, and JSCA members to examine systems of oppression in the United States as well as the Pacific. By speaking largely of imperialism and its negative effects on the world, Chinese, Japanese, and Filipino students all had a large stake in understanding and analyzing the Second Sino-Japanese War. During lectures and talks of the underlying causes of the conflicts in Asia, students at these meetings tried to think concretely about the abstract ideas of peace, love, and brotherhood in relation to war, prejudice, and inequality. Since most students identified the problems of Asia as part of a larger problem in the Pacific basin, many of the meetings (apart from two successful ones in Buffalo and New York City) were held at colleges and universities along the West Coast, drawing attendees from various institutions to the Stanford and University of California campuses, to name a few.[54] During the annual YMCA/YWCA-sponsored Asilomar Conference of 1938 in California,

Asian students formed breakaway groups to devote time to the Second Sino-Japanese War and its global effects. Often, these discussions spilled over into the plenary events of the conference. Attendee George Savage observed how CSCA, FSCM, and JSCA delegates successfully blended the problems of the Pacific with the problems of racism in America. Specifically, "the large number of Japanese, Chinese, Hindu, Philippine, and Hawaiian students helped focus attention on angles of problems, especially the coast racial problem, that created a new interest and understanding among other delegates." Asian and Hawaiian students drew a strong connection between "the horrors of war abroad and the horrors of prejudice in America" that resulted in "un-Christian ideas of white superiority . . . racial superiority, and injustice in the Western cities and states." Savage's report from the conference also included references to the Japanese students' "insistence on fighting against imperialistic motives and designs as a means to greater acceptance of all of God's peoples in the United States and around the world," a statement that spoke to the concern among Christian students about the dangerous connections between imperialism and racism.[55]

Many students identified parallels between unchristian acts in the Pacific and the equally unchristian acts toward racial minorities on the West Coast. At a time when racial discrimination against Filipinos was rampant in agricultural centers of California, Oregon, and Washington, and when sociologists and psychologists were still analyzing the second-generation problem, CSCA, FSCM, and JSCA members were not shocked that these events occurred within the larger context of political and military crises in Asia and Europe. JSCA member Shuichi Harada argued during a 1936 meeting at Stanford that it should come as no surprise to Americans that because of the "immigration problem" of the United States (meaning the Asian exclusionary acts), Japan wished to demonstrate its own strength on the world scene.[56] Harada did not justify Japanism by referencing American immigration policies; rather, he used this phenomenon as an example of chickens coming home to roost after discriminatory immigration and naturalization laws, anti-Asian sentiment, and racism in the United States. Harada and other JSCA members argued in publications and at conferences for an end to immigration discrimination in order to promote equality in America and greater Christian goodwill to prevent future conflicts. The push for repealing anti-Asian immigration policies would gain speed during World War II and the following years of the Cold War, but this was a topic that many Christian association members passionately addressed during the 1920s and 1930s.

Other students suggested they use the problems of deteriorating inter-ethnic relationships that result from global crises to build stronger connections between the Christian associations and larger Asian communities in West Coast cities. CSCA member David Toong suggested that his organization should work more closely with the East Bay Youth Work group in San Francisco so that "we can best further our program of soliciting moral and material aid for China in her present struggle and to educate the public on racial tolerance."[57] It is interesting that Toong connected the two problems, one across the Pacific and one among Chinese immigrants and Chinese Americans living and working in California. Toong's plans suggested the CSCA's potential to correct its practice of generally remaining distant from citizens of Chinatown, bridging gaps between student and community organizations and repairing fault lines between foreign students and the working-class Chinese. For the CSCA, JSCA, and FSCM, the Second Sino-Japanese War and international conflicts were not distractions from their work on the problem of racial injustice in the United States. Rather, they were opportunities to preserve panethnic networks while creating new ones by using the goals of ending prejudice and striving for Christian peace. While the impact of Toong's strategy on the CSCA remained unknown, other Christian students made bold moves in applying their views on international conflicts to West Coast race relations.

As a result of the growing concerns over the Pacific crisis as well as possible solutions, student conferences evolved from largely interethnic to interracial gatherings. One of the most visible examples of this transition in conference demographics occurred on May 12, 1938, when Chinese, Filipino, and Japanese student Christian groups at the University of Washington organized an interracial conference that attracted students from all ethnic and racial groups and was open to everyone, Christian and non-Christian. The subjects the students discussed at the conference were wide-ranging and represented the different backgrounds of those in attendance. JSCA members as well as African Americans brought to the forefront what they identified as the most pressing concerns for students of color in Washington and along the West Coast: the racial discrimination against the largest minority groups on campus, Japanese, Filipino, and African American students. Students shared reports of racism among campus groups as well as troubling surveys of white students who admitted that they would never room with an "Oriental or Negro" student. Attendees were concerned that these forms of what some would call mild prejudice might carry over into university policies in dormitory living. In response, the students developed an official stance on discrimination among student organizations, vowing to "call attention to those student groups guilty of denying equality for Asian and Negro students" and "lead boycotts against any fraternity or academic group which practices un-Christian behavior and discriminates against Negro and Asian students."[58] One JSCA member also argued that the racism against Japanese in Seattle would only become worse as a result of both "the insatiable quest for dominance by Americans and Japan—two peoples unfettered by true Christian love— . . . and destroy any chance for the second generation to advance beyond the prejudice that left our parents in fear in the United States."[59]

Racial issues beyond campus also received attention from conference attendees, and the problems of anti-miscegenation and anti-alien land laws were of particular concern. JSCA members stressed the unfortunate connections between racism in the United States and American immigration policies. In response, attendees drafted a petition during the conference to send to local representatives in the Washington legislature protesting the Immigration Act of 1924. The JSCA received support from many of the students in attendance (a few students opposed the petition because they "feared . . . for the treatment of Japanese in Seattle" during the heightened tensions with Japan) for their written denouncement of the United States' attitudes toward Japanese and other Asian immigrants. Filipino students also contributed to the discussion of international and American domestic issues by inviting opinions from other students on how American imperialism compared with Japanese expansion and other oppressive regimes that challenged Christian fellowship. Overall, the conference drew together students from various ethnic and racial backgrounds to approach the entanglement of racism, imperialism, and turmoil in the Pacific.[60]

The meeting also had lasting effects on interethnic and interracial activism at UW and in Seattle. While in attendance, the students formed what would come to be one of the most influential interracial groups at the University of Washington: the Committee on Interracial Relations (largely made up of Chinese, Filipino, Japanese, and African American students), a group that would continue to operate with the assistance of FSCM member Victor Carreon during and after World War II. The University of Washington YMCA was so inspired by the action of the students that leaders provided financial backing and administrative support to the committee and allowed the group to continue to meet in the YMCA building. After the initial interracial meeting in 1938, the committee and the YMCA sponsored joint programs and discussions on creating relationships between races in order to fight discrimination along the West Coast and across America.[61]

Although the reports on the conference from association members and the YMCA are limited in detail, this 1938 gathering is significant for the possibilities it represented in interracial and interethnic activism. As the war continued, more foreign- and American-born Asian Christian students convened with other racial and ethnic groups to analyze military and political problems in Asia within the context of their own lives in America. Asian Christian students were able to create a transnational activist identity that spoke to the influence of transpacific issues at the time. Along the West Coast, where there were large numbers of Asian students and the problems of the Pacific appeared more pertinent, anti-Asian sentiment was no longer simply a domestic problem; it was an international peril that required Christian solutions.

The University of Washington interracial conference is important for the glimpse it provides of the influence of the student associations on interracial and interethnic organizing before World War II. Historians of civil rights and activism have long argued that such forms of activism existed during the 1930s through the support of the Communist Party of America, labor unions and organizations, and other radical members of the Popular Front. The Great Depression and the economic, social, and political challenges that characterized this moment encouraged, as Michael Denning explains, artists, actors and actresses, authors, and other left-leaning believers in the chance for a new United States to come together and emphasize reaching hands across racial and ethnic lines.[62] While these groups are certainly necessary for understanding the rise of interracial activism for labor, civil, and political rights, the contributions of the students to the growth of civil rights networks on the West Coast should not be underestimated.

The fact that the Christian student associations were key organizers of larger campus and regional meetings speaks to the place of Christianity in activism during the 1930s. Although the students may not have viewed themselves as radical in the sense that most historians use the term, their combination of Christian critiques of imperialism and nationalism and the connection of these problems to racism and prejudice in the United States were unique and revolutionary for the time. The Christian base provided for a wider appeal to students and additional opportunities for in-depth analyses of the causes of international prejudice and racism. The radical groups of the Popular Front had greater success in applying theories to economic and political circumstances, but for the students, the risks of political action may have outweighed their desires for education and success, particularly among foreign-born members. Also, the students in attendance did influence later social movements in Seattle with the formation of the Committee on Interracial Relations, which would become an important component of the growth of a postwar civil rights movement in the city. The students' Christian approach to interracial and interethnic networks called for an all-inclusive movement that transcended the often black/white view of race relations at the time. Perhaps these students cannot be considered as part of Denning's Cultural Front or the broader Popular Front of the 1930s; however, their connections of racial inequality to global issues of nationalism and war did carve a space for them in the interracial and interethnic activist movements of this era.

A Gathering Storm: The Coming of World War II and Growing Ethnic Tensions

By 1940, political, ethnic, and racial tensions from all sides challenged the previous levels of cooperation among the Christian associations in the United States. The publications and decreasing numbers of Oriental student conferences after Japan's alliance with the Axis nations initiated a ripple effect that was felt among all in America, including the JSCA and CSCA. It became more difficult for Chinese and Japanese students to embrace Christian tolerance and brotherhood as they shifted their attention from building the Kingdom of God to creating strategic identities during rising anti-Japanese sentiment. Whereas the Manchurian conflict once presented opportunities for greater cooperation, such avenues narrowed as the Pacific crisis grew into a World War. Although cooperation among Christian students from different racial and ethnic backgrounds grew, the networks the students sustained would again be challenged as the military aggression in Asia and Europe engulfed the world during the late 1930s and early 1940s.

The Second Sino-Japanese War forced JSCA members to recognize once again the vulnerability of the Nisei during the conflict and the continued presence of discrimination and racism. Despite their Issei parents' strong support of the Japanese, the Nisei, as American citizens, had a more difficult time openly accepting Japan's actions.[63] Japanese American organizations such as the Japanese American Citizens League (JACL) often supported the Issei and their dedication to maintaining ties to the homeland through donations to the Japanese and speeches to "counteract the American public's overwhelming support for the Chinese."[64] Nisei members of the JSCA, however, faced a different conundrum: how could they support their families while maintaining their roles in a worldwide Christian kingdom that renounced imperialist and nationalist actions? Leaders of the JSCA recognized that their Nisei members found themselves in unique circumstances and encouraged them to speak out in the *Japanese Student Bulletin* about their experiences.

The majority of JSCA Nisei who expressed their opinions favored the more Christian or international approach to the conflict, arguing for fellow JSCA members and Japanese Americans to remember that above all, they were Christians and had a duty to realize the negative consequences of Japan's actions. Many Nisei remained taciturn when it came to the Second Sino-Japanese War, often revealing that they knew little about the turmoil or the politics and history behind the violence in Asia. However, Nisei in the JSCA had a desire to share the conflicts they faced as both Japanese Americans and Christians in the United States.[65] Kay Uchida wrote an article for the *Japanese Student Bulletin* in 1938 describing his position on the Second Sino-Japanese War and returned to the concept of "bridge building." "Especially today, with the conditions in the Orient as they are," he explained, "we Nisei in the midst of pro-Japanese feeling within our homes and anti-Japanese feeling in the outside society, can be an important link in fostering better understanding." Nisei were not to "make excuses" for Japan, but to "state the facts which induced the actions" and "help our parents, who naturally are likely to be strongly biased to see the situation in a Christian way."[66] In another article, an anonymous JSCA member argued that the "average Nisei is not stirred to the quick by every report that trickles in . . . [and] to most Nisei, the war in China is just so much Greek." But the author warned that "whether the Nisei like it or not, he is looked upon by Americans as Japanese" and "people don't take the time to ask whether a Japanese is born over here or not; moreover, they don't care." This member concluded that if a boycott of Japanese-made goods (a reaction to the Sino-Japanese War that was rapidly becoming more favorable among Americans and Chinese) became a reality, Issei and Japanese American businesses would see a downturn in business from those who refused to patronize such establishments.[67] Just as CSCA, FSCM, and JSCA members connected the racial inequality in America to worldwide oppression, Nisei JSCA members understood that an Asian conflict could only exacerbate existing prejudices against Japanese in the United States.

Foreign-born members of the JSCA grew increasingly concerned over not only the possibility of a war between Japan and the United States but also the impact such a war would have on minorities in America—particularly those who were pacifists. Genuine fear of the complete dissolution of the students' progress with building Christian coalitions in America influenced the writing of members during this uncertain time. Many articles published in the *Japanese Student Bulletin* still maintained that as horrific as the actions of the Japanese in Manchuria and China were, Americans had no place to criticize the Japanese or any other nation until they analyzed their own wrongdoings. In March 1940, editor and JSCA president Toru Matsumoto opened his article "On America and Japan" by assuring readers of all backgrounds that foreign-born members of the JSCA, though Japanese, "speak . . . as Christians, because only by doing so we may be on permanent grounds," but he continued by explaining that Japanese students in America had a unique vantage point of the Second Sino-Japanese War. He argued that Japanese students were "familiar with the whole recent history having to do with America and Japan in Asia . . . and up to the present decade, one has not done anything the other has not."[68] Later that year, Matsumoto contributed a more pessimistic article titled "A Lost Cause?" which, despite describing pacifism and international cooperation as an increasingly difficult path, advised JSCA members and other readers of the *Bulletin* to continue to work toward increasing international goodwill and to "let the nations suspect and hate each other; it still cannot destroy the soul of good citizens in them."[69]

CSCA and FSCM members shared the concerns of Matsumoto but turned their attention toward recruiting more Asian American and white students to join their groups and discussions. While such groups and conferences still focused on a pan-Asian theme, there was a more concerted effort (particularly among members of the CSCA and JSCA) to reach out to their American colleagues. CSCA member Al-Li-Sing returned to the cultural bridge theme to support his belief that "we who have recently come from China can act as a bridge between the American-born Chinese and their native country," adding that "both parties have a great deal to contribute to each other and to the interpretation of China to our American friends."[70] Similarly, JSCA members also wished to conduct outreach opportunities to American classmates by sponsoring conferences, including the University of Oregon JSCA chapter's creation of the International Goodwill Club, designed to help build better relations among Japanese, Chinese, and American students on campus.[71] JSCA members—including Michiko Yasumura (University of Washington), Kyoko Matsui (Reed College), William Ito (Oregon Medical School), and others—also participated in the 1937 America-Japan Student Conference at Stanford University (sponsored by the Institute for Pacific Relations as well as the Japan Student Association), a meeting held annually since 1933 that had grown in significance since the escalation of the Second Sino-Japanese War. The six-day event brought together faculty, religious leaders, and over a hundred American, Japanese American, and foreign-born Japanese students from Japanese and West Coast universities to discuss topics such as "the strength of nationalism," "the force of international law," "labor and law in Japan and America," "American expansion in the Pacific," and "the rights and duties of liberal democracy."[72] The conferences and groups were important during a time when ethnic, racial, and national tensions threatened to destroy the pan-Christian cooperation these students had worked to create for nearly twenty years.

But the efforts of students to preserve their panethnic and interracial relations as well as promote Christian goodwill would become more strained. In September 1940, Japan entered into an often-shaky and tense alliance with Germany and the Axis powers, changing the Sino-Japanese War from an Asian conflict into a looming global disaster. Suddenly, the Pacific problem over Manchuria was a global war that placed Japanese students in the United States in a new politically and racially uncomfortable position. It became increasingly difficult for students such as Matsumoto to argue that Japanese militarism could be countered with Christian love and acceptance. The Axis alliance with Japan rattled Americans who viewed the crisis in Manchuria as a chance to support Chinese with donations and voluntary forces, all the while with a cautious eye turned toward the growing economic and political tensions between Japan and the United States. Japan's expansion across Asia appeared to be growing larger and more threatening, increasing anti-Japanese sentiments in America. In light of the growing political tensions, the bridge-building meetings and conferences were small bastions of Christian cooperation amid an international crisis.

Although relations between CSCA and JSCA members did not become immediately tense or appear to deteriorate with Japan's entrance into an Axis alliance, there was a shift in themes and issues in both the *Chinese Christian Student* and the *Japanese Student Bulletin*. There were few shared discussions on the evils of imperialism and nationalism, and joint and pan-Asian conferences received little attention from writers or editors. More specifically, members of the JSCA and CSCA largely adopted defensive positions as a strategy for surviving the growing ethnic and political turmoil in the United States.

For many Christian Chinese students, maneuvering around the Pacific crisis meant recruiting more support for China and pulling away from the JSCA. At the beginning of 1940, CSCA members used their newspaper to build support among Americans and fellow colleagues for a boycott of Japanese goods in America and a Non-Recognition Doctrine of Manchukuo from the US government.[73] Hanson Hwang, the new, second-generation president of the CSCA and editor of the *Chinese Christian Student*, also shifted the social programs of the CSCA back to a cultural bridge format, using Bowls of Rice parties to build support for China among American colleagues and raising donations for Chinese refugees rather than assisting with Sino-Japanese meetings.[74] Similarly, the Pacific Coast branch of the CSCA began an active campaign to gather signatures for a petition to show support among Chinese and Chinese American students for a bill that opposed renewing an existing trade agreement with Japan.[75] The students were not alone in turning their attention toward supporting China, but this support had a negative impact on the desire for panethnic cooperation. Despite the hard work in maintaining open friendships with the JSCA and FSCM during the 1930s, the CSCA moved away from the establishment of a Kingdom of God by 1940. These actions were also important in that they reflected the agreement between both the second-generation and foreign-born Chinese of the CSCA that a defensive position was perhaps the best way to proceed.

While China was the recipient of American sympathies and charitable donations, many Japanese students in the United States tried to separate themselves from Japan. Just as FSCM members were acutely aware of their status as colonials in the metropole, Japanese students became increasingly anxious about their status as potential enemies in the United States. Unlike Filipino students, however, many JSCA members (particularly those who were foreign-born) did not hesitate to speak out against what they viewed as a hostile environment in America and the hypocrisy of Western nations in accusing Japan of unwarranted action in the Pacific. Often, Japanese students denounced American imperialism without turning that same critical eye toward Japan, signaling an attempt to draw attention away from their homeland's aggression by discussing the perils of expansion and nationalism at large. These topics were similar to earlier discussions among Christian association members, but with a different goal of deflecting anger toward Japanese instead of promoting panethnic relations in the United States.

JSCA President Toru Matsumoto personified the defensive position of the JSCA in his writings. A particularly disturbing turn of events for foreign-born Japanese students and members of the JSCA was the emergence of American aid to Britain. In a January 1941 article, Matsumoto explained that England's "fight to preserve her Empire is essentially imperialistic—a war in defense of imperialism," and that "when America endeavors to give England sustenance, she is no less innocent and is partly to blame for the blood-plunder of the Empire builders."[76] "More sinister than the factor of America saving the British empire," he continued, "is her subtle yet ignoble intentions in South America and other parts of the globe," using aid to the British in an attempt to disguise future imperial projects in the name of American liberty and democracy. While he agreed that "non-belligerent aid" to victims of warfare was a Christian duty, he doubted that America provided aid solely for benevolent purposes. In the same edition of the JSCA *Bulletin*, Matsumoto also worried that House Bill 1776, an act authorizing President Roosevelt to use the means necessary to protect the United States in war but also to provide lend-lease assistance to Europe, would possibly endanger the personal freedoms of all Americans who spoke out against the war effort. Matsumoto expressed his concerns that there were "no restrictions which may restrain the head executive from uprooting democratic institutions as they exist in America."[77] It was impossible for Matsumoto to know how right he was in predicting the "uprooting" of American democratic institutions in the name of self-defense during World War II; his words serve as a chilling prediction of what was to come for the Japanese population in the United States during the war.

Conclusions

By recognizing their shared status as Christians with connections to the social, economic, and military problems across the Pacific, both foreign- and American-born students turned an event (the Second-Sino Japanese War) with the potential for disruption into an opportunity to examine the core values of their organizations and the challenges they faced. CSCA, FSCM, and JSCA members used their preexisting panethnic networks to connect the goal of achieving world peace to the concerns of prejudice and racism on the West Coast, helping to broaden the influence of the associations. But the war also emphasized transnational connections to political developments in Asia that threatened the students' coalitions. Issues of nationalism and imperialism during wartime were complex topics that exposed underlying tensions between students of different nationalities. The outbreak of World War II challenged the high levels of cooperation the students achieved during the 1920s and diverted attention away from fruitful discussions of race relations and oppression. However, the CSCA, FSCM, and JSCA continued to push for panethnic and interracial cooperation, actions that contributed to a sustained effort for promoting human and civil rights on the West Coast and abroad during the Second Sino-Japanese War. The students' efforts to band together during international unrest, however, would soon face the ultimate test from changing social, political, and racial landscapes on the Pacific Coast and across America during the emerging world war.

5

Christian Citizenship and Japanese American Incarceration during World War II

• •

Toru Matsumoto's use of the term "uprooting" to explain the radical changes that would accompany World War II was perhaps the best way to describe life for all living in America at the time, including the Christian association members. Employment opportunities in wartime industries changed the racial and ethnic map of the United States, particularly along the West Coast, as African Americans, southern whites, and others left their homes and migrated to cities such as Los Angeles, San Francisco, and Seattle. While movement was voluntary for many, Japanese and Japanese Americans faced a tragic form of uprooting under President Franklin Roosevelt's Executive Order (EO) 9066 of 1942. Roosevelt and other state and local officials (including then California attorney general and later governor Earl Warren) supported "evacuation"[1] as a "military necessity" for the declared western defense zone following Japan's attack on Pearl Harbor and the United States' declaration of war. However, historians have since reevaluated the wartime policy as a deeply racist maneuver that rested on anti-Japanese propaganda produced by groups such as the Native Sons and Daughters of the Golden West, the California State Grange, the Japanese Exclusion League of California, the American Legion, and others before and during World War II.[2] Those already suspicious of the clannish nature of the Japanese and their enclaves argued that Japan's proximity to the West Coast placed California, Washington, Oregon, and other western states in danger of further attacks propagated by Japanese subversion.[3]

By January 1942, Lieutenant General John L. DeWitt of the Western Defense Command encouraged federal and state officials to view the 288,000 Japanese "enemy aliens" in the United States and particularly the 117,000 people of Japanese descent along the West Coast (including American-born Japanese) as disloyal and potentially dangerous agents.[4] During the late winter and early spring of 1942, the War Relocation Authority (or WRA, the government agency staffed by military and other bureaucratic officials in charge of the process) circulated pamphlets and flyers in an attempt to explain the process as well as encourage voluntary movement from the West Coast states to temporary "relocation centers" or "camps." Assisted by the US Census Bureau (which provided background information on the occupations and activities of Japanese communities), the federal government relocated and imprisoned (or "interned" as the WRA described the process) approximately 120,000 Japanese, including 80,000 American citizens.

Just as the war uprooted West Coast Japanese, World War II was also a transformative period for the Christian student associations. The changes the students and their organizations underwent during the war were complex and reflective of the challenges and shifts for Asian communities along the West Coast. Ethnic and racial tensions among various Asian groups and between Asians and whites that were heightened during the Second Sino-Japanese War increased after Pearl Harbor. This instability and inter-ethnic/interracial tension during the war challenged the goals and operations of the student associations in dramatic ways. The JSCA disbanded after the Immigration and Naturalization Service detained Matsumoto in Fort Meade, Maryland, following his refusal of their offer of repatriation to Japan; the imprisonment of their leader was demoralizing for many members and also disruptive for day-to-day operations. The cohesion of the CSCA and FSCM also suffered during the war when the groups lost administrative and financial support from the YMCA (now focused more on war relief efforts) and were not able to produce student bulletins to build communications between different campus chapters. The relationships between foreign-born and American-born members also suffered, as the stifling of Christian student networks during the war prevented a free exchange of ideas. The associations fractured as war fever swept through Asian America.

Although the Christian associations splintered during the war, individual members continued to apply Christian principles and strategies they developed earlier to the racial problems that EO 9066 exposed and created. Similar to the upheaval during the Second Sino-Japanese War, World War II forced Asian and Asian American students to consider what Christian citizenship meant for them, but within the troubled framework of American democracy and freedom. While not as strong as it was prior to the war, the CSCA continued to operate in a limited manner, with Chinese Christian students meeting at smaller conferences to discuss the removal of Japanese from the West Coast and its impact on Chinese communities and other minorities. JSCA members and former students also continued to build interracial relationships on college campuses outside of the defense zone and participated in nationwide groups that called for an end to discriminatory anti-Asian naturalization and immigration laws. These activities, though not as large or panethnic as before 1941, represented the strength of the students' commitment to social and Christian justice.

For these students, the US government's imprisonment of Japanese Americans was a high-water mark in the long history of discrimination against immigrants and Asian Americans. The forced removal was an awakening, a powerful event that made them think about how to apply their vision of Christian fellowship and their goals of building solidarity across racial and ethnic boundaries beyond campus. Prejudice and racism from sororities, fraternities, YMCAs, and employers paled in comparison to the systematic abuse of power by the War Relocation Authority, backed by the Supreme Court's decision to uphold the constitutionality of imprisoning US citizens without due process. Christian students could not ignore this tragic turn of events and viewed EO 9066 as a painful consequence of America's previous failures in addressing anti-Asian discrimination.

The students' writings and meetings also demonstrate how important the Christian associations were for carrying forth the ideas of interracial and interethnic solidarity. The students were part of a changing racial landscape during the war, as well as a burgeoning civil rights movement that would use the hypocrisy of America's racial turmoil to push for legislative change. Many others, including members of the federal government and the various social workers who worked within the prisons that held Japanese, also questioned the motives behind the forced removal of Japanese as well as worried over the lingering effects of EO 9066 on race relations. The disconnect between America's war against fascism abroad and its own discriminatory policies and denial of justice at home was palpable and a strong incentive to capitalize on this contradiction in the name of civil rights. Greg Robinson describes this period as one of dramatic change as white liberal Americans and minorities came to view the war as a "racial revolution" that would shape postwar civil rights activism. Similarly, Matthew Briones has used the life of Charles Kikuchi—a Nisei who recorded his experiences with imprisonment in the Tanforan detention center and his later interactions with various activist figures—to chart the growing interest in interracial cooperation for both a better United States and a better world. Leftist, secular organizations such as labor unions, campus student groups, and various civil rights organizations viewed the war as both a challenge and an opportunity for bringing whites and minorities together to fight for equality. This form of interracial or "culturally pluralistic" engagement for the benefit of integration and equality was a new type of "racial liberalism" that historians argue was a product of World War II.[5]

But these were not new ideas for Christian Asian students. The push for interracial solidarity to provoke social movements and change existed well before World War II along the West Coast, as evidenced in the conferences, discussions, resolutions, and publications of the CSCA, JSCA, and FSCM. The students' focus on creating a Kingdom of God on Earth that resulted in the earlier formation of interracial, panethnic, and interethnic groups also sheds light on a specifically Christian element of the wider prewar civil rights movement. Executive Order 9066 and the war were not the spark for racial liberalism but rather an important moment for Christian Asian students to assess the impact of their own interracial and interethnic networks in the racially charged atmosphere of the 1940s.

This chapter explores the effects of wartime upheaval on Christian association members, former members, and Asian students in addition to its impact on social and political developments between 1941 and 1945. These students brought their interracial and panethnic ideas with them to new settings, albeit with varied results and outcomes. As before, there were limitations to the influence of discussions and conferences as well as Christian fellowship on race relations beyond campus. However, the war was not a complete rupture with the past for the students who continued their activism outside the boundaries of the associations. This was not easy to accomplish during what Scott Kurashige has identified as the "shifting grounds of race" during World War II.[6] Both voluntary migration and forced removal brought Americans of various races and ethnicities into contact with one another, showcasing the difficulties as well as the possibilities of interracial solidarity. Uprootings, ethnic tensions, and limited resources resulted in new student attempts at panethnic cooperation that were more detailed in comparison with those of the prewar years. Although the Christian associations unraveled, individual students began a process of integration into larger forms of civil rights activism along the West Coast and across the nation. Christian students redefined their goals and strategies for equality during the war, challenging their previous notions of ending prejudice by building a Kingdom of God and encouraging them to think of the legal and political implications of these views.[7]

West Coast Colleges and EO 9066

The reactions of college and university students of all races and ethnicities to the Japanese after Pearl Harbor were complex, ranging from suspicion to tolerance to sympathy. One of the most important differences between student responses and those of other communities was the students' tendency to promote meetings and conferences to openly discuss the backlash against Japanese on the West Coast. As early as December 16, 1941, a group of over two hundred Japanese American students at the University of Washington met with other classmates and members of the administration to discuss their course of action in the wake of Japan's attack. Japanese American students joined with Dean Robert O'Brien, who was also the Japanese Club advisor, to "discuss pertinent problems" such as an increase in anti-Japanese attitudes and the ideal amount of money that Japanese nationals should withdraw from their bank accounts in case of emergency.[8] While college campuses were not immune to prejudice and patriotism-tinged hatred during the war, they did offer spaces for open communication between Japanese students and others about the challenges of forced removal.

Once news arrived in early March 1942 that the federal government and the army required American- and foreign-born Japanese to leave their schools—stopping first at temporary holding centers for screening and then moving on to prisons managed by the War Relocation Authority—Japanese students wasted little time in using campus newspapers to express their opinions of EO 9066. Japanese reactions to removal were naturally varied. In many cases, Japanese American students responded with a stoic certainty that the forced removal, though unfair, was not a complete surprise considering the history of anti-Japanese sentiment. "Don't feel sorry for us," a University of Washington Japanese Club member explained in the *Daily*, "we have expected this for some time and are taking the whole thing calmly."[9] Similarly, Berkeley student and JSCA member Tom Shibutani demonstrated quiet acceptance in a 1942 *Daily Cal* editorial, acknowledging that "true, we are being uprooted from the lives that we have always lived, but if the security of the nation rests upon our leaving, then we will gladly do our part."[10] Japanese students' initial acceptance of removal appeared to be in line with the Japanese American Citizens League's controversial support of cooperation with EO 9066 in order for Japanese Americans to prove their loyalty to America. Students professed faith that the process would be fair and that they would return to campus when the chaos ended.[11]

However, other Japanese American students were more cautionary and pessimistic. In the April 1942 edition of the YMCA's *Intercollegian*, JSCA member and leader of the student YMCA at the University of Washington Kenji Okuda warned "this mass movement" of Japanese students "may arouse racial antagonism and unfortunate situations are almost inevitable." "We must settle somewhere," Okuda explained, "but will the resettlement process be accompanied by tyrannical expressions of Hitleristic mob action, or will the Christian principles which we members of the Student Christian Movement endeavor to practice prevail?"[12] Daiki Miyagawa, another University of Washington student, could not answer Okuda's haunting question but insisted that "the evacuee has rights" regardless of the wartime hysteria. In a 1942 editorial for the *Daily*, Miyagawa argued that while "some of the clamor for a mass exodus comes from those who hope to gain from the evacuees' losses, others are impelled by racial reasons," identifying EO 9066 as the ripening of hatred for the Japanese along the West Coast. For Miyagawa, forced removal was simply "business-and-prejudice as usual," but this prejudice "had no place in our war effort," making it necessary for the WRA and the government to assess equally individuals for subversion "whether their family trees reach back to Benedict

Arnold or the Tokugawas [of Japan]."[13] Both students were concerned about the underlying motives behind and possible outcomes of EO 9066, considering it a racist outcry from West Coast residents hiding behind the pretense of wartime necessity. Although these were only written warnings in campus publications, Japanese American students called on classmates of all racial and ethnic backgrounds to be on guard lest Christian and civil rights be violated.

Did students such as Okuda and Miyagawa receive support from their fellow classmates on campus? In many cases, students rallied with their Japanese American classmates and decried the tragedy and undemocratic nature of EO 9066. In editorials submitted to campus newspapers, students were quick to defend those who questioned the process. In early March 1942, two University of Washington students, Oleg Kur and *Daily* editor Russ Braley, exchanged heated words over the topic. Braley was not shy when it came to expressing his anger and disappointment in the US government for issuing the executive order. Kur accused Braley of being oblivious to the necessity of incarceration for Japanese and Japanese Americans, claiming that "in defending the 'defenseless Japs,' our honorable Mr. Bradley [*sic*] forgot his own brothers and sisters. What would the great humanitarian Mr. Bradley say had he seen his fellow schoolmates and neighbors oppressed by the Japs?"[14] Braley retorted that after reading Kur's letter to the editor, he "phoned immediately to see what the Japanese American[s] . . . had done to my little brothers and sisters. But the little tykes were alright, so I settled down to write you." "Look chum," Braley snapped at Kur, "what conceivable good is it going to do to persecute loyal American citizens because their ancestors were born in a country which we are at war? What do you think they are going to do, burn down the school house?"[15]

Although the back-and-forth newspaper debate between Kur and Braley ended with this saucy exchange, other students voiced their more serious disagreements with evacuation. Two University of Washington students and YMCA/YWCA members Hildur Coon and Curtiss Adler testified before the House Select Committee Investigating National Defense Migration (known as the Tolan Committee) during a series of hearings on the nature and purpose of evacuation held in Seattle in February of 1942. Headed by Representative John Tolan (a Democrat from Oakland, CA), the committee—charged with investigating various wartime issues, including migration and German and Italians in the United States—held a series of meetings in Los Angeles, San Francisco, Seattle, and Portland in February and March following EO 9066. These hearings featured testimonies from local and state officials and members of the public on the potential impact of mass Japanese American removal. Many of the white local and state officials as well as other members of the cities spoke in favor of the order, while others denounced the measure. Coon and Adler "urged that evacuation be used only as a last resort" and, if necessary, to be done in an expedient and humane manner (e.g., by making time in relocation centers brief and finding similar occupations for evacuees in other towns and cities). Both students also requested that "Nisei students now at the university be excepted [*sic*] from any evacuations" since "these students would be able to help Americanize their parents and would be useful in peace work following the war."[16]

Surprisingly, given how supportive many of the students were of their Nisei classmates, there was no mass moral or political outrage on West Coast campuses against this blatant violation of civil liberties. While individual students wrote editorials and other articles, the forced removal of hundreds of foreign- and American-born Japanese failed to garner front-page attention or any in-depth coverage in campus publications. Executive Order 9066 did not even make the "Top Ten" list of events from 1942 at the end-of-the-year edition of the University of Washington *Daily*. Just as students such as Russ Braley believed that removal was unjust and would only create more problems in the future, other students admitted that evacuation was a tragedy but ultimately a defensive necessity. While West Coast students were active in peace movements and radical groups on campuses during the 1930s and into the early years of the war, there was relative silence on the topic of EO 9066. Most tellingly, a Berkeley administrator's statement that there was little left for Berkeley to do besides "wish all [Japanese students] well" and hope that regardless of where the students might find themselves, Americans "will regard them as the sons and daughters" of California and the United States elicited no response from the students on campus.[17]

The likelihood of other Americans viewing Japanese Americans as their sons and daughters, however, appeared slim. While students along the West Coast were often shocked at the sudden and extensive effects of EO 9066, for Nisei students such as Kenji Okuda, this was a culmination of discrimination against Asian immigrants and Asian Americans. The forced migration of thousands of Japanese was a carefully planned mass violation of both civil and human rights, but the racism inherent in this act was no surprise. Executive Order 9066 was a large-scale example of the hypocrisy of democracy in twentieth-century America as well as a turning point for Asian Christian activists and their allies. Similar to the way FSCM members turned to labor organizing to fulfill their needs, many individual students returned to larger Christian organizations such as the YMCA when the CSCA, JSCA, and FSCM floundered during the war years.

Christian Citizenship and Civil Rights

At times, as in the case of University of Washington sociology major Gordon Hirabayashi, protest against EO 9066 assumed a more defiant stance than editorials and publications. A Christian, YMCA member, and pacifist, Hirabayashi openly protested warfare, but in a life-altering decision in early May 1942, he became a crusader for equality through civil disobedience. He first defied a curfew imposed on all those of Japanese descent, choosing instead to remain in the library to finish his studies, and later refused to board the last of the buses transporting Japanese from Seattle to the temporary assembly center at Puyallup Fair Grounds in Washington. Hirabayashi then reported to the local US district attorney in the fall of 1942 and submitted a written statement explaining that if he "were to register and cooperate" with the order, he would be "giving helpless consent to the denial of practically all the things which had given [him] the incentive to live."[18] He argued that it was necessary during wartime to maintain his "Christian principles" and considered it his "duty to maintain the democratic standards for which this nation lives."[19] Hirabayashi's surrender to the district attorney resulted in multiple court cases and appeals until his defense team (with assistance from groups including the American Friends Service Committee, the American Civil Liberties Union, and the YMCA) presented the case to the Supreme Court, where the justices ruled in 1943 that both the curfew and EO 9066 were constitutionally sound during times of war. Hirabayashi based his rejection of the forced removal of Japanese and Japanese Americans on principles of both Christian and civil rights, ideas that reflected earlier activism in the Christian student associations. Overall, the *Hirabayashi* case ushered in a new phase of questioning of EO 9066 among students, one that required more analysis and awareness of the hypocrisy of American practices. (See figure 4.)

FIGURE 4. Gordon Hirabayashi (seated, front right) with YMCA/YWCA friends at the University of Washington in 1941. Kenji Okuda is also present (back row, second from left). University of Washington Libraries, Special Collections, UW23241z.

Hirabayashi's protests were part of a growing concern among Christian activists that EO 9066 represented a negative turning point in American democracy. Many Christian groups had little faith that either the federal government or their fellow Americans would view forced removal as an injustice rather than a necessity of war. In fact, organizations such as the YMCA/YWCA and the Quaker-led American Friends Service Committee (AFSC) were among the most vocal of groups to speak out against the constitutional injustices of Japanese incarceration. In a report on the University of Washington YWCA's earliest reactions to EO 9066, the executive secretary of the organization explained that "because many Nisei were YMCA members and because, as a Christian organization we were professionally concerned, [forced removal] became a dominant factor in the Association," and, based on the articles published and actions taken by the organization, this was certainly true.[20] As the report indicated, because many Japanese Americans were Christians, leaders of the YMCA/YWCA assumed responsibility to assist those imprisoned. In a July 1942 article titled "The Church and Japanese Evacuation," YMCA regional secretary Gordon Chapman cited a statement from a "certain

Congressman" which "said that the Japanese in America 'are pagan in their philosophy, atheistic in their beliefs, alien in their allegiance, and antagonistic to everything for which we stand.'" Chapman vehemently disagreed with the congressman, arguing that "fully half of the Japanese Americans and a quarter of the non-citizens are Christians or pro-Christianity. . . . this constitutes their claim to our Christian sympathy and interest and support."[21]

While many members of the YMCA argued that it was their duty to protect Japanese and Japanese American Christians, others were also concerned about what EO 9066 meant for the rest of the nation. In April 1942, Los Angeles branches of the YMCA held a conference and issued a report on "the Japanese evacuation situation" that highlighted the organization's warning that "we may see the day when our own citizens will be taken from their enforced idleness to do forced labor of a 'patriotic nature'" now that the federal government had evacuated Japanese Americans from the West Coast.[22] Like the Los Angeles YMCAs, Edna Morris of the AFSC also issued a memo in which she explained that "all constitutional guarantees during war time are threatened by Evacuation Orders" and warned that "if Japanese can be deprived of both property and law without judicial procedure . . . [it] established a dangerous precedent."[23]

After the initial phase of removal in early March, however, YMCA and AFSC leaders and members expressed disappointment in themselves and other Christians for not speaking out more forcefully against EO 9066 and its racial underpinnings. In a March 1942 letter to Galen Fisher (leader of the Northern California Committee for Fair Play for Citizens and Aliens of Japanese Ancestry), YMCA national administrator Arthur Jorgensen explained that "while it was proper and necessary for the Christian forces to collaborate with the Government in this evacuation . . . it would have been more to the point to have declared the fundamental question of the constitutional rights of the Nisei more vocally and from the very beginning of evacuation."[24] Edna Morris also described "another serious phase of the situation [of evacuation] from the standpoint of democracy is that these Evacuation Orders were issued and executed with almost no protest or opposition from responsible people, the general public, the church or the press."[25] Both the YMCA and AFSC lamented that neither they nor many Americans took any serious actions against forced removal and waited too long to begin questioning the constitutional violations of EO 9066. In other words, there were stark differences between the response of

Christians like Hirabayashi and the response of large Christian organizations to the injustice suffered by the incarcerated.

As opposed to the administrators of the YMCA and AFSC, the student branches of these and various other Christian organizations were more vocal and more concerned with how EO 9066 would shape the future of American race relations. The National Intercollegiate Christian Council (or NICC, a student organization associated with the World Student Christian Federation and the Student Christian Movement associations in the United States) strongly denounced the undemocratic and unchristian nature of EO 9066 and was particularly concerned about its effects on Japanese American students. Edmonia White Grant, an African American program secretary for the NICC as well as a member of the NAACP and a research sociologist at Fisk University, encouraged Christian students to carefully analyze the racism at the heart of forced removal. Under Grant's guidance, NICC members identified incarceration as "a racial problem" based on the fact that "inasmuch as Japanese Americans and alien Japanese have been treated differently from German and Italian-Americans and aliens who are white, this in part becomes a racial issue."[26]

Executive Order 9066 exposed racial injustices that existed outside of a white/black binary. "Too often in the past," Grant declared in a 1942 pamphlet, "our attention has been directed only to minority problems as they relate to Negroes and we have not faced the total problem of minority groups within our country." Forced removal showcased what Christian Asian students had been arguing all along: "the crux of our present minority problem lies in the attitude of the majority not only to Negroes, but to all colored peoples: mixed blood, Indian, Chinese, Hindu, Japanese, African and others." America's "constitutional amendments which made racial bars to citizenship illegal have failed to achieve political democracy in the United States," with incarceration being the end result. "If our conception of a genuinely Christian brotherhood society is a true concept," Grant informed readers, "we must direct ourselves toward the furthering of a world order which provides every individual, regardless of race, creed, or national origin, the opportunity to participate in and share alike all the relationships of life." In a time of war against fascism abroad, "the unjust treatment of minorities within the U.S. not only contributes to national but international division and must be corrected if the U.S. is to lead the struggle for freedom."[27] As Grant's work with the NICC suggests, forced removal was not the beginning of massive racism or xenophobia directed toward Japanese (particularly along the West Coast), but rather a pivotal point in a legacy of hatred. However, just as local battles for civil rights among Africans Americans in the South would meld into a growing national fight for equality following World War II, EO 9066 also forced Americans to confront the plight of Asian immigrants and Asian Americans as part of a larger problem. Other Christian organizations would come to embrace what the members of the Asian student associations were working toward before the war: an interracial, interethnic, and Christian-based approach to achieving rights through youth leadership. Forced removal, though painful, reflected changing race relations that would create both challenges and opportunities for future activists.

Grant's leadership in the NICC represented an important shift in both Christian and student attempts to place incarceration in a larger racial framework. Not only did the NICC urge American Christians to look upon EO 9066 with shame for its success in stripping American citizens of their civil liberties, but the organization also identified the uprooting as a denial of basic human rights. The NICC made no distinction between American-born or immigrant Japanese when discussing the devastating effects of the order; after all, true Christians did not distinguish between citizens and noncitizens in need of help. In the Kingdom of God, removal was unjust because it intensified and promoted discrimination and prejudice. Grant's timely words prompted NICC members and other students to contribute articles to the YMCA's *Intercollegian* that focused on the duty of Christians to assist Japanese and Japanese American war victims and denounce EO 9066 as an inhumane process.

One powerful piece was the April 1942 article titled "American War Victims," which placed Japanese and Japanese American evacuees in the category of tragedies brought about by World War II, "reducing these thousands of uprooted peoples to the status of refugees and peons." The author explained that "as a Student Christian Movement, it is not our place to sit in judgment on the imperatives of national defense . . . but when we see clear violation of the fundamental principles of human brotherhood and individual justice, we feel qualified to speak for such principles are at the heart of our movement and such imperatives, not luxuries, to a democracy at war . . . we believe we are seeing such a violation."[28] Following the article, the Student Christian Movement passed a resolution formally protesting the "mass evacuation order and the principles of racial discrimination and denial of human rights on which it is based" and stressing the "vital importance of government subsidy or provision for continuing higher education and secondary education for the American-born Japanese torn from West Coast schools and colleges."[29]

Christian students also argued that EO 9066 and anti-Japanese racism were devastating to America's reputation as a Christian and democratic nation. Dean Leeper, a graduate student at the University of Washington and a YMCA staff member, "spoke on the need for a world out-look and world and racial fellowships" to help understand and navigate evacuation and incarceration.[30] Just as China's alliance with the United States made anti-Chinese sentiments among Americans something of an embarrassment during the war, others argued that incarcerating American citizens based on racism was a terrible contradiction in a war built on fighting fascists.[31] Leeper stressed that EO 9066 "may lose us the war because China, India, and all the darker-skinned people are watching our treatment of colored folk in this country" and urged "that every effort be made to relocate the Japanese American college students so that this leadership may be saved for Christianity and democracy."[32] Christian students identified forced removal as a hindrance for democracy as well as worldwide fellowship. Getting Nisei as well as foreign-born Japanese out of the camps and back into schools would not only benefit the students but also help to restore faith in American democracy, equality, and Christian values.

Student Resettlement

"Resettlement" (as the government officials and Christian leaders identified the process) of students was part of a larger process of removing Japanese Americans from the detention centers and placing them in cities and communities away from the West Coast. Beginning as early as 1942, the WRA cooperated with organizations like the YMCA, YWCA, and the AFSC to identify Japanese who were eligible for leaving the centers and to assist them with finding homes and jobs. While Issei and students who did not repatriate to Japan were held in higher-security Department of Justice internment centers, Japanese Americans had an opportunity to leave their prisons. As a result, those remaining foreign-born Japanese students were not easily resettled due to their alien status. Most candidates for resettlement were well-behaved, Christian, and patriotic (as demonstrated in questionnaires and psychological evaluations) Nisei with established outside connections either through a job or outside sponsor, generally a religious or community organization. In its most basic sense, resettlement assured Americans that incarceration was temporary and that reentry of Japanese Americans into society was already under way.

But white liberals in charge of resettlement also viewed the process as a way to dismantle Japanese enclaves and break down barriers to assimilation. By steering Nisei toward cities like Chicago (one of the areas with the largest increase in Japanese American populations during the war), the resettlement program sought to refashion Japanese Americans as culturally and socially assimilated citizens. If Japanese and their descendants faced difficulties under the racial limitations of West Coast society, these problems could be addressed by properly integrating them into communities outside of California and breaking up ethnic enclaves that prohibited advancement. Mike Masaoka, the head of the JACL, also supported resettlement as a way to promote leadership and social mobility among the Nisei. Leaders in Japanese communities hoped resettled Japanese Americans would choose to remain in their new homes and prevent the rebirth of close-knit Japanese neighborhoods by becoming more American (white) and less Oriental/other after the war. Overall, approximately 36,000 imprisoned Japanese resettled in Midwest and East Coast cities, adding to the changing racial makeup of urban landscapes during the war. While resettlement placed Nisei in the crosshairs of existing racial tensions between blacks and whites, it also facilitated, as Ellen Wu explains, Japanese Americans' complex transition from "yellow peril" to "model minority."[33]

Stemming from the concern for Nisei in the detention centers, Japanese American students were the earliest group to be resettled. WRA officials and social workers who interacted with the second generation argued that education was paramount to ensuring students' loyalty and full participation in American society. Assisting incarcerated Japanese students in returning to college became the primary task for the Student Christian Movement as well as other Christian students and groups. As early as May 1942, the National Japanese American Student Relocation Council (or NJASRC, founded by a variety of Christian groups, including the AFSC, Committee on Friendly Relations among Foreign Students, and the YMCA with assistance from the War Relocation Authority) found campuses to sponsor students who were continuing their high school and postsecondary studies.[34] Since West Coast schools were located in the military defense zone, colleges and universities in the Midwest and along the East Coast became the primary recipients of resettled Nisei. In order to leave the centers, students (with the help of the NJASRC) were required by the WRA to be qualified for admission at an approved institution and be able to finance their education (either through savings, scholarships, work, or aid from an organization such as the YMCA). Letters of recommendation, good grades, and evidence of excellent character (as described in worksheets provided to universities by the NJASRC describing religious background, "friendliness," "obedience," and other favored qualities) were the usual requirements for leaving the centers. By the spring of 1943, the WRA had cleared over two hundred colleges and universities as "reception schools" and 550 students had left detention centers and resettled in institutions mainly in the Midwest, along the East Coast, and in some instances the South (at smaller private schools).[35]

In many ways, the work of the NJASRC appeared to be both a wartime necessity to boost morale among Nisei and a humanitarian effort. As the historian Allan W. Austin explains, reports on the detention centers revealed dispiriting conditions for young Japanese Americans.[36] In September 1943, a field director for the NJASRC warned, "when a person visits a project for just a few days or so, he can easily fail to realize that he is seeing only the people who are sympathetic to the cause of the Japanese." The NJASRC's write-up was in direct contrast to the *Time* and *Life* magazine articles that displayed glossy photos of Japanese American families at home in the modest yet comfortable furnishings of the prisons or young Nisei playing games and socializing at dances. Instead of these idealized press treatments, NJASRC reports indicated that racism and discrimination were daily facts of life in the camps: "There [were] many people . . . who [were] not sympathetic to the Japanese and specifically hostile to the idea of Japanese Americans getting a college education," ideas that were a mixture of racism and "realism" in that "it [was] a mistake for a Japanese American to think in terms of a college education since he is destined to be only a manual laborer anyway." One internee lamented that "the Caucasians on the WRA staff [were] setting up a whole Jim Crow system of their own" in the relocation centers.[37] Even the WRA admitted that the "Nisei as a group [were] dissatisfied with the treatment they have received from the government" and becoming "disillusioned . . . frustrated . . . and bitter." Conditions in the camps turned loyal, successful Japanese American students into resentful individuals losing faith in American democracy.[38]

Imprisoned Christians also expressed both anger and frustration at their isolation from interracial and interethnic fellowship. During a Christian student conference in 1944, JSCA member Tek Sakurai (a student originally from California who left the Manzanar detention camp for Worcester College in Massachusetts) recalled how his "long hibernation in the [internment] center" had allowed him to forget "much of the problems of other races and groups—the Negro, the sharecroppers, the migratory workers, the Mexicans, the Indians, and the Jews."[39] In 1943, JSCA member Kenji Okuda explained in a letter to Mary Farquardson, a member of the AFSC in Washington who assisted with the resettlement of Japanese, that he and fellow interned students felt that "more interracial understanding" was needed in the camps. Okuda requested "more Negro speakers . . . and also other minority speakers" and demanded "more action and less talk" from the organizers of the camps and the AFSC.[40] Students engaged with campus organizations and familiar with social issues before EO 9066 forced them from their homes found the camps dehumanizing. They were removed from the social problems of other groups and the rest of humanity—a terrible position for Christian students devoted to worldwide fellowship.

Fortunately, for students seeking integration into campus life and activism, university presidents and administrators such as Robert Sproul of the University of California supported the resettlement of students. However, Sproul (who was also on the NJASRC) cared more about ensuring that Nisei were able to seamlessly integrate back into society than about promoting Christian activism. "As a university administrator," he began in a 1942 letter to the Tolan Committee, "I am particularly interested in the fate of those young citizens of Japanese ancestry who are being forced to leave colleges and universities in the restricted areas. . . . they, above all others, will provide the leadership for their racial minority group in the future years." Like other West Coast Americans, Sproul (correctly) believed that the Nisei would serve as the leaders for the Japanese community and argued that the incarceration centers damaged young Japanese Americans and their capacity for leadership. "It is essential to the welfare of the nation," Sproul pleaded to the Tolan Committee, "that these leaders be given every opportunity to complete their preparation for responsibility in a way which will insure wholehearted loyalty to this country."[41] Resettlement for students was not only a way to ensure that loyalty would prevail but also a way to prepare for life after the war. In general, the WRA,

NJASRC, and other organizations argued that Nisei could fully assimilate into a white, American culture and assume the former leadership positions of the Issei when the war ended.

The response to Sproul's concerns were mixed, with schools around the country either embracing, cautiously accepting, or denying admission to students. Some institutions, such as the University of Tennessee, the University of the South (in Sewanee, Tennessee), the University of San Francisco, and Susquehanna University in Pennsylvania, were either hesitant to accept or refused to have Japanese Americans in their institutions, fearing the local community's reaction to accepting "enemies of America." The University of Tennessee issued a more direct reply to the NJASRC's plea by stating that "this war has given evidence of character in the Japanese" that made Nisei students an uninvited group on campus.[42] Others, including those West Coast schools cleared by the army for accepting relocated Japanese American students, were eager and welcoming. James E. Edminston, a member of the NJASRC, was happy to report to the council in April 1945 that despite lingering anti-Japanese feelings, Stanford University, San Jose State College, and the high schools of Santa Clara County in California were "warm and enthusiastic" in their acceptance of Japanese students.[43] Similarly, Robert Galbraith, president of Westminster College in New Westminster, Pennsylvania, expressed his hope that even a small number of resettled students would erode the "pride in the fact that there are no 'foreigners' in the neighborhood" and that "the presence of these boys will help break down a definitely un-American tradition and . . . do us all good."[44] While some schools balked at the idea of accepting students, other universities across the country recognized that admitting Nisei might bring a worldlier atmosphere to their campuses as well as assist resettled students in finishing their educations. Regardless of the mixed receptions, by 1943, approximately six hundred students enrolled in colleges and universities across the United States.[45]

As the historian Gary Okihiro has argued, the effect of resettlement on Japanese American students reveals both the promise and turmoil of wartime migration and changing racial identities and relationships. As minorities (and, in many cases, the only Japanese) on campuses hundreds and thousands of miles away from their homes, Japanese students encountered reactions from other students that ran the gamut from conciliatory to cold to curious. In many cases, whites welcomed their new classmates, reaching out to Japanese students and wishing to incorporate them into campus life.

Okihiro describes the integration of clubs, sports teams, and other social and cultural organizations once Japanese students arrived, signaling a certain level of acceptance. However, at times suspicion characterized interactions between resettled students and their hosts. Whites held Japanese students at arm's length for racial reasons or due to wartime prejudice. It was often easier for Nisei students who were either the only one of their kind on campus or one of only a handful of Japanese Americans to merge if not blend with other students. In other cases, receiving students were wary of Nisei who congregated together at lunch or in dormitories.[46]

On campuses in the East and Midwest, relocated students often found that reaching out to others was as much a strategy for social survival on campus as it was for building interracial friendships. The NJASRC as well as other student groups often advised resettled students to resist the urge to seek out other Japanese and form cliques, for such actions were sure to draw unwanted attention. Connecting with students from a variety of racial/ethnic backgrounds may have been the only way that resettled students could socialize while at their new institution if they were the only Japanese on campus. Depending on where they attended school across the country, resettled students, known as "tumbleweeds" in popular periodicals, were treated as threats, curiosities, or "potential Americans" who could fully assimilate. Regardless of the reaction, resettlement contributed to the challenging transformations of race relations in the United States as groups migrated across the country during the war.[47]

For Christian Nisei, the experience of resettlement was confusing, yet also promising. JSCA members and other Japanese American Christian students did not abandon their desire for fellowship and equality while incarcerated but viewed resettlement as an opportunity to transfer their mission of creating interracial friendship and Christian understanding to new locations. Although the JSCA ceased operations during World War II, Christian Japanese American students still had the opportunity to form their own groups while in the detention centers. In March 1943, the Pacific Southwest branch of the World Student Christian Federation assisted Japanese in forming a Student Christian Association at the California Tule Lake "segregation center," a strict prison reserved for those deemed to be of a higher threat to American security. Later that same year, the Tule Lake Christian Japanese students invited California college students to attend a "Little Asilomar" conference a few weeks before the big yearly YMCA-sponsored Asilomar conference.[48] Problems of racism, discrimination, poverty, and the role of Christianity in social problems in the United States and around the world were topics of conversation at the Little Asilomar meeting, just as they were at conferences and discussion groups the Japanese students previously attended.[49] Incarcerated students were eager to reestablish their pre-EO 9066 lives, which included outreach, Christian discussion groups, and promotion of interracial and interethnic harmony.

With the assistance of the AFSC as well as the NJASRC, many Christian students and former JSCA members resettled at schools in the Northeast. The students' Christian status and good behavior in camps made it relatively easy for the committees to find colleges and universities in Pennsylvania, New York, New England, and even in the Southeast that were willing to accept them. Once on campus, students immediately found the cosmopolitan clubs, the YMCA/YWCA, or other Christian organizations to begin their process of integration. Interracial and Christian groups also provided opportunities for engaging in the fellowship-building activities the students embraced. In many ways, resettlement broadened the students' experiences with interracial interaction and brought their Christian-based activities into the fold of changing race relations during the war. These tumbleweeds, like the African Americans who migrated to the West Coast, also faced the new challenges of settling into unfamiliar territory and working to adapt to their new environments, with varied results.[50]

As students' writings indicate, being the only Japanese American student on campus was difficult and at times isolating, which made personal connections with white students a psychological and social necessity. In a March 1945 letter to the Relocation Council, Sumiko Fujii (a student transplanted to Vermont from Washington) explained, "I realize that since I will be the first Japanese to ever attend Bennington or to ever be seen by most of the people in Vermont, my job will not only be one of studying hard, but also one of creating good public relations with the Caucasians who I will be in contact with, so that I may pave the way for more Japanese Americans who might be interested in attending schools in Vermont." While at Bennington College, Fujii was an "ambassador of goodwill" who was singly responsible for "trying very hard [to] . . . not commit any blunders which will be detrimental to . . . attitudes toward other Japanese Americans."[51] Similarly, Tamio Kitano, a former JSCA member who received his undergraduate degree from Harvard University and attended graduate school on the West Coast, advised other Japanese students who had resettled at Brigham Young University in Utah to be sure to attend religious assemblies on campus every Tuesday and Thursday. Though not a Mormon and unsure of how to proceed during services, Tamio believed that this would "make the Caucasians think that we are at least loyal to the assemblies, although it may be dry, which it usually is."[52] Readjusting to campus life meant trying to form friendships with others and, when necessary, attending dull church services in the name of ambassadorship.

Other resettled students viewed their time on campus as a way to erase misunderstandings about the Japanese and create cultural connections. Japanese American students described their attempts at interracial friendship in ways that echoed the early missions of cultural bridge-building. Campus organizations and local religious groups from the nearby community invited students to speak about their culture (perhaps an uncomfortable position for Nisei), racial discrimination, and the incarceration experience at discussion groups and gatherings. Masaye Nagao was one such student who relayed to the Relocation Council that "many of the organizations in Kansas City have asked the Park College Nisei to speak about evacuation and their experience" and that "it has been interesting to me to know how much of the misunderstandings and prejudice had arisen because of lack of information and knowledge."[53] Nagao's remarks were in contrast to the rash of racial intimidation and harassment that other students encountered in the Kansas City area and surrounding communities. One student at Park College (located in Parkville, Missouri, near Kansas City) described having no problems while on campus with other students, but being harassed and taunted one night by a group of men when returning to her dorm after having dinner in town.[54] Despite the racial problems near Park College, Nagao was determined that "our little bit will help in clearing up some of the misunderstandings in this community and elsewhere."[55]

The experiences of resettled students were different from those of other Japanese Americans, who ended up relocating to the Midwest or other areas of the United States for employment rather than education. As Charlotte Brooks explains, in the larger urban communities such as Chicago, racial discrimination in housing and employment often led to interracial tensions between Nisei and both whites and African Americans who shared the same space.[56] Similarly, protests against forced removal and imprisonment assumed many forms, including rebellious Nisei both in the camps and in cities as well as more direct political forms of opposition, such as the "No-No Boys," who refused to serve in the armed forces and renounce their supposed foreign allegiance. When placed next to these overt reactions, building cultural and racial bridges may appear as if students were simply giving in to the demands placed on them by various organizations. By attempting to settle into their new colleges through outreach and interracial friendships, Christian students appeared to follow the desired plan for resettling Japanese at large: full participation in American society beyond ethnic enclaves.

However, Japanese American students still recognized their precarious positions as both racial minorities and descendants of the enemy when they arrived on campus. Their attempts at building bridges reflected the resettlement program's larger goals of assimilation, but creating opportunities for interracial and interethnic outreach were longtime goals of JSCA members and Christian Japanese. As with other changes in race relations at the time, EO 9066 and the forced removals and migrations that resulted emphasized trends and trajectories that were already in place prior to the war. Many Christian students who came to different campuses and attempted to build connections with white students did not see themselves as assimilating but rather using tactics and strategies of Christian fellowship and networking to navigate their new terrain.

Wartime suspicion, combined with a general lack of knowledge about the Japanese Americans and their plight during the war, often presented challenges to Christian students, but also opportunities for exchange. Some students were delighted to have the chance to educate their peers but were also shocked at how little students knew of the Nisei experience as well as of EO 9066. Yutaka Kobayoshi relocated to Alfred University in New York in 1942 and excitedly wrote a letter to the NJASRC, explaining that the university chaplain "tells me that the Hi-Y[57] group in Cornell would like to hear something about the YMCA on the West Coast, so I may have a chance to speak there."[58] However, Kobayoshi was disappointed to learn of "the ignorance of people on the East Coast. Most of the students know nothing about evacuation . . . one of them actually asked me whether the rest of the Nisei spoke English and another history teacher asked me why the Isseis were not citizens!"[59] For Kobayoshi, the opportunity to speak to a student group at Cornell on the history of the YMCA along the West Coast was also an opportunity to educate East Coast Americans on the realities of life as a Japanese American.

Christianity served as a means for resettled students to build social capital while spreading Christian messages on campus and around their new communities. Grayce Kaneda, a Nisei student, JSCA participant, and future JACL leader who resettled at a college near Richmond, Virginia, described an encounter she had with the mother of an American prisoner of war held in Shikoku, Japan. While the encounter had the potential to disintegrate into an awkward and troubling affair, Kaneda explained that "the mother, after meeting me and talking with me, felt much more secure about her son as she saw that all Japanese are not cruel pagans" and that she enjoyed "this opportunity to say the things that need to be said, which makes up for whatever loneliness I feel due to the scarcity of Japanese in this community." While Kaneda expressed her belief that "much hatred is based on ignorance and not realizing what true democracy means," she also argued that by speaking with other students and members of the community, she was "trying to make people understand what practicing Christianity is and what it can mean for our post-war world." "I think many of us do not realize that what we want in our post-war world, must be started today within our own hearts," Kaneda poignantly concluded, "to respond to the needs of people . . . in other words, 'Dare to be Christians.'"[60]

From detention centers to new campuses, Christian Nisei students attempted to continue their work in building interracial relationships as well as the Kingdom of God. Whereas others viewed resettlement as an opportunity to get vulnerable Nisei out of the prisons before they became completely disillusioned with American democracy, Japanese American students viewed relocation as a chance to spread their message of Christian principles beyond the West Coast. Amid the tragedy and the uncertainty of the fractured Christian campus associations, JSCA members expanded their reach to other schools and universities across the United States. There were limits to the interracial bridge-building approach (resurrected during the war), but World War II allowed the students to view integration and education as more important than ever during an international crisis.

Divergent Paths to Community Activism

Because it was a wartime measure, many other minority groups often viewed EO 9066 as an injustice but did not vocally oppose the process. Just as many Nisei showcased their devotion to the United States and embraced a model minority identity, other Asian groups also saw a chance for a fresh start that would bring them out of the shadows and into American society during the war. For Chinese, the war created opportunities to emphasize their loyalty to America while distancing themselves from the Japanese, leading to a certain degree of acceptance among Americans (although this did not mean full integration or a complete disposal of racism and prejudice). As a result of China's alliance with the United States during the war, not only did the federal government lift the Chinese Exclusion Act, but it also granted naturalization rights to some Chinese already residing in the United States under the 1943 Magnuson Act.[61] The historian K. Scott Wong has explained that many Americans associated the Chinese and China with a heroic struggle against the ruthless Japanese, reflecting America's own struggles for democracy abroad.[62] As many Chinese joined the war effort through patriotic campaigns, jobs, and varying levels of military service, Chinese Americans often emphasized the differences between them and the Japanese in hopes of building beneficial relations with white Americans. In response, both Issei and Nisei (with the assistance of the JACL) also sought to prove their loyalty by promoting the US war effort once they resettled or by serving in the armed forces (as the men of the 442nd Regimental Combat Team did). As time would show, these attempts at integration met with varying degrees of success both during and after World War II. Many Asian Americans juxtaposed their own courage and dedication to the American cause with Japan's violence against China and the Philippines. By using this strategy of what Ellen Wu identifies as "disaggregation" (or separating from the Japanese), many Asian communities hoped to achieve some level of equality (with often disappointing results) in the United States and end the long tradition of anti-Asian sentiment.[63]

While the story of assimilation and adaptation are important concepts for understanding the changes in Asian American identity during the war, Chinese Christian students offered a glimpse into a unique response to EO 9066 and its effects on the United States. These students recognized the incarceration of Japanese Americans as part of large-scale, government-endorsed violation of civil rights and believed that although they were minority students, they could speak out against this injustice. Drawing on their identities as Christians, they separated themselves from larger Chinese communities that were not interested in or willing to protest EO 9066 (similar to those Japanese Christian students who distinguished their goals from those of imperial Japan). Despite the interethnic tensions that resulted from the Pacific atrocities during World War II, Christian Chinese students continued to work for an end to discrimination and prejudice by using religious networks to target EO 9066 as the ultimate symbol of American and Christian hypocrisy.

Although the Christian student associations were in shambles during the war, CSCA members continued to meet with other Christian students on the West Coast and around the country. In order to finance travel to and from the conferences as well as provide refreshments for attendees, students would hold fundraisers to continue where they had left off with their work before the war. Topics at the meetings were varied, but discussions usually circled back to the detention centers and the fate of Japanese Americans. In August 1943, former CSCA member and University of Chicago student Beulah Ong Kwoh helped to lead a Christian Chinese student retreat at Lake Tahoe, where incarceration was a vital concern for attendees. After discussing the unchristian nature of EO 9066 and Americans' disappointing compliance with the measure, the students passed a resolution "asking for fair play for loyal American citizens of Japanese descent."[64] This initial focus on Americans of Japanese descent reflected the larger trend of those who spoke out against EO 9066. However, the resolution from the Chinese students represented the views of Asian Christian students, a unique group whose views on forced removal differed from that of other Asian communities at the time. The Lake Tahoe retreat reflected the traditional distance that CSCA members kept from other members of the Chinese and ethnic communities, but it also highlighted the group's commitment to using Christian connections to meet and discuss American social, political, and racial problems. Despite the resolution and its attempts to provide interethnic support for imprisoned Japanese, the students in attendance did not drastically depart from the reactions of many other Christian and civil liberties groups during the first Tahoe conference.

Two years later, however, the tone of the Lake Tahoe meeting and the discussions of the devastating impact of EO 9066 took a more radical turn. With many of the formerly imprisoned Japanese resettled in either schools or communities far away from the West Coast and the threat of subversion from both Nisei and Issei agents in the United States under control, the WRA announced that the organization would close the detention centers in the late fall of 1945.[65] The 1945 Lake Tahoe meeting reflected the concerns of Americans and foreign leaders with what shape the postwar world and postwar relationships would assume with the foreseeable end to EO 9066. Not only was this conference, with 107 in attendance, larger than the 1943 meeting, but attendees also focused more on connecting the problems of the Japanese with the problems of Chinese and Chinese Americans more generally. How would Japanese and other Asian communities fare following the war? How did EO 9066 change the lives of not only Japanese but also other minority groups? American organizations, civil rights groups, and government agencies were already looking toward potential problems in these areas as Japanese Americans would return to the West Coast and CSCA members and Chinese students were no less concerned with such topics.

The future of West Coast race relations weighed heavily on the minds of the conference attendees. Wilbur Choy (a CSCA member as well as student chairman of the College of the Pacific's Nisei Relocation Committee) turned the conference into a sounding board for students to voice their ideas on "interracial relations, churches in our community, post-war employment, housing for our people, and social agencies." In the resolution passed by the attendees, Choy emphasized that "whereas the world has been ravaged by war and persecution and dominated by hatred and suspicion[,] and whereas . . . this state of the world is contrary to the principles of humanity and the teachings of our Master, Jesus Christ, be it resolved that we . . . dedicate ourselves to work for the elimination of war and militarism and for the building of Christian democracy in this world." As in past student conferences, attendees connected the global problems of war with the domestic issues of race relations and postwar uncertainty in America. During the 1945 Lake Tahoe conference, CSCA members and other Chinese Christian students looked at these issues through the lens of Christian democracy and were able to see just how far their ideas of Christian interracial fellowship could go in the new racial environment of the United States. Whereas students had tended to focus on campus issues in the past, they now expressed wider concern for the working class and the poor. In general, though, the topic of the return of uprooted Japanese shifted their attention to problems with racial discrimination in larger communities.[66]

Students also paid particular attention to the problems of resources for Asian minorities along the West Coast. Far too often, anti-Asian sentiment and cultural misunderstandings produced friction between the white social workers and Christian leaders and the Asian communities they tried to serve. Attendees at the conference cited language barriers, racism, and a lack of Christian principles as causes for breakdowns in relationships between whites and Asians and feared that these problems would only increase after the war. This "lack of understanding causes unresponsiveness and suspicion" but also interrupted the growth of "inter-racial relationships." There was concern that Japanese American returnees would have difficulties in "re-entering neighborhoods and communities . . . and building fellowships with other races who had moved into their homes and businesses" and "learning to work with white agents who were not fully capable or wanting to understand the problems the evacuees and the Japanese had experienced both before and during the war."[67] These were certainly valid points, considering that the war created a massive shift in demographics on the West Coast, with various ethnic groups and especially African Americans moving into neighborhoods and homes once occupied by the Japanese in areas of Los Angeles and San Francisco. While resettled Japanese experienced prejudice and racism in cities such as Chicago as a result of migration, the racial mix on the West Coast and the potential for clashes among whites, blacks, and Asian Americans prompted fear among residents, the WRA, local planning committees, and Chinese Christian students alike.[68] The concern of CSCA members over these issues brought Christian students into the fold of broad racial changes and a growing civil rights movement.

Whereas Christian Asian students in the past had tended to focus on campus issues, they now sought greater immersion in the social and political problems of their larger communities. Students at the 1945 Lake Tahoe conference argued that the problems that returnees were bound to encounter on the West Coast reflected the racism that "all of Oriental lineage have encountered and will continue to encounter from an American government which does not care to examine its own politics [sic] towards other races and peoples." "With all these problems in mind," the student attendees asked themselves, "what can we as youths do to lessen or eliminate them?" At the most abstract level was the suggestion that students "look beneath the surface and attack the intrenched [sic] social problems with a view toward long-range improvement," but students also offered suggestions that were more concrete. Some solutions to promoting better interracial relations included joining in "with other minority groups and by cooperative efforts and actions [to] achieve better racial relations," promoting "closer relations with Interracial churches," and encouraging more Chinese and Chinese American students to enter professions such as "social work, medicine, and ministry to address community problems for all minorities."[69] While the attendees were clearly devoted to understanding how they could improve their own communities, they were also interested in addressing the underlying discrimination against minorities along the West Coast. The topics of EO 9066 and Japanese resettlement brought the need for Christian, interracial cooperation to the forefront in the battle against inequality and poor social conditions.

The students offered suggestions on using the church as a means of promoting interracial cooperation and activism, topics that CSCA members had discussed for years during student conferences, Asilomar meetings, and group get-togethers. The Christian roots of the Lake Tahoe conference served to bring the students together as well as inspire them to think broadly about how they could use Christianity to build a more inclusive social movement after World War II. Also, the war forced the students to think in tangible ways about developing strategies for bringing their groups closer to other minorities and civil rights organizations. This was a new approach for these activists, who had relied in the past on network building with other students rather than the populations outside of their colleges and universities. Like other civil rights groups, CSCA members underwent a transformation in their discourse and approach to ending prejudice, seeking to use interracial and interethnic integration to achieve new standards of equality. Executive Order 9066 galvanized Christian association members to engage in civil rights battles and apply their traditional interracial fellowship approaches to new wartime situations.

However, other ethnic groups were not as interested in assisting the Japanese with resettlement or their problems with race relations. While CSCA members were eager to use EO 9066 to examine preexisting discrimination and civil rights violations, there are few written sources indicating that Filipino students felt the same way. During World War II, a lack of funds had forced the FSCM, like other Christian student associations in the same situation, to cease publication of the *Filipino Student Bulletin*. As a result, it is difficult to uncover exactly what Filipino students, and particularly those who identified as Christians, thought of the forced removal policy. In Filipino communities, the attitudes toward EO 9066 and Japanese Americans in general were not pleasant or favorable. Off campus and outside of meetings like the Lake Tahoe conferences, Japanese and Filipinos did not always engage in positive or cooperative relationships, reflecting the larger climate of interethnic tensions. The forced removal of Japanese was a topic that Filipinos either avoided or, in some instances, advocated. In October 1944, leaders of West Coast Filipino organizations met in Fresno, California, during the Fourth Filipino Inter-Community Conference where the attendees discussed a pre-circulated and advertised resolution that "advocated the permanent exclusion of American citizens of Japanese ancestry and their parents from California, noting that some Filipinos have made substantial economic gains in taking over production of certain farm crops previously produced by farmers of Japanese ancestry."[70] Like the Chinese, Filipinos viewed the war as an opportunity for greater acceptance in America as well as independence for the Philippines. As Filipinos served in the armed forces and worked on the home front in similar ways to the Chinese, the reputation of Filipinos among Americans changed from that of suspicious outsiders to tragic victims of Japanese violence such as the Bataan Death March.[71]

In this regard, Filipino students often shared the same views as other members of their communities. As early as January 1942, a Filipino student, Aquileo Leander Dongallao of Washington State University, published an article in *The Evergreen* (the student daily) outlining both his appreciation for American governance of the Philippines and his homeland's duty and honor in defending American democracy at war. Dongallao was thankful that "the Philippines are a democracy acquiring her teachings from the United States" and argued that Filipinos "owe America our government, our education, our economic system, our commerce, and all elements necessary for democracy." As "repayment for [their] indebtedness," Filipinos "offered to America all the armed forces of the islands and her vast resources, . . . [for they] are loyal to America and . . . bow to the Stars and Stripes, which are a symbol of democracy and justice." Dongallao informed readers that "in this present war, we Filipinos will have our chance to show our loyalty and help America defeat the evils of Japanese barbarism and Paganism, which are trying to engulf us."[72] Dongallao's article was a departure from those that had previously appeared in the *Filipino Student Bulletin*, in which authors decried American imperialism and discrimination against Filipinos in the United States and in the Philippines. His classification of the Japanese as harbingers of "barbarism and paganism" was a far cry from the messages of tolerance and cooperation that had brought Christian Asian students together at the height of the Sino-Japanese conflict. Filipinos identified World War II as an opportunity to prove their loyalty and hopefully promote the needs of Filipinos, not to attempt to create a pan-Asian identity that included their homeland's aggressors. Rather than an opportunity for examination of larger patterns of racism against Asians on the West Coast, EO 9066 and wartime politics further exacerbated long-held tensions between Filipinos and Japanese.

While Filipino Christian students remained for the most part removed from the problems of EO 9066, former JSCA leader Toru Matsumoto created an important organization to assist Japanese Americans with resettlement during the war. After spending time in an alien detention center, Matsumoto was released in late 1943 and went on to form the New York–based Committee on Resettlement of Japanese Americans (CRJA) while waiting to return to the West Coast. The CRJA was an interracial and interethnic organization that brought together various church leaders and volunteers to assist Japanese seeking resettlement. However, activists associated with the group also worked to ensure the safety of those who returned to their homes along the West Coast by disseminating informational pamphlets and establishing interracial groups to discuss the difficulties faced by the uprooted. Matsumoto enlisted the help of Chinese, African American, and white students in welcoming resettled Japanese American students to their new college campuses and creating interracial groups to encourage acceptance of the Japanese and promote Christian fellowship among all races. Although the CRJA was not limited to Christians, Matsumoto made former Christian association members central to his goals for improved postwar race relations. The war weakened the student associations, but their former members and leaders carried over the work of the 1920s and 1930s while adding Christian principles and modes of activism to a growing, interracial West Coast civil rights movement. (See figure 5.)

Matsumoto's approach to the problems of incarceration was similar to that of the students at the Lake Tahoe conference. Executive Order 9066 and the devastation it caused threatened all minorities but also called attention to the legacy of anti-Asian sentiment and discrimination in the United States. The CRJA used questions surrounding resettlement to initiate a larger discussion of discriminatory immigration and naturalization laws. Here was a continuation of the JSCA's earlier attempts at connecting Christian principles of equality to the unjust laws of the United States. In terms of immigration restriction, the CRJA urged "the repeal of the Oriental Exclusion Act of 1924, directed at immigration from China and India, as well as Japan." Just as Matsumoto and other members of the Christian student associations had pointed out decades before, the Exclusion Acts and other restrictions on Asian immigration represented a "denial of freedom and democracy to Asian immigrants." Although concern over the plight of internees and resettled Japanese was "admirable" and indicated a general "feeling of sympathy for those who had been ripped from their

FIGURE 5. Toru Matsumoto speaking at a CRJA meeting in New York City, 1944. Bancroft Library, University of California, Berkeley.

homes ... with their rights violated," there were still "large issues concerning the rights of Japanese, Chinese, Filipino, and Hindus in America" and the "prejudiced laws that prevent these people of God from becoming true participants in American democracy and citizenship."[73]

Matsumoto and other members of the organization connected EO 9066 with larger problems of citizenship and rights for Asian Americans, representing a form of racial liberalism that went beyond what white liberals would identify as the "Negro" problem, or the binary composition of race relations as white/black. While the CRJA was not the only group that addressed the concerns of Asian communities (the JACL as well as the Chinese Citizens Association and the Citizens Committee to Repeal the Chinese Exclusion Act were also active in these pursuits), Matsumoto's organization argued for panethnic participation from Chinese, Japanese, and other Asian American groups. When activists like Carey McWilliams and former detainee Ina Sugihara proclaimed that "the Oriental Problem is not a Pacific Coast one . . . [but] it is now bigger and far more destructive than the evils existing in any one region alone," they touched on a form of interracial activism already embraced by Christian

Asian students.[74] This panethnic form of solidarity was a reflection of the type of racial liberalism that was already in place for the Christian student associations before the war and an indicator of an emerging Asian American movement that would mature in the postwar years.

But political and social change did not come easy for Japanese after they left the detention centers. Along with the racism that many Japanese Americans faced from hostile groups and organizations upon their return, they also often encountered difficulty finding jobs, reclaiming their property and possessions, and basically beginning their lives from scratch.[75] While organizations such as the YMCA and the AFSC provided them with financial and community support, they discouraged Japanese Americans from returning to the West. Many (including Japanese Americans) had hoped that both Issei and Nisei could emerge from the devastation with a new opportunity for integration, thereby transforming tragedy into upward economic, social, and political mobility through assimilation. Many more argued that in order to achieve these goals, Japanese Americans should remain far away from the West Coast to avoid the racism and prejudice that characterized life before the war. There were also fears that a mass return of Japanese Americans to the West Coast would create a "race war" between the Japanese returnees and the African Americans who had moved into Japanese neighborhoods and businesses during incarceration. In many ways, as the historians Ellen Wu and Matthew Briones explain, American officials, Japanese American organizations, and even Christian groups viewed Issei and Nisei as pawns in the attempt to realize a greater vision of a more racially integrated society. Here was an opportunity to remake the racial composition of the United States by downplaying racial differences and melding all minorities into true Americans. The problem with this noble plan was that those who believed they had the best interest of the Japanese in mind rarely analyzed the larger consequences of the changes in race relations brought about by the war.[76]

Attempts at encouraging Japanese to move beyond their communities and assimilate into larger American society unintentionally supported nativist and racist groups. Organizations such as the Native Sons of the Golden West and other "concerned citizens" in California proposed pieces of legislation that would codify the 1920 alien land law in the state constitution and also strip both Issei *and* Nisei of voting rights as a result of lingering fears among whites of Japanese subversion. While these propositions were ultimately defeated in referendums or died in the state legislature, there were few attempts by larger Christian associations like the AFSC to protest such measures or help those who refused to relocate to cities outside of California, Oregon, or Washington. White liberal groups and many Japanese Americans lost the larger issues of racial inequality or civil rights violations in the drive for assimilation.[77]

Whereas many resettlement organizations failed to take into account the radical impact of the war on all minorities, the CRJA gained attention from other circles and venues for its Christian, interracial approach to building a more integrated society. Matsumoto's work with the CRJA and other organizations caught the attention of the editors of the *Journal of Social Issues*, a quarterly publication established in 1945 by the Society for the Psychological Study of Social Issues, which issued a special edition "Race and Prejudice in Everyday Living" in May 1945. Japanese resettlement received special attention in the periodical and featured a number of brief articles and responses by different individuals arguing either for or against the Japanese returning to the West Coast. While most arguments against resettlement focused on the better living and working conditions for Japanese Americans east of the Rocky Mountains, others argued that a mass return would only exacerbate racial tensions among whites, African Americans, and other Asian communities.[78] In contrast, Matsumoto outlined why the problems of Japanese and Japanese Americans in the United States were part of the larger structure of racism and discrimination in America rather than problems of assimilation. He believed that "the problem of Japanese-Americans must be solved as part of the total problem of social justice for all minorities" and that "things like fair employment for Negroes applies to all other minorities. Segregation of housing against Negroes applies to all other minorities. Segregated churches for Negroes applied to Japanese as well. Any of these discriminatory practices against any minorities affect the Japanese."[79] Like Charles Kikuchi and other civil rights advocates and groups, Matsumoto connected the plight of Japanese Americans to the problems of other minority groups within the United States and wished for the growth of networks that would embrace interracial solidarity. Matsumoto approached the wartime issues of race relations as an extension of the drive for interethnic and interracial network building that characterized the activism of Christian association members since the 1920s.

Matsumoto also urged Japanese Americans not to forget the struggles of other minorities in their attempts to rebuild their lives and gain acceptance in American society. During and after the war, Asian ethnic groups tended to form organizations devoted to the protections of rights of specific ethnic populations. Matsumoto argued against this trend and explained that "Japanese Americans ought to do their full share in solving interracial problems in America, by not identifying themselves with the prejudice pattern of majority segregation as the line of resistance, but rather cooperating with all liberal elements, within both majority and minority groups, for a total solution of the problem."[80] Matsumoto's analysis of the growing "model minority" stance of the Japanese and other Asian groups revealed a concern for the very patterns of ethnic isolation that the Christian associations fought against for so long. Although the war was an opportunity for Asian Americans to make demands and capitalize on the hypocrisy of the United States, it could also lead to self-interested racial politics that would deepen existing racial and ethnic tensions.[81]

The work of activists like Matsumoto and the CSCA members who attended the Lake Tahoe conferences on promoting interracial and interethnic cooperation are not typically part of the larger story of race relations during the war. Their absence in the narrative stems from how we generalize the "civil rights activist" that emerged during World War II. As students and minorities, they had limited opportunity to directly influence the policies and actions of the federal government in carrying out EO 9066; however, their discussions of interracial and Christian fellowship preceded the type of racial liberalism that historians argue was a product of the war. Although Asian Christian students did not engage in more radical forms of protest as leftist organizations before or during the war and were not connected with emerging groups such as the Congress for Racial Equality, they embraced interracial networks that went beyond black and white. Interethnic, panethnic, and interracial fellowship characterized their Christian approach to civil rights, while the war helped students and former students to see how influential their strategies could be in a climate of growing interracial outreach. The students' use of discussions, conferences, and publications were not the same tactics used by other groups, and there were limitations to what the students accomplished by not engaging with other community groups. Nevertheless, the Christian association members were at the forefront of an inclusive interracial movement along the West Coast that brought together students seeking to build networks for civil rights activism. Like more radical and left-leaning ideas, Christianity also contributed to the social and political movements that emerged during the war, and the Asian Christian students were key activists in promoting these ideas.

Conclusions

Despite appeals from various organizations to remain far away from the West Coast, many students and other Japanese and Japanese Americans such as Matsumoto chose to return to their former communities. Not only were the cities and towns in California, Oregon, and Washington their homes, but these places also represented areas that desperately needed those who were dedicated to interracial civil rights activism. Following the end of World War II, race relations became volatile as various ethnic and racial groups competed for jobs and housing. Recalling their own experiences with racism along the West Coast, many Japanese chose to remain in the Midwest and along the East Coast to begin new lives and refashion themselves as Americans rather than be ethnic outsiders. Others, such as former student Yori Wada who graduated from the University of California, Berkeley, in 1940 and would later become a leader of the San Francisco YMCA, enthusiastically chose to return to the West Coast and explained that "I return gratefully to 'my California life.' . . . I must go back, for my home is in California."[82] Wada's devotion reflected the passions of those Christian Chinese, Filipino, and Japanese students who viewed the West Coast as an area in desperate need of interracial cooperation to end racism and prejudice. And who better to lead this movement than the students who were seasoned veterans in using Christian fellowship to build networks and promote equality?

6

Christian Social Action
in the Postwar Era

● ●

The changes in race relations and racial identities ushered in by World War II were drastic, with perhaps the most striking evidence of these transformations found in an evolving civil rights movement. While racial liberalism and interracial activism became more prominent goals during the war, white liberals, African Americans, and other minority groups turned to legal activism and civil disobedience to achieve justice during the late 1940s and 1950s, building on strategies established by black civil rights activists during the 1930s in cities like New York City and Los Angeles.[1] After African American groups migrated to northern and West Coast cities and Executive Order 9066 forced thousands of Japanese out of their homes and into desolate prisons, more Americans became aware of the extent of racial inequality. Thanks in part to the challenges that the war exposed, civil rights battles went from regional problems for Asians on the West Coast and African Americans in the South to a nationwide confrontation with a legacy of injustice. With housing covenants, discrepancies in pay based on race (despite the prohibition of discrimination in defense industries under FDR's Fair Employment Practices Commission), and other forms of de facto and de jure segregation throughout the country came the realization that the hypocrisy of race relations was no longer confined to southern states. Along the West Coast, where a mix of racial and ethnic minorities created a racial frontier, interracial cooperation assumed a new meaning.

Following the war, interracial solidarity was needed to overturn discriminatory laws on the books. In order to truly reform race relations on the West Coast and across America, interracial groups targeted individual acts of racial discrimination and broader inequalities in housing, labor, and education. African Americans' use of nonviolent protest and the Double V Campaign (victory against fascism at home and fascism abroad) to pressure the federal government to intervene became major organizing tools for the postwar era. As the historian Mark Brilliant suggests, a general "shift away from antidiscrimination initiatives that emphasized 'understanding, proper education, co-operation, and good will'" characterized the "new" civil rights movement.[2] Racial discrimination along the West Coast required swift and direct action through legislative reforms rather than the cumbersome and time-consuming task of creating cultural exchange through education and racial understanding.

If the old ways of interracial cooperation through education and exchange were no longer suitable for the volatile civil rights scene, where did this change leave Asian students' use of Christian fellowship to end prejudice? More specifically, as Toru Matsumoto asked in 1946, "what remains for the churches" in this new era of activism?[3] While former students like Matsumoto and the attendees at the Lake Tahoe Chinese Christian Student Conferences were able to adapt by applying their Christian ideas of interracial cooperation to a larger, more community-based framework, questions about the role of Christianity in interracial civil rights groups on the West Coast abounded. Matsumoto admired the fact that the "membership in these groups [ACLU, Civic Unity Councils, Congress of Racial Equality] is splendidly representative of all kinds of people" including "liberals and 'reactionaries,' church people and non-church people, workers and industrialists, and Negroes, Mexicans, Orientals, and Caucasians," but the secular nature of these organizations appeared to challenge the goals of ending prejudice through fellowship.[4]

The interracial and panethnic solidarity that the student Christian association members worked to build, however, did not disappear after the war but rather evolved into what Matsumoto identified as "Christian social action." This form of activism connected fellowship with the drive for legislative change. For Matsumoto and others, education and cultural/racial outreach were neither forgotten nor ineffective concepts: they were necessities for achieving legislative change. Relationships in interracial organizations would be tenuous at best if there was not a true form of Christian brotherhood and understanding among the members. Ending prejudice through education and exchange would create organic cooperation for legal victories, not vice versa. As Matsumoto explained, "enter into a genuine fellowship and you will forget that you are promoting better race relations."[5]

As the historian Shana Bernstein has argued, interracial and interethnic groups along the West Coast during and after the war are important for understanding the changing nature of civil rights activism. Organizations such as the California Federation for Civic Unity (a statewide coalition of civic unity councils in cities such as Los Angeles, San Francisco, Sacramento, and San Diego founded in 1946) brought Japanese, African American, Mexican American, and Jewish inhabitants of California together in what Bernstein has called "interracial pragmatism." With so many ethnic and racial minority groups in California, there was a need to cooperate "through coalitions made both possible and mandatory by the war-induced influx of racially diverse populations that strained local resources and revealed a stark option: work together or suffer from the resultant discord."[6] But interracial organizations on the West Coast often suffered from differences in goals and ideas. The path of racial liberalism could only go so far in alleviating ethnic and racial tensions, which led to difficulties in creating solidarity for legal action. Breakdowns in communication and strategies often resulted in disagreements between leaders and lay members in identifying and prioritizing the most pressing issues. While Christian organizations were not immune to these problems, Matsumoto believed that encouraging interracial, religious fellowship created an incentive for people to maintain solidarity when they are faced with challenges. Although the role of the church is ingrained in the historiography of leadership and tactics in the African American civil rights struggles, few scholars have identified the influence of Christianity in West Coast movements.[7]

By following the postwar work of former Christian association members, including Chingwah Lee, Toru Matsumoto, Victor Carreon, and Victorio Velasco (among others), this chapter argues that the goals of the associations and students continued to influence a changing civil rights movement on the West Coast. While the student associations disintegrated as a result of changes in Asian American communities and identities during and after the war, former members continued to argue for the importance of cultural exchange and Christian fellowship as precursors to legal activism. Historians of Asian America illustrate the rocky assimilation of Asian Americans into white, mainstream society as model minorities during the postwar years, but this chapter tells a different story. Former Christian association members and Asian Christian activists in general were not removed from the changes in American perceptions of Asian Americans as assimilated individuals rather than part of a yellow peril. As educated Christians, former Asian students viewed themselves as leaders in the push for equality in West Coast communities despite rarely interacting with the working class, and this pattern continued following the war. However, former Asian students did not distance themselves from the "Negro Problem" that defined civil rights after the war but rather used their past organizing experience and identities as Christians to join the fight for African American equality. Although Matthew Briones argues that some Asian Americans rejected "whiteness" for "situational Blackness" to move closer to radical forms of protest and activism, this chapter shows that Christianity provided an alternative option for Asian participants in the civil rights movement, one that was not constrained to a black/white model.[8] In many ways, former association members like Lee, Matsumoto, and Velasco became acculturated to a growing social and political consciousness in addition to assimilating into white society, two trends that characterized life after World War II in Asian America.

This form of civil rights acculturation did not come without a price. As former Christian association members joined different community organizations in cities like Seattle and San Francisco as well as nationwide groups, their views on racism changed. The language of human rights that members of the CSCA, FSCM, and JSCA used before the war became less prominent, with former students discarding the larger discussions of Christian citizenship and worldwide justice. Also, an increasingly radical civil rights movement challenged the acculturation and bridge-building approaches of men like Velasco, Lee, or Matsumoto. Fighting class inequality, exposing the misconceptions surrounding the idea of a model minority, working for access to social services for Chinatowns and other communities, and protesting against the Vietnam War would become the mantle of the student activists of the late 1960s. While calls for yellow power defined a rising Asian American movement, the former Christian students became less central to political activism on the West Coast.

Despite the setbacks that Christian Asian activists experienced, the perceived gap between the supposedly apolitical identities of Asian Americans during the nineteenth and early twentieth centuries and the later activists of the 1960s is not as wide as historians tend to believe. The connections between the student Christian associations, former members, and postwar civil rights are crucial to understanding the varied terrain of social movements on the West Coast.[9]

Assimilation, Cold War Politics, and the End of the Christian Association Groups

The changing identities of Asian Americans in the postwar and early Cold War eras had a direct impact on the further decline of the Christian student associations. As historian Kevin Allen Leonard explains, the phenomenon of "race" disappearing from media outlets to encourage equality and democracy began during World War II, but ideas of successful assimilation among Asian Americans in the years after the war made the student groups appear outdated and unnecessary.[10] Christian associations came under attack from both students and outside observers who viewed groups like the CSCA, FSCM, and JSCA as limiting and ethnically isolating for young Asian Americans. The Christian organizations' focus on panethnic cooperation clashed with the desires of Nisei, other second-generation Asian Americans, and immigrant groups to integrate into American society.

The JCSA suffered the most as a result of the war and its aftermath. Already in shambles by 1941, the organization came to represent everything that prevented Japanese Americans from advancing in American society. After EO 9066 challenged the foundations of Japanese communities as well as their Issei figureheads, the Japanese American Citizens League urged the Nisei to bring other Japanese into American political, social, and cultural life. During the postwar years, Japanese Americans debated whether assimilation meant an increased presence in activism and the political process or a more traditional approach that encompassed cultural, economic, and social integration into the mainstream. Regardless of which definition of assimilation Japanese Americans chose, when Nisei assumed leadership positions in Japanese communities, they proudly displayed the ability of Japanese Americans to integrate rather than remain culturally tied to Japan.[11]

This focus on assimilation also triggered similar movements on West Coast college campuses. Following World War II, a group of Japanese American students from California joined together to create the California Intercollegiate Nisei Order (CINO). Inspired by the JSCA and the earlier student associations, CINO was designed to serve as a California-wide attempt to support the "furtherance of racial tolerance towards Japanese-Americans."[12] Although CINO was more socially oriented than the JSCA (organizing beauty pageants and dances, rather than discussion groups and conferences), the group provided students with a way to regain a sense of community and belonging following World War II.[13] Despite the initial popularity of the group, by 1955, many members of CINO doubted the necessity of the organization for creating "further racial tolerance," and just four years later, the leaders of the organization voted to disband during its annual meeting in Fresno. Citing "negligible" occurrences of intolerance against Japanese following the war, the leaders and members believed that the "serious work" of CINO was complete, since few students reported incidents of racism or discrimination on or off campus.[14]

Others came to believe that ethnic student associations hindered acceptance and assimilation. Samuel I. Hayakawa, a semantics scholar and, in the late 1960s, the president of San Francisco State University, was one of the leading proponents of the move to end Asian ethnic organizations during the postwar era.[15] In 1958, a year before CINO disbanded, Hayakawa (a Nisei from Canada) officially declined an invitation to come speak at the group's annual meeting, explaining that such groups only served as "social crutches" for Nisei and prevented them from intermingling with other students.[16] Hayakawa's belief that "the Nisei and Sansei [third generation] should give up their organizations and cultural patterns and try to assimilate with the general public" resonated with young Asian American students who emerged from World War II with an optimistic outlook on race relations in the United States.[17] As a result, members of the second generation no longer viewed ethnic student organizations as essential to their college experiences. Whereas African American youth organizations (such as the Student Nonviolent Coordinating Committee and groups associated with the YMCA/YWCA in the South) blossomed in the era of civil disobedience and protest during the postwar years, Asian American students celebrated a perceived acceptance among white Americans and an assimilation to American cultural, social, and political life that had been out of reach prior to World War II.[18]

A series of limited postwar legislative victories for Asians and Asian Americans also led to faith in the power of assimilation. The repeal of racist immigration/naturalization policies and prejudicial land laws aimed at Asian immigrants became a token of postwar-era acceptance. In 1952, Congress lifted bans on naturalization for Asian immigrants with the approval of the Immigration and Nationality Act, legislation that sought to limit communist infiltration by deporting those suspected of subversion while simultaneously granting access to citizenship for previously excluded racial groups. The act also modestly increased the number of visas for Asian immigrants but ultimately maintained the nationality-based quotas of the Immigration Act of 1924. Along with the immigration laws, Asian American lawyers and various interracial supporters also denounced the wartime process by which state and local governments justified seizing land purchased illegally by the Japanese under the alien land laws. In turn, Asian Americans and Asian immigrants celebrated when the California Supreme Court declared such measures to be unconstitutional in the 1952 *Masaoka v. California* and *Fujii v. California* decisions.[19] While such legal changes did not create a clean slate for Asians Americans in terms of acceptance by the majority, they did signal a shift in how Americans saw Asians: as model minorities rather than perpetual foreigners.[20]

Although the JSCA and FSCM disappeared, the CSCA continued to operate following the war; however, members and administrators raised important questions concerning the role of the association in the postwar world. The number of Chinese students coming to American colleges and universities actually increased following the war when compared with those from Japan and the Philippines. More Chinese students enrolled in graduate programs with the assistance of "cultural ambassadorship" programs such as the Fulbright Exchange (initiated with China in 1947 as a Cold War measure).[21] As a result, foreign-born and older students became the core members of the CSCA, and discussions within the organization reflected this change. As the historian Timothy Tseng argues, the politics of the CSCA took a decidedly transnational turn after World War II, with members focusing on "rebuilding" China after the war and working to "better the nation."[22] Postwar Chinese nationalism and the role of Protestantism in rebuilding China became popular topics of conversation for

CSCA members at conferences and in the *Chinese Christian Student*. At the 1948 Western Conference, panels on "the propaganda programs of the U.S. and Russia," "what factors contribute to the popularity of Communists in China," and "in what ways will Americans aid further Sino-American relations" were well attended by members. Similarly, a CSCA conference in New Hampshire later that year featured discussions on how Chinese students in America could help "those Chinese students at home" who were attempting to rebuild their nation amid a civil war between the Kuomintang and the Communist Party of China.[23] In fact, Tingfu F. Tsiang, a former CSCA member who worked for pacifism and interethnic peace between Chinese and Japanese during the Second Sino-Japanese War, became an ambassador of China, representing the influence of those Asian students who returned home after receiving their educations.

The CSCA's postwar focus on China did not, however, completely overshadow the group's concerns for race relations and civil rights. In fact, the organization's 1948 Western Conference combined both international and domestic concerns, with an entire panel devoted to "education" and "racial justice." While CSCA members continued to focus on issues of race relations, these discussions were quite different from the prewar discussions. Following a panel on "inter-exchange of American and Chinese influence on both cultures—advantageous or not," conference attendees debated whether or not "education" should be the solution to "community problems, racial justice, political effectiveness, and economic justice." These heated discussions reflected uncertainty about the role of cultural education and Christian fellowship in postwar society.[24] Questions relating to the usefulness of education and fellowship were a far cry from the large panethnic conferences of the prewar days, when members embraced cultural exchange for its potential to end prejudice.

YMCA administrators were also unclear about the purpose of the CSCA in the United States following World War II. In 1948, Tom Moore, co-chairman of the Pacific Southwest branch of the Student YMCA, published an announcement in the *Chinese Press* (an outgrowth of the *Chinese Christian Student* following World War II) that outlined his desire to see the CSCA merge with the YMCA and the National Intercollegiate Christian Council. Since "the members of the Student YMCA and YWCA have many times affirmed . . . that the barriers which at present separate persons because of color, national origin, and religion . . . should be removed," Moore did not understand why the CSCA should continue its operations.

The YMCA administration hoped that "the CSCA shall move toward the position of being chiefly a Student Christian Association rather than a predominantly Chinese SCA."[25] Similar to Samuel Hayakawa's arguments that ethnically oriented student groups prevented the Nisei from fully assimilating to American culture, the YMCA hoped that the CSCA could abandon the "Chinese" component of its organization, making it either a general student Christian association or simply another branch of the YMCA.

Concerns about the ability of foreign-born Chinese students to adapt to American life also prompted administrators to push for an end to the CSCA. Reflecting the larger push for assimilation from Asian Americans and other organizations, Moore urged "Chinese students studying in this country to enter American life rather than Chinese-American student life."[26] Despite the CSCA's history of panethnic and interracial cooperation with other student Christian associations, the organization's emphasis on Chinese students not only deterred the postwar image of America as racially inclusive but also went against the Christian principle that "all men are brothers." Many American-born Chinese students were also uninterested in participating in the foreign-dominated CSCA and chose to join emerging national and intercollegiate Christian groups such as the American Students Association. As a result, a general decline in membership of the CSCA justified the YMCA's decision to direct funds to other programs that were more popular, such as the growing Student Summer Program, a civil rights and social movement initiative.[27]

Moore's questioning of the purpose of an ethnic-focused students' association echoed larger fetishes for "Americanness" and belonging during the Cold War era. Growing international tensions with the Soviet Union and the communist Mao Zedong's rise to power in China created a frenzy of paranoia in the United States over the possibility of communist infiltration. With the Immigration and Nationality Act's deportation provisions in place, many Asian Americans and particularly the Chinese wondered if another measure like EO 9066 would become a possibility during the rise of McCarthyism and the second Red Scare. In response, Chinese and other Asian American groups defined their loyalty to the United States through public displays of patriotism and support for American ideals and democracy. For example, in larger Chinese American communities, many leaders and organizations such as the Chinese Consolidated Benevolent Association responded to the rise of communism in China with anti-Mao rallies and benefits during the early 1950s.[28]

This climate of Cold War loyalty also affected the CSCA. The organization became a point of concern for the US government, with the Central Intelligence Agency and Federal Bureau of Investigation keeping track of activities and publications and the CSCA's own general secretary Paul Lin fleeing to Canada after accusations of communism in 1948. Charles Hurrey described a sense of fear among Chinese students in the United States after the war, particularly during a 1947 CSCA conference in Chicago where, according to Hurrey, there appeared to be "two conferences: one that was 'open' [to CSCA members and nonmembers] and another [just for members] with a deep natural concern of what was ahead for the Chinese students in the United States . . . with unscheduled sessions that lasted far into the night." Hurrey also described "instances of persecution [of Chinese students] on campuses and in some communities," "expulsion," and, in some instances, "students who simply dropped out of existence with no record of their return to China" after being expelled from college for communist activities. Eventually, the organization disbanded by 1951, when accusations of communist infiltration and the organization's postwar emphasis on Chinese affairs provoked federal investigations.[29]

In general, the postwar era was not kind to the Christian student associations. The heightened fear of otherness and the push for assimilation among whites and Asian Americans accelerated the disintegration of the organizations. Appearing outdated and disconnected from larger trends in American social, political, and cultural life and blind to the optimism of Asian American communities, the CSCA, JSCA, and FSCM faded from the college scene. Many Asian students abandoned panethnicity (until more radical Asian students picked it up once again in the 1960s) when the focus on using Christianity to build networks fell out of favor with a changing civil rights movement. Ironically, the student associations' emphasis on interracial and interethnic solidarity failed to adapt to the postwar climate of racial liberalism.

Chingwah Lee: "Mr. Chinatown" and Chinese Identity in a Civil Rights Era

With the end of the student Christian association era, former members, such as the prominent Chinese American and onetime CSCA secretary Chingwah Lee, continued their interracial and panethnic work in broader venues. Lee's transformation from Christian student activist to a promoter of Chinese culture and education as "Mr. Chinatown" offers interesting examples of postwar Asian American and West Coast social, cultural, and political activism. In her article on Lee, the historian Atha Fong described the man who was well known in San Francisco's Chinatown as well as across the nation for his part in the 1937 movie *The Good Earth* (an adaptation of Pearl Buck's 1931 novel) as an "influential, yet historically forgotten man."[30] As a co-founder of the Chinese Historical Society of America as well as the *Chinese Digest* (the first English-language periodical for Chinese American communities), Lee holds an undoubtedly important position in Chinese American history. However, while his presence in the historiography is growing, his work in promoting equality has not been placed within the context of West Coast trends after World War II. His work in changing the negative image of Chinese Americans through cultural exchange and education in San Francisco's Chinatown is well known, but he also participated in the new wave of civil rights movements to influence and supplement legal action. Lee's story is complex and provides an interesting case study in the postwar activities of former Christian association members that complicates our understanding of both West Coast and Asian American activism.

Lee's background as both a leader and a member of the CSCA and other Christian organizations created a foundation for his later work in San Francisco's Chinese community following World War II. Lee was born in 1901 to immigrant parents who settled in San Francisco during the 1870s, prior to the enactment of the Chinese Exclusion Act. Despite Lee's comfortable upbringing as a merchant's son, he discovered at a young age when he attended a segregated school in San Francisco for Chinese and Korean students that class and money could not break through all barriers. Lee was not alone in his experiences with West Coast anti-Asian sentiment, and he developed a strong sense of duty as a second-generation Chinese American to work to improve both his community and the Chinese image. Lee's desire to represent Chinatown as well as improve relations between Chinese and others in San Francisco prompted his involvement in a variety of groups and organizations, including leading a Chinatown Boy Scout troop prior to World War I, serving as a staff volunteer for the YMCA in 1919, and later joining the CSCA when he enrolled at the University of California, Berkeley. By 1927, Lee was the general secretary of the West Coast division of the CSCA, a status that placed him in an excellent position to work on behalf of not only the second generation but all Chinese. Like other members of the CSCA, Lee used the organization and other opportunities to create lasting connections and bridges between Chinatown and the rest of San Francisco.[31]

Lee's role in the CSCA earned him a reputation of leadership, outreach, and interracial cooperation that would place him in the midst of civil rights reform during and after World War II. In 1944, Lee's work with the YMCA caught the attention of the Pacific Coast Committee on American Principles and Fair Play, a group composed of white, mainly Christian leaders who argued for the constitutional rights of incarcerated Japanese. The organization, headed by Berkeley provost and vice-president Dr. Monroe Deutsch, served as an unofficial liaison between the War Relocation Authority, the Department of Justice, the Department of State, and other associations addressing the potential problems of Japanese Americans returning to the West Coast. Deutsch and the other members of the committee were concerned that returning Japanese would find themselves in competition for labor and housing with not only African Americans but other groups including Chinese, Filipinos, and Koreans. One member feared the unfriendly receptions that returning Japanese might receive in "urban centers, where the immigrating Negroes had taken over the previous Japtown dwellings" and "showed no disposition to welcome any return."[32] There was also anxiety about those Japanese who wished to come home to the Watsonville-Salinas region of California, where anti-Japanese sentiment remained strong among nativist organizations. For the committee, the return of thousands of Japanese to the Pacific Coast represented potential problems in race relations, mainly in the form of negative reactions from other minority groups.

In order to address these issues before the end of the war, Pacific Coast Committee leaders set to work planning a Conference on Interracial Coordination, or Interracial Conference, in late 1944 and invited leaders from various minority groups and organizations to attend. The committee also contacted representatives from religious groups, labor unions, and state and federal government bureaus and agencies to join the meeting and offer their own views on the impending racial problems on the West Coast. The main focus of the conference was to "study housing, employment, farm, legal, and other problems facing the Japanese Americans who would return to the Coast communities," with Dillon Myer of the WRA, A. J. McFadden (chairman of the California State Board of Agriculture), and representatives from labor unions to elaborate on the specific work-related problems of Japanese returnees. McFadden explained in a news release announcing the conference that "it is evident that Japanese Americans are needed for war essential work in Pacific Coast industries and farms" and that "practical steps need to be taken now to give the Japanese-Americans full opportunity for useful citizenship." Accounts of discrimination against Japanese Americans seeking employment disappointed committee members as well as labor and government representatives, who worried that racist employers rejected much-needed laborers based on race.[33]

But the committee also emphasized that the conference would investigate issues for all minority and racial groups, hoping to create a diverse and representative event. Dr. Deutsch echoed this goal in another press release from early January 1945 when he publicly described the meeting as "an attempt to evolve a coordinated post-war race-relations program for the Pacific Coast" and "an attempt to coordinate the efforts of some 300 West Coast groups making efforts to improve race relations . . . and seeking to present a unified front against bigotry and intolerance." Referring to the West Coast as a "laboratory in which post-war models of race relations will markedly affect the whole world," Deutsch emphasized that "the conduct of Pacific Coast residents towards returning Japanese-Americans may provide the clue as to the relations between the white peoples of the world and Orientals for generations to come." The committee designed the Interracial Conference to address the problems of all racial and ethnic groups along the entire West Coast, seeking to draw together representatives from all organizations and "benefit [from] an interchange of facts and point of view." By focusing on creating an inclusive space for discussions of race relations, the Interracial Conference, an event planned by white activists to attract a diverse audience, was the epitome of the racial liberalism that grew during the war.[34]

Since the committee sought leaders from a variety of racial and ethnic backgrounds, they turned to religious and civic organizations and, consequently, often recruited leaders who were former student Christian association members. To make the conference a success, committee members called on individuals within West Coast communities who they knew would understand the importance of such an interracial and interethnic meeting. Deutsch drew from organizations (particularly religious groups such as the YMCA) that had reputations for tackling problems of inequality and injustice through cross-racial discussions and activities. It was no coincidence that some of the more vocal leaders and prominent members of such organizations were, in fact, former student Christian association members. The roster of attendees at the conference included Julio Espiritu and Juan Dulay, two former FSCM members who became leaders of the San Francisco–based Filipino Community, Inc., an organization devoted to securing Filipino rights as well as promoting interracial and interethnic relationships in the city. The committee also invited Antonio Gonzalez, another former FSCM member who became a leader of the Western Filipino Communities and played a key role in promoting the 1946 Filipino Naturalization Act.[35] Leaders such as Espiritu, Dulay, and Gonzalez had expertise in organizing and guiding interracial and interethnic meetings and working to build solidarity, skills that helped them to become well-known leaders of their own community organizations and catch the eye of the committee leaders. Other invited attendees were representatives from the WRA, West Coast YMCA branches, West Coast chapters of the National Association for the Advancement of Colored People, and Seattle and Portland committees on racial equality.[36]

The committee also identified Chingwah Lee as a powerful community leader who would be a valuable asset to the conference. Lee's previous experience with outreach and close cooperation with other Christian organizations made him a perfect representative for Chinese communities. Also, his high-profile image and reputation reflected the committee's desire to create a top-down leadership structure to promote better race relations on the West Coast. In many ways, the conference served as a microcosm for a changing Asian American identity: Lee, like others, straddled the line between model minority and racial liberal. Many of the ethnic and racial community leaders who attended the conference were engaged in this elite form of civil rights activism, which reinforced the politics of respectability that so many Christian students clung to during the early years of the Christian associations. Lee's involvement with the Interracial Conference also reinforced the growing recognition among white liberals of the model minority status of Asian immigrants and Asian Americans following the war.

When the conference commenced on January 10, representatives centered their conversations on ways in which the members of their respective communities would respect and assist the returning Japanese. Notes from the meeting indicated that "the Negro, Filipino and Korean spokesmen all expressed eagerness to safe guard the rights and liberties of returning evacuees and said that any attempt to make capital for their own racial groups at the expense of the Japanese would be sawing off the limb on which they themselves sat." They "recognized that all minorities . . . are in the same boat and that to deny full constitutional rights to any racial or religious group would weaken the rights of all." Likewise, Espiritu and Dulay "declared they would not allow indignation over atrocities by the Japanese military [in the Philippines] to betray them into taking revenge on innocent and unfortunate persons of Japanese descent here." Antonio Gonzalez also used the history of discrimination against Filipinos on the West Coast to call for an "Oriental" version of the Square Deal, involving legal interventions for government protection and ensuring civil and human rights.[37] This exchange of ideas among the former Christian association members harked back to the larger panethnic conferences of the 1920s and 1930s. However, because of the war, discussions of Christian fellowship had given way to a more direct attention on the need for outreach, interracial cooperation, and legal intervention.

As an attendee, Chinatown leader, and activist, Lee contributed to the changing postwar conversation on the place of Asian Americans in civil rights movements. Along with Dulay, Lee recommended that the committee "ask and urge the WRA to become a clearing house for information on housing, employment, and all other problems relating to various communities along the West Coast." The desire to have a government agency such as the WRA work to address problems of discrimination spoke to the growing desire among activists for legislative action to ensure racial equality. Lee also requested that the committee continue to work closely with the various community leaders present at the conference to create a "coast-wide coalition" devoted to analyzing and addressing issues of race, equality, and discrimination. More specific recommendations included that "each community be encouraged to organize an overall committee of outstanding citizens from every walk of life—labor, capital, business, religion, and so on—to study the problem of racial discrimination from two angles: investigating individual cases of discrimination that may lead to major tensions if unchecked and working out a program in adult education."[38]

After Lee's remarks, the attendees passed a resolution containing references to an adult education program as well as Lee's recommendation for a "coast-wide committee to be set up which will collect data on the progress of the cultures of minority groups and distribute this data to people who will be qualified to make effective use of such material."[39]

Lee's recommendations and the suggestions of other former students who attended the conference represented the types of activism that Christian student associations embraced in the past: education, outreach, and the role of gathering information to pass along for creating structural change. These resolutions (although missing the larger discussions of human rights and imperialism) were not altogether different from those approved during earlier student association meetings. The contrast was in the conference attendees' growing desire to work with a variety of racial and ethnic leaders to prompt legislative change.

Although the lack of Christian language represented a break with the past activism of the student associations, Lee's presence at the conference is an example of the power of the student Christian associations' interracial and interethnic networks. The use of education and fellowship in activism did not disappear in the later years of the war or after but rather evolved alongside other strategies for achieving equality. Lee's legacy as an activist goes far beyond advocating for an end to prejudice against the Chinese. He was also an important contributor among other former students to the multicultural and interracial movements that grew during the postwar years in California. Lee's experience with the Interracial Conference opens up possibilities for exploring the multifaceted roles of other Asian Americans during the postwar years as well as the impact of the past experiences of Christian association members on the rise of a West Coast civil rights era.

However, Lee's participation in the interracial conference differs from his work in later years and offers insight to the multifaceted nature of the former students' activism and their experiences with postwar identity. Following the war, Lee continued to draw on his leadership status to improve the image of Chinese in America. As an actor, Lee knew all too well the prejudice and stereotypes that Asian Americans and Chinese faced in the United States. Rampant Orientalism characterizing Asian immigrants as dirty, treacherous, pagan, and licentious "others" persisted well into the twentieth century. In essence, the Cold War offered both limits and opportunities for Asian Americans to refashion themselves as the model minority, but this did not undermine the ingrained, racist tendencies of Americans to embrace Asian stereotypes.[40]

Lee was particularly concerned with the negative image of San Francisco's Chinatown and set out in the 1950s to revamp the enclave's image. Typically seen as an adventure-filled, yet dangerous lair of iniquity, San

Francisco's Chinatown attracted tourists who wished to "slum" among immigrants and take in exotic food and entertainment during the early twentieth century. Lee identified the negative image of Chinatown as the root of prejudice and discrimination directed toward Chinese communities. While Lee's recommendations at the Interracial Conference demonstrated a desire to transform outreach and education into legislative change, Lee again returned to the idea of bridge building to create more opportunities for interaction between whites and Chinese. In the 1950s, Lee developed a number of programs for Americans to learn about Chinese traditions rather than Chinese stereotypes, using his experience as an appraiser for the US Army Alien Property Custodian Bureau following the war. Lee used pieces of Chinese art and other artifacts during Saturday symposiums to invite Americans to visit Chinatown for culture and history rather than Orientalist curiosity.[41]

Lee's work in improving the reputation of Chinese people as well as enhancing relationships between residents of Chinatown and outside communities speaks to continuities in Asian American activism. In 1963, Lee, Thomas W. Chinn, C. H. Kwock, H. K. Wong, and Thomas W. S. Wu formed the Chinese Historical Society of America and trained younger generations of Chinese Americans to invite visitors to the society and provide tours of Chinatown. The Historical Society was the fruit of Lee's work in cultural outreach and correcting the long-held anti-Asian attitudes directed toward Chinese on the West Coast.[42] The desire to educate Americans and Chinese alike on the long history of Chinese communities as well as the discrimination and prejudice Asian immigrants encountered was part of a growing movement to create spaces for learning and self-discovery (a trend that would increase following the rise of the Asian American Movement in the late 1960s). As Daryl Joji Maeda explains, "Asian American arts and culture blossomed" throughout the 1960s and 1970s, with more Asian Americans becoming aware of their unique cultural heritage and using it to create a new identity of pride and social and political mobilization.[43] The same can be said for the rise of Asian American history and historical societies (as a result of a turn to social history and the study of peoples and movements rather than government officials or leaders) during the same time period, with scholars such as Betty Lee Sung, Royal Morales, Him Mark Lai, and Yuji Ichioka working to establish Asian American history and studies as necessary fields. In this way, Lee's activism continued his earlier involvement with groups like the CSCA but brought education and exchange into the postwar civil rights era by using the often unspoken history of Chinese and Asian Americans to inspire change.

Just as Lee serves as an example of the integration of other Christian association members into larger social movements, his emphasis on changing the image of Chinese also played into the model minority identity. By showcasing the admirable traits of Chinese, including a history of business ownership in the United States as well as Chinese culture and art, Lee (as many other Asian American leaders during the 1950s and 1960s) paid less attention to the plight of the working-class, impoverished residents of Chinatown, or the continued presence of segregation for Asian groups in housing, employment, and other areas of life. Also, improving Chinese Americans' image was different from the panethnic focus of the Christian associations on the problems of all Asian minorities on the West Coast prior to the war. As a result, Lee's postwar activities speak to the changing role of Asian Americans in both their visibility as assimilated Americans and their place in a changing civil rights movement. While Lee's actions were still interracial in the sense that he sought collaboration between whites and Chinese, he did not make interracial action or the explicit use of religious networks with other minorities or other ethnic groups a central goal in his work, as he did during the Interracial Conference of 1945. In general, Lee's place in the context of changing urban and racial landscapes during the postwar years highlights the complex place of Asian Americans as both model minorities and activists for justice.[44]

Toru Matsumoto and Christian Social Action

Like Lee, Toru Matsumoto continued to be an active presence in the postwar world of civil rights, but his approach was different from that of Mr. Chinatown. During the late 1940s and the 1950s, Matsumoto not only penned books and publications that spoke to the need for Christian principles in social action and cultural outreach but also became a leader in interracial religious organizations. Similar to Lee's tactics for promoting better understanding between Chinese Americans and whites, Matsumoto's Christian social action approach (i.e., applying Christian brotherhood and the methods of education that the Christian student associations embraced to the changing nature of civil rights activism) represented both the limits and the possibilities of interracial and interethnic solidarity.

Matsumoto was a firm believer in the need for outreach, racial understanding, and fellowship before moving on to legislative measures, a stance that was both useful and problematic in movements along the West Coast and across the country.

Matsumoto's postwar writings provide the best insight into the ideology that shaped his activism as a student and continued to mold his experiences in the postwar era. In his 1946 best-selling book *Beyond Prejudice*, an account of the role of the church in supporting incarcerated Japanese and the responsibility of Christians to remake the world after World War II, Matsumoto observed that many civil rights groups used the courts without first building interracial solidarity and understanding to end prejudice.[45] Published jointly by the Federal Council of Missions and other Christian organizations, *Beyond Prejudice* recounted the history of early Japanese settlement along the West Coast and Christianity's fight against the devastating effects of racism and EO 9066. The book, however, did not merely describe the triumph of Christianity over the injustices of imprisonment in America. It also contained Matsumoto's opinions on how Christianity could continue to influence the push for racial equality and civil rights for all minorities in the United States, particularly along the West Coast. Most importantly, Matsumoto's timely book spoke to his strong belief that the battle for civil rights did not end or necessarily begin with legislative victories.

In the introduction to *Beyond Prejudice*, Matsumoto informed readers that "with the return of peace, the Christian churches in the United States face a rare opportunity and a heavy responsibility for healing the wounds of mankind." While Matsumoto conceded that the formation of postwar civil rights groups such as California's State Council of Civic Unity and the heightened awareness of groups such as the American Civil Liberties Union to legal violations along the West Coast showed progress in the struggle for equality, he argued for the renewed role of the church in supporting a lasting interracial civil rights movement. "Thanks to the painful experiences in race relations during the war," Matsumoto said, "the larger community is now more conscious of its responsibility to its different smaller ethnic communities within itself," explaining that "on the Pacific Coast—the focal point of the evacuation controversy—communities are organizing for civic unity . . . made conscious of their responsibility by the evacuation and being desirous of curing causes of interracial tension." Like others on the West Coast, Matsumoto used *Beyond Prejudice* to analyze the impact of EO 9066, examine changes in demographics during the war, and outline the emerging problems in race relations. However, he argued for the necessity of Christian fellowship for creating deep cultural and racial understanding even among those who were unable (for a variety of reasons) to participate in the more radical or active civil rights groups. In many ways, Matsumoto offered a Christian, Asian American, and immigrant's perspective on issues that other authors, like Carey McWilliams, presented to American readers.[46]

Creating legal change was important for guaranteeing civil rights, but Matsumoto argued that "legislation is essential, but education is basic." If those along the West Coast desired true interracial and interethnic cooperation, "the general and pressing problem of race relations in the country . . . require[ed] Christian social action." Since churches as well as religious organizations were prominent in many ethnic and racial minority communities, Christianity had the potential to build strong and diverse networks. In his final chapter, Matsumoto described interracial and interethnic Christian social action by outlining the various projects that the churches and religious organizations designed, such as "special studies of race relations," conferences, lectures, and interracial workshops. In other words, the "best education for better race relations" was achieved through interaction and "personal contact." Whereas Christian student association members used such forms of education and fellowship before the war to build cultural and social bridges, these tactics would continue to shape interracial and religious activism during the postwar era as well.[47]

But Matsumoto also warned that interracial movements would fail to be truly egalitarian and representative if one denomination, ethnic/racial congregation, or socioeconomic class assumed leadership and failed to recognize the interests of all. In order to create a level playing field during interracial meetings, "paternalistic treatment must be avoided" in the church's attempts to build solidarity, allowing individuals to meet each other on equal ground and use Christian fellowship to understand and appreciate both the similarities and variations in experiences. By emphasizing the need for equal leadership in any network or interracial group, Matsumoto presented a more complicated picture of Asian Americans in postwar civil rights activism. To make Christian social action as inclusive as possible, he argued against Asian Americans or any racial, ethnic, or class group of Christians assuming the lead in interracial organizations without consulting the other members. Matsumoto explained that true civil rights activism required neither a top-down nor a bottom-up approach to organizing but rather an organic coming together of various races and ethnicities for the purpose of social justice.[48]

Matsumoto did more than simply write about the power of Christianity in civil rights; he also rose to national recognition as a religious leader and a promoter of interracial church youth organizations, camps, and meetings during the postwar years. In October 1946, the *Afro-American* (based in Baltimore, but with a wide readership among blacks) reported on a Metropolitan Christian Youth Council Session held at Riverside Church in New York and planned by the "renowned religious leader" Matsumoto. "Youth United for Christ" was the theme of the annual conference in 1946, and attendees from New York, New Jersey, Connecticut, and other Northeast and mid-Atlantic regions gathered together to "carry out interracial fellowship in every phase of its program." The Metropolitan Christian Youth Council worked to increase interracial membership in New York churches and religious institutions across the country, with leaders calling for churches to promote interracial relations and civil rights in America. Matsumoto collaborated with the Reverend Ralph Rowse, an African American minister in New York and founder of the New York–based Interracial Fellowship program for Christians interested in race relations, to establish a "social action committee" and an "interracial committee" as part of the Christian Youth Council. Although Matsumoto reveled in this opportunity to work with Rowse in organizing the conference, he supported committees in order to ensure that responsibilities and ideas were shared with others in the council. During the 1946 conference, Matsumoto also worked with the other attendees and leaders to establish a "committee on legislation." This group introduced Christian youth to the process of raising awareness of racial discrimination through Christian fellowship to inspire political activism.[49]

Although the Christian Youth Council was based in New York, Matsumoto also lectured widely on the West Coast. The former student activist agreed with other leaders in the civil rights movement that the demographics of cities such as Los Angeles, San Francisco, and Seattle required special attention to develop interracial cooperation and solidarity.[50] In order to strengthen such relationships, Matsumoto supported the Race Relations Sunday program, an initiative established by churches across America in 1922 that encouraged church leaders and members to attend the services of different racial and ethnic congregations. Ideally, these measures would lead to fruitful discussions during coffee hours, seminars, and roundtables following services and hopefully result in the creation of permanent inter-racial groups. Although the program lost steam during the war, Matsumoto lectured to California, Oregon, and Washington residents that the revival of Race Relations Sunday would invigorate Christian activists and help them to see how a West Coast "interracial force depended on a Christian foundation for further action . . . against prejudice and those who oppose understanding and fellowship."[51] It is difficult to know how many West Coast Christians responded to his call, but Matsumoto visited hundreds of churches and Christian groups during the late 1940s to preach that religion was necessary for creating an equal and just society.

Matsumoto's work with other Christian and civil rights leaders reflected his commitment to using the church to build interracial foundations for legal change, but his goal of shared leadership was difficult to meet. Despite his push for egalitarianism in interracial groups, it was difficult for any Christian civil rights organization to promote full equality in decision making and leadership. As in the earlier days of the student Christian asso-ciations, Christianity provided a certain level of political respectability to the battle for equality and justice during the postwar years. The focus on Christian morals catapulted the most respectable members of civil rights groups (based on education, community involvement, and morals) to lead-ership positions. As a result, such leaders developed a tendency to overlook working-class and larger community issues. Despite his emphasis on shared leadership in Christian associations, Matsumoto argued in 1949 that "the most crucial problem in the church is that of the place of the leadership of minority groups."[52] For Matsumoto, leadership had a distinct definition that rested on the ability of church officials to call lay members to action. In order to build interracial coalitions, the church was required to pro-mote such relationships by engaging and encouraging notable members of minority religious communities to "lead the way in creating opportunities for solidarity."[53]

In practice, Matsumoto preached a top-down form of organizing, with church officials from each ethnic and racial community taking the lead in drawing groups together. Not only did this reflect the same limits that the student Christian associations faced before the war in their inability to reach beyond student populations, but this tactic also distanced Christian interracial organizations on the West Coast from other religious and more secular groups. Christian activism and network building, as demonstrated by the Christian association members in the past, were powerful tools for interethnic and interracial solidarity; however, the emphasis on using ethnic and minority church leaders to train students (or the more educated and elite members of Asian American and other ethnic and racial communities) to carry forth justice could be limiting in its scope. Race Relations Sundays and social change committees were noble activities but also problematic. How to apply these initiatives in order to bring forth political and social change was a difficult question, partly because of the disconnect between church leaders and other members of Christian groups that varied in socioeconomic status and racial/ethnic backgrounds. How could an interracial organization ensure that one group would not overshadow others? If Christianity was bound to concepts of morality and respectability, how far would the influence of Christian interracial activism reach in the religiously diverse states of the West Coast? Realistically, there was no way to answer these questions, presenting Christian groups with the same challenges as secular activists along the West Coast.

While Matsumoto attempted to integrate into a postwar civil rights culture, his emphasis on top-down leadership also spoke to the assimilation of Asian Americans into respectable roles in society. Although Matsumoto's work with the Race Relations Sunday and youth groups was part of his larger plan for Christian social action, his reliance on writings, discussion groups, and church services did not consider the wide variety of minority experiences. Interestingly, the majority of individuals who praised Matsumoto's work were white liberals, Christian students, and African American religious leaders, illustrating those whom Matsumoto reached as well as those he did not. These accolades reflect both the appeal and the challenges of Matsumoto's tactics for ending prejudice through Christian fellowship before developing legal strategies. Matsumoto's argument for creating interracial solidarity before creating plans for social and legal change connects him to other former students, such as Lee, who attempted to balance assimilation and activism.

Though limited, Matsumoto's plans for establishing interracial Christian organizations across the country were examples of the continuing influence of the students' interracial, interethnic, and Christian-based activism. The need for interracial activism was not new among former students, like Matsumoto, who were leaders in this area well before the postwar civil rights movements. By becoming active in different groups during the war and branching out after the demise of the JSCA, Matsumoto represents many ethnic and racial minorities who were awakened to a nationwide problem of racial inequality. As a result, he continued his activities in faith-based organizing, particularly on the West Coast, where the need for interracial and interethnic cooperation was crucial for reform. More importantly, the ideas and plans that he implemented also place Asian Americans in the context of civil rights history and vice versa. Other former students and association members shared his ideas and would go on to apply Christian principles more effectively in interracial West Coast civil rights organizations.

The Christian Friends for Racial Equality and Christian Social Activism in Seattle

Matsumoto's philosophy for faith-based legal change was reflected in one of Seattle's most important civil rights organizations, the Christian Friends for Racial Equality (CFRE). Following the YMCA interracial campus meeting at the University of Washington discussed in chapter 4, FSCM member Victor Carreon and Seattle native and missionary Edith Steinmetz met with other interested members in 1939 to build an inter-racial group to "welcome all peoples to our churches and strengthen those bonds which unite us all as one people in our democracy."[54] Just like the student Christian associations, the CFRE was framed around a Christian understanding of democracy and cooperation in America. The organiza-tion grew to 500 by 1944 and later, after World War II, to 745 members. By 1956 the CFRE was a large and active interracial group in the Seat-tle civil rights movement.[55] With the guidance of Steinmetz, Carreon, and former FSCM members Victorio Velasco and Grandino Baaoa, the CFRE became an integrated and interracial group that attracted members from the Seattle and University of Washington branches of the YMCA/YWCA, the Chinese Baptist Church, the Temple de Hirsch, the Filipino Community Church, and the First African Methodist Episcopal Church of Seattle.[56] Membership in the CFRE, despite racial and ethnic varia-tions, was largely representative of the middle class of Seattle, possibly because of the Christian and "nonconfrontational" nature of the group.[57]

The impressive growth of the organization after World War II was the result of a rising African American population in the city (where migrants took advantage of wartime employment with ship and airplane manufacturers such as Boeing) and, as city councilmen believed, rising racial tensions. After the war, Seattle's mayor Gordon S. Clinton maintained an active interest in analyzing and addressing issues of racial inequality and civil rights violations, primarily in housing and employment. Gordon formed a variety of city councils to investigate incidents of racial injustice and raise awareness of the problems that Japanese returnees, African American migrants, and other minority groups encountered in the city. Chapters of both the NAACP and the Congress of Racial Equality in Seattle also responded to increased discrimination and segregation in the city following an influx of African Americans from southern states (despite some middle-class Seattle blacks' initial hesitance to assist working and lower-class migrants). While the CFRE consisted mainly of white and African American members, other ethnicities, races, and members of various religious groups (including Asian Americans and Jews) joined the organization.[58]

The rise of the CFRE following World War II represents an understudied aspect of the history of West Coast civil rights. During the late 1940s and into the 1950s, historians have argued that the Cold War focus on anticommunism in the United States drastically derailed budding civil rights movements in cities such as Los Angeles. Activist organizations, including the California Federation for Civic Unity (CFCU), feared Americans' perceptions that civil rights advocacy was coterminous with subversion or attempts to incite racial warfare in order to promote a communist takeover. As a result, the CFCU and other groups placed a greater emphasis on anticommunism and community "betterment" programs rather than openly promoting a civil rights legislative agenda. The California equivalent of the House Un-American Activities Committee particularly suspected Mexican immigrants, members of Hollywood's Jewish community, and African Americans such as the famous activist-lawyer Loren Miller of subversion for their participation in labor organizing and civil rights protests. Unlike the seemingly radical groups and organizations mentioned above, the CFRE and its Christian-based notions of fellowship, exchange, and cultural education continued to operate through the Cold War era without drawing attention from red-baiting legislators or suspicious community members. In the middle of an anticommunist attack on groups that advocated for legal change or labor rights, organizations such as the

CFRE appeared to be innocuous and even model organs for the promotion of American and Christian notions of interracial cooperation.[59] (See figure 6.)

While the CFRE was based on a social understanding of how best to combat racial prejudice and intolerance, the organization also forayed into legal action during the 1950s and early 1960s. In many cases, CFRE members tackled issues that government agencies overlooked in the larger battle for racial equality and civil rights. During the early 1950s, Velasco and the other members worked to end discrimination in cemeteries, in which some churches and privately owned lands refused to accept the burial of certain racial minorities or segregated the deceased with separate plots according to race or ethnicity. Both African American and Japanese American inhabitants of Seattle brought complaints of discrimination to the CFRE during the late 1940s and early 1950s when local cemeteries refused to bury their family members (including one World War II veteran) because they were not white. The CFRE launched extensive letter-writing, petition, and pamphlet campaigns against the discrimination in Seattle's cemeteries "in order that practices within our country be brought into closer harmony with our pronouncements of foreign powers concerning justice and equality."[60] Members delivered hundreds of materials to residents, churches, and local businesses decrying the blatant discrimination that was present in Seattle.

As a result of the religion-based framework of the CFRE, much of the activism centered on cultural exchange and "the procedures of investigation, persuasion, and when advisable, by publicity to foster equality and understanding." More specifically, the 1944 CFRE Constitution listed "endeavoring to promote understanding by social acquaintance" and "developing understanding rather than resentment" among Seattle's minorities as its main goals. Reflecting the group's Christian influence, the former FSCM member and CFRE activist Victorio Velasco also worked to build relations between the Filipino community of Seattle and other minority groups by promoting interfaith and interracial/multicultural social and church events. In 1950, the CFRE "cooperated with Thalia, Allied Artists Inc. (of Seattle) in presenting its productions with interracial casts" to integrate the arts and culture scene in Seattle, and it also worked closely with the Church of the Fellowship of All Peoples (an interracial San Francisco–based nondenominational church) that came to Seattle to host a special meeting for addressing racial issues through church services. Later, Velasco and Baaoa encouraged the CFRE to sponsor the civil rights section of the

NO=MAN=IS=AN=ISLAND

ANNUAL MEETING · MAY 19 · 1953
CHRISTIAN FRIENDS
FOR RACIAL EQUALITY
PLYMOUTH CONGREGATIONAL CHURCH

FIGURE 6. Cover of the CFRE Annual Meeting program, May 19, 1953. University of Washington Libraries, Special Collections, UW36378.

Annual Institute of Government at the University of Washington as well as a project titled "American Conversations," a slate of student conferences and seminars on how to respond to "racist thinkers with Christian suggestions" and "explain away stereotyped ideas." Like Matsumoto, the former FSCM members and leaders of the CFRE recognized the prominent role that students could play in the movement for racial equality and understanding, drawing on an earlier tradition of organizing. During its early years, the CFRE offered a Christian and cultural angle to interracial organizing amid the growing civil rights movement in Seattle.[61]

Carreon, Velasco, and the other members of the CFRE saw cemetery discrimination in Seattle as a disturbing racial injustice. Discrimination in housing for the living was bad, but why allow such a disgusting display of unchristian behavior to deny the right of the deceased to rest in peace? Here was an issue that touched on all of the principles of the CFRE: equality, Christian fellowship, and religious practices. As the religious scholar Randi Walker explains, the issue of cemetery segregation was particularly disturbing for members.[62] In a 1950 article in the University of Washington *Daily*, Velasco (writing on behalf of the CFRE) decried the church leaders who refused to speak out against segregated burial plots, asking students if there was "no greater denial of Christian brotherhood and upholding of hypocritical prejudice than to insist on placing the burdens of this life on the dead" while insisting that Christian students join with the CFRE and other groups to "lend a hand to replace the foul state of Seattle inter-group relations with love and understanding . . . where our own church leaders have failed to see the error of their ways among the cemeteries and headstones" in the city.[63] Velasco's approach to the problem reflected the old student association strategies of using publications to raise awareness and building support among various racial and ethnic groups to initiate change. But the fact that even church officials and other Christians in Seattle failed to see how far segregation seeped into the religious aspects of life left some questioning how far writing about and discussing this problem could go in solving it. A change was needed, one that combined education and Christian interracial fellowship with a more demanding stance.

By late 1950, the CFRE, galvanized by Christians' ignorance of racism in burial grounds and Velasco's passion, moved beyond the abstract ideas of fellowship and faith. As a response, the organization based its fight against cemetery discrimination on legal principles, demonstrating the group's combination of social and political action. In one pamphlet, the CFRE argued that the recent 1948 *Shelley v. Kraemer* Supreme Court decision (which made housing covenants based on race illegal) also applied to cemeteries. Velasco enlisted the help of local churches, the Civic Unity Committee, and the NAACP to battle discrimination in cemeteries and, by 1951, was engaged in a number of conversations with the assistant to the

Washington state attorney regarding the issue. CFRE members as well as local ministers argued that discrimination in cemeteries was no different from restrictive housing covenants: both acts represented "a denial among policy makers that racial injustice . . . had come to characterize inter-race relations in Washington following a war where America's sons had fought to bring democracy to the world."[64] The efforts of the CFRE in the fight to end cemetery covenants resulted in a 1953 Washington statute that made it "unlawful for any cemetery under this act to refuse burial to any person because such person may not be of the Caucasian race."[65] Members of the CFRE celebrated their victory in Seattle and the triumph of Christian equality over worldly prejudice. The success in rallying Christians to protest cemetery discrimination and resulting legislative action represented the powerful forces of education, religion, and legal outcomes in Christian social action.

Inspired by their success with cemeteries, Velasco and Baaoa turned their attention to the problems of employment discrimination in Seattle in 1956 and created a committee to branch out to others in the community with concerns or experiences in this area. The CFRE was particularly concerned that rampant employment discrimination discouraged minorities from even considering positions in certain occupations like factory work, clerical work, and other white-collar positions. Velasco and Baaoa designed the committee with the assistance of other CFRE members to survey the hiring practices of local employment agencies and assist job seekers in applying for positions regardless of their racial or ethnic status. Later that year, Velasco also sponsored and chaired a public panel discussion at the University of Washington bringing together civil rights activists on and off campus to discuss ways in which Seattle citizens could push for fair employment practices. Although the employment committee did not directly call for legal change to guarantee equality, the former FSCM members used their strategies of interracial cooperation, or "intergroup" cooperation as the CFRE often described it, to organize for change in the day-to-day violations of civil rights in Seattle.[66] The focus on employment also connected the CFRE to campus groups and organizations like the NAACP and CORE during the 1950s, demonstrating the integration of Christian activist groups into a larger civil rights movement.[67] Application of abstract goals of ending prejudice through interaction and Christian principles to daily struggles against legal segregation signified a maturation of many of the former students and an acceptance of the changing struggle for racial justice. Spiritual and interracial fellowship and cultural understanding were still important, but they could be used to create a new form of activism that was grounded in Christian principles.[68]

Velasco's participation in CFRE's employment committee also prepared him for his later work with the Seattle Citizen's Advisory Committee on Minority Housing during the late 1950s through the early 1960s. The Citizen's Advisory Committee was an initiative founded during the late 1940s by Mayor Clinton and designed to analyze and address problems with housing, ranging from segregation to landlords overcharging minority renters. By the early 1950s, de facto discrimination in property sales and rentals had become prominent issues for various civil rights organizations along the West Coast. As a result, there were many ill-fated attempts at interracial, interethnic, and multicultural cooperation to address these problems and provide suggestions. In Los Angeles, for example, the return of Japanese evacuees created tensions with African Americans who had moved into many of their homes and businesses.[69] For minorities in Seattle, however, frustrations with the longstanding problem of housing discrimination dating back to the late nineteenth and early twentieth centuries reached fever pitch by the early 1960s. In counteraction, the CFRE, NAACP, and local churches supported multiple bills to address the problem through state legislation; unfortunately, however, these bills failed first in 1959 and again in 1961. Disappointment and anger mounted among these groups as the struggle against housing segregation became increasingly difficult. In response to opinions stated by lawmakers and Seattle realtors that there was nothing that could legally be done about white renters and homeowners "simply not wanting to live amongst Negroes and other minorities," the Citizen's Advisory Committee resolved in 1962 to "study whether there is a need for federal, state, or local legislative aid or governmental assistance to minority families in securing adequate and suitable housing in Seattle."[70]

Velasco actively assisted in designing the proposed study, representing the role of former students in legal activism during the postwar years. Drawing on his past experience as a journalist, labor organizer, and FSCM member, Velasco suggested that the Citizen's Advisory Committee "study minority housing problems in other states and review the information reports" from other cities.[71] After canvassing Seattle's housing market and comparing the results with other cities like Los Angeles, San Francisco,

Chicago, and Philadelphia, Velasco revealed the findings of the CFRE's survey (including rampant discrimination against black renters in certain districts and realtor discrimination against potential Asian homeowners) to the citizen's committee in 1963 and joined other committee representatives in calling for government intervention. In response, the Seattle City Council and sympathetic legislators introduced bills in the 1963 legislative session that would create legal provisions for fair housing. Unfortunately, the 1963 bills died in the House Rules Committee, with similar losses again in 1964 (following on the heels of the disappointing repeal of California's fair-housing Rumford Act the same year). Velasco and the CFRE continued to work with local civil rights groups to bring about legal change in housing when, in 1965, the Seattle Real Estate Board announced its compliance with a voluntary Washington State Board of Realtors nondiscrimination code (possibly as a result of pressure from civil rights groups).[72] Later, in 1968, the Seattle City Council finally passed an open housing policy outlawing racial discrimination. Although the work of Velasco and the CFRE had not achieved the desired effect in terms of enforceable legislation, the adoption of the code by Seattle in 1965 was hailed as a victory for the widespread organization of multiple civil rights groups in the region, including the CFRE.

The work of the CFRE in promoting fair housing, however, did not stop in 1965. Maintaining their belief in the idea that "though you can legislate against discrimination, you can cure prejudice only by social acquaintance," Velasco and other members of the CFRE pushed to change racist hearts in Seattle in addition to its housing laws.[73] The CFRE encouraged pastors and other religious figures in various neighborhoods to promote integrated housing and the benefits of "mixed-living" for children and families of various racial and ethnic backgrounds. Velasco also headed a committee that would meet with individuals who were moving and urge that they remain committed to nondiscriminatory selling practices. Despite the voluntary and legal steps toward equality in housing during the 1960s, the CFRE continued to see restrictive covenants and housing discrimination as part of a larger problem of prejudice in Washington and along the Pacific Coast. Although laws could help limit the legal effects of discrimination, only education, understanding, and "social acquaintance," the main principles of the CFRE, could bring about a real change in the racial atmosphere of Seattle by promoting interracial interaction based on Christian values.[74]

Velasco and the CFRE's devotion to utilizing Christian leaders and community groups to enforce equality in housing adds another layer to the interracial civil rights movement on the West Coast. Housing discrimination was a prominent issue in California and prompted African American, white, and Japanese Americans (among others) to work together to promote fair practices among realtors as well as interracial and interethnic cooperation. However, such interracial ties were often tenuous, particularly as the rise of suburbia in the postwar era and white flight further complicated the struggle for space in West Coast cities as well as solidarity among these groups. As African Americans, Asian Americans, and working-class whites vied for a new middle-class identity and perfect homes in up-and-coming developments and well-manicured neighborhoods, segregation in housing became self-enforced despite government or social steps to prevent discrimination. For Japanese Americans, Chinese Americans, and Korean Americans, obtaining "whiteness" and model minority status during the early Cold War meant temporarily abandoning panethnic and interracial activism for access to fair housing in favor of using education and economic status to move up the socioeconomic ladder.[75]

In contrast, the work of activists like Velasco offer an alternative account of Asian American participation in the changing urban and suburban landscapes as well as race relations following the war. Although Velasco (like Lee and Matsumoto) used his identity as an educated Christian and prominent member of the Filipino community to assume leadership in the CFRE and other organizations, his focus on housing placed him within a larger world of civil rights activism. While achieving success and integrating into American society may have been concerns for Velasco, he still clung to the ideas of fellowship and Christian equality and continued to involve students in the process of ending prejudice in Seattle. Christian Asian activists were not always forced by changing racial, social, and political climates after World War II to choose situational blackness or whiteness to make their way through the complex and challenging urban terrain. They could also, as Velasco suggests, call on Christian activism to provide them with a way to participate in the call for racial equality while also remaining respectable. Though there were legal and economic ways to maneuver and address the problems of housing discrimination as well as racism in other facets of life for minorities, Velasco and the CFRE (like African American activists in the South and in northern cities following the war) often relied on other Christians and religious leaders in the community to initiate change through discussions and outreach. In other words, the former students did not forget their roots following the war but rather adapted (albeit unevenly) to evolving concepts of civil rights and civil rights activism by arguing that Christian interracial fellowship should be at the heart of any social or political movement. Ending prejudice, promoting education and cultural exchange, and building large networks among Christians were still goals for former association members like Velasco, but the postwar world encouraged them to view interracial and interethnic relations as the organic foundation for more direct legal and political activism.

For all of Velasco's and the CFRE's efforts, however, the organization would begin to decline by the mid-1960s as the civil rights movement in Seattle reflected the growing radicalization of the next generation of activists. There was a widening gulf between the type of activism that the former Christian association members embraced before, during, and after the war and the growing student movement by the 1960s. The Free Speech Movement that began at the University of California, Berkeley during the early 1960s quickly morphed into the Students for a Democratic Society's radical attacks on both socially unresponsive institutions of higher education and the unchecked power of university administrators. The Berkeley movement coincided with America's increasing involvement in the Vietnam War, resulting in protests against nationwide and global issues such as poverty and inequality, imperialism, and America's growing military presence in Vietnam. The rise of the Black Power Movement among African Americans in Seattle also challenged the cultural exchange and fellowship approach of the CFRE. In 1965, the CFRE further distanced itself from this sweeping wave of activist change with a publication that questioned the tactics of nonviolence protest, claiming that interaction rather than confrontation was the correct path for improving racial relations and creating legal changes. This demonstrated the CFRE leaders' muddled interpretations of concepts of civil disobedience that often rested on Christian-oriented themes of peace.[76]

Also, by the late 1960s, the growing Asian American Movement, or poet Amy Uyematsu's "yellow power" struggle, led by students in San Francisco and other West Coast campuses represented new goals for equality and rights.[77] Students called for repudiating the model minority myth, securing more access to social services for impoverished Asian Americans, protesting America's involvement in Vietnam, and building connections with new immigrant groups that arrived following the lifting of race-based quotas after the Immigration and Nationality Act of 1965. The Third World Liberation Front (an Asian American student-run group representing peoples previously colonized or repressed by the United States) led strikes in 1968 and 1969 at San Francisco State University and Berkeley for more ethnic studies courses, which represented an important event in this growing movement, one that combined radical goals with a desire for a more integrated curriculum. As Asian American activists such as Grace Lee Boggs (a participant in civil rights and labor groups in Detroit) and Yuri Kochiyama (an activist alongside Malcolm X) became more radical in their ideas and actions, men such as Velasco appeared to be stuck in the past. Compared with these more ambitious and wide-reaching critiques of American race relations and other global issues, former Christian association members were out of touch with a new type of student activist. The Asian American students of the late 1960s focused on the damages of Orientalism and denounced "bananas" (a derogatory term for people who were "yellow" on the outside but "white" on the inside) who failed to challenge the image of the model minority and worked within the system of oppression rather than outside of it. In this drastically changing world of civil rights movements, the CFRE struggled to stay alive.[78]

Even Velasco and the CFRE could not keep pace with the changing nature of Christian activism. Former association members found themselves unable to keep pace with the influences of the New Left on faith-based rights movements. The idea of existentialism and humanitarianism that many students embraced raised questions about the stifling moral codes of Christianity and its potential to do more harm than good. These themes were not completely absent from the student conferences of the 1920s and 1930s, but the more radical forms came across as somewhat distasteful, blunt, and aggressive to former student association members like Velasco. Also, other Protestant and Catholic organizations turned toward larger global goals and missionary works and moved away from cultural exchange at home in the United States. The politics of respectability and the reliance on Christian networks to create lasting interracial change were not faring well by the late 1960s. Unfortunately, former Christian association members who were no longer youthful students but out-of-date "old-timers" found themselves unable to assimilate into this new wave of social, political, and cultural activism.[79]

The CFRE's foundation of education and cultural exchange, while useful in creating an interracial base for civil rights in Seattle during the immediate postwar years, was their eventual undoing by the late 1960s. With the problem of racism in housing solved (legally) and groups such as the NAACP and the Civic Unity Council growing in importance for legal battles in Seattle, the CFRE was becoming less relevant on the civil rights scene, and the membership numbers reflected this decline. Meetings that once attracted hundreds of Seattleites from a variety of racial and ethnic backgrounds waned to mere dozens of white, middle-class women in the late 1960s. By 1968, the CFRE was also experiencing financial difficulties, facing steep cuts in revenue from vanishing membership dues and faltering financial support from local churches for social events (the mainstay of the organization).[80] The CFRE's middle-class, older, and less confrontational nature, combined with the belief of many Americans that the Civil Rights Act of 1964 and the Voting Rights Act of 1965 did away with discrimination, made the organization a relic of the past rather than a key component of newer, more radical civil rights movements.

Conclusions

The eventual decline of the CFRE speaks to the legacy of Christian activists such as Lee, Matsumoto, Velasco, and Carreon as well as the broader evolution of the West Coast civil rights movement. Throughout the 1960s, the CFRE continued to work with growing civil rights groups such as the NAACP and the Civic Unity Council. Velasco and other prominent members of the CFRE encouraged cross membership between the NAACP and the CFRE, often meeting at affiliated churches for events and planning. Members of the CFRE maintained their strategies of education and social interaction, attempting to revive membership by raising donations for scholarships to the University of Washington for local African Americans. Velasco, in a well-intentioned yet old-fashioned manner, also worked with adoption agencies to place minority orphans in Christian homes. Attempts to realign the CFRE's agenda to the changes in the civil rights movement failed, however, and by 1970, membership in the organization had declined so rapidly that it was more a gathering of lingering Christian liberals than an activist group. In many ways, the death of the CFRE was symbolic of the struggles of former Christian Asian students to embrace new tactics and move beyond Christian ideas of fellowship.[81]

What, then, is the legacy of the CFRE and, more generally, of the Asian Christian activists who pushed for panethnic and interracial cooperation both before and after World War II? Despite its eventual decline, the CFRE does not represent a complete disjuncture between pre- and postwar struggles for racial rights but rather a continuation of the ideas of the Christian student associations in West Coast civil rights battles. Although education and cultural exchange alone did indeed become relatively outdated modes of social action by the late 1960s, the principles of interracial and interethnic cooperation created a foundation for the later civil rights tactics. Legislation did, in many cases, trump education as the most important means of creating social and political change after the war, but the former students continued to argue for ending prejudice as well as ending discriminatory laws. Individuals such as Matsumoto and Velasco and groups such as the CFRE argued that legal change could only do so much without true interracial understanding and compassion. An emphasis on the importance of education, fellowship, and the ideas of interracial/interethnic solidarity continued to attract activists who may not have identified with other activist groups in West Coast cities. The ideas and influences of the student associations continued after the war as former members moved the struggle for racial equality off the campuses and into larger political and social movements.

The activities of the student Christian associations before World War II and the former members who went on to become prominent figures in state and local civil rights groups speak to the long genealogy of West Coast civil rights. This lengthy tradition was bolstered by the adherence of Asian students to Christian and spiritual ideas of belonging and panethnic cooperation in their fight for racial equality. While this chapter focused on Lee, Matsumoto, Velasco, Carreon, and other former students and activists, their importance in the creation of interracial movements, as well as their difficulty in adapting to changing ideas, represents the challenges that characterized racial liberalism and interracial activism before, during, and after the war. Were the former students who formed a core of middle-class, older, and Christian activists in places like Seattle exceptional and therefore not representative? Was their trajectory so exceptional when compared with other trends at the time as to render their experiences incapable of informing larger narratives of both Asian American and civil rights history? Former foreign- and American-born Christian student association members certainly were not representative of all Asian Americans and activists, but then again, neither were individuals like Boggs or Kochiyama who contributed to different movements while utilizing similar ideas of interracial activism and panethnic cooperation. What Matsumoto, Velasco, and Lee challenge historians to do is to think about how we tend to identify an activist by using certain standards (such as radicalism and leftism) that limit the complex and fascinating image of West Coast and American civil rights movements and their connections to Asian American history.

Conclusion

● ●

"Although Asians in the United States have long been engaged in political action," the Asian American Studies scholar Yen Le Espiritu explains in her groundbreaking 1992 work, *Asian American Panethnicity: Bridging Institutions and Identities*, "their efforts never drew public attention until the 1960s." Espiritu continues by arguing that along with the impact of "civil rights and Black Power movements . . . on the consciousness of Asian Americans, sensitizing them to racial issues," a panethnic Asian movement in the United States was impossible before World War II because "the predominantly foreign-born Asian population did not share a common language," and most Asian Americans were too preoccupied with ethnic-specific issues to build Asian solidarity.[1] There is no doubt that events and circumstances such as the Vietnam War, the unprecedented number of Asian American students on college campuses, the arrival of new Asian immigrant groups, and the results of African American, Native American, and Latino struggles for rights strengthened Asian American commitments to justice. However, the history and known presence of Asian civil rights activism predate the protests and strikes of the 1960s.

Foreign-born Asian students used Christianity to form coalitions with American-born students and connect immigrant rights with racial equality in the United States, highlighting the interracial, interethnic, multicultural, and ideological roots of American civil rights movements. Well before the war in Vietnam and the racial activism of the 1960s, Chinese,

Filipino, and Japanese students worked to build panethnic, interethnic, and interracial solidarity on and off campus. They pursued racial justice and raised awareness of the devastating effects of racism and prejudice in America and around the world.

More importantly, however, the long record of Asian students' activism and interracial organization suggests Asians should be more visible in the history of the early civil rights movements in the United States. Asian students' interracial and interethnic cooperation contributed to a growing civil rights movement along the West Coast during the early to mid-twentieth century. Although there are merits to discussing the specific problems that Asian Americans faced, there has been a tendency in the historical study of racial relations during the twentieth century to separate the struggles of Asian Americans from those of other racial groups. The struggle for Asian American rights appears to run parallel to other racial rights movements—rarely intersecting with the goals of other minority activists. The case of Christian Asian students in my book demonstrates that Asian activism in the United States was integral to the growth of civil rights activism rather than an offshoot of a larger social movement during the 1960s. The experiences of these students evince not only the story of a "long Asian American Movement" but also the integration of Asians into the history of a nationwide movement for racial justice.

The struggle for Asian American rights constitutes an important part of the larger struggle for racial equality in America, which is constantly reframed and redefined as the "long civil rights movement" by historians of race. Asian Christian students' activism before the post–World War II period encourages scholars to understand how the continuing fight for racial justice in the United States is as wide as it is long.

Notes

Introduction

1. "Important Historical Dates for the University of Washington YMCA and YWCA," folder 2, box 1, Young Men's Christian Association, University Branch Records, University of Washington Special Collections, Seattle, Washington; "YW Cabinet Will Hold Discussion" (April 1938), folder 2, box 1, Young Men's Christian Association, University Branch Records.

2. "Important Historical Dates for the University of Washington YMCA and YWCA," 2–3.

3. See Shana Bernstein, *Bridges of Reform: Interracial Civil Rights Activism in Twentieth-Century Los Angeles* (New York: Oxford University Press, 2011); Mark Brilliant, *The Color of American Has Changed: How Racial Diversity Shaped Civil Rights in California, 1941–1978* (New York: Oxford University Press, 2010); Scott Kurashige, *The Shifting Grounds of Race: Black and Japanese Americans in the Making of Multiethnic Los Angeles* (Princeton, NJ: Princeton University Press, 2007); Quintard Taylor, *The Forging of a Black Community: Seattle's Central District from 1870 through the Civil Rights Era* (Seattle: University of Washington Press, 1994); and Quintard Taylor, *In Search of the Racial Frontier: African Americans in the West, 1528–1990* (New York: W. W. Norton, 1999).

4. Chih-ming Wang, *Transpacific Articulations: Student Migration and the Remaking of Asian America* (Honolulu: University of Hawaii Press, 2013), 112. See also Sheng-mei Ma, *Immigrant Subjectivities in Asian American and Asian Diaspora Literatures* (Albany: State University of New York Press, 1998); and Shu-mei Shih, *Visuality and Identity: Sinophone Articulations across the Pacific* (Berkeley: University of California Press, 2007) for their interesting analyses of what Shih describes as transnational ideas of belonging in Asian student publications and their impact on the identity of foreign students in the United States and in Asia.

5. Eiichiro Azuma, *Between Two Empires: Race, History, and Transnationalism in Japanese America* (New York: Oxford University Press, 2005), 7–8.

6   Wang, *Transpacific Articulations*, 112–113.
7   William Wei, *The Asian American Movement* (Philadelphia: Temple University Press, 1993), 20–22, 126–128. Yuji Ichioka was also an eminent historian of Japanese American history, and his seminal work *The Issei: The World of the First-Generation Japanese Immigrants, 1885–1924* (New York: Free Press, 1990) and his edited volume *Views from Within: The Japanese American Resettlement Study* (Los Angeles: Asian American Studies Center–University of California at Los Angeles, 1989) helped to establish the historical study of the Japanese American experience before and during World War II. See also Eiichiro Azuma, Gordon Chang, and Yuji Ichioka, eds., *Before Internment: Essays in Prewar Japanese American History* (Redwood City, CA: Stanford University Press, 2006).
8   See Weili Ye, *Seeking Modernity in China's Name: Chinese Students in the United States, 1900–1927* (Redwood City, CA: Stanford University Press, 2001); and Larry Clinton Thompson, *William Scott Ament and the Boxer Rebellion: Heroism, Hubris, and the Ideal Missionary* (Jefferson, NC: McFarland Publishing, 2009), 34–38, 40.
9   The overwhelming majority of *pensionados* and self-supporting students were male, but select females from elite families also took part in educational opportunities abroad. See Emily Lawsin, "*Pensionados, Paisonos,* and *Pinoys*: An Analysis of the Filipino Student Bulletin, 1922–1939," *Filipino American National Historical Society Journal* 4 (1996): 35–50, for a more in-depth discussion of this educational program.
10 Azuma, *Between Two Empires*, 7–8.
11 "Notes and News on International Educational Affairs," *Bulletin of the Institute of International Education*, 3rd ser., 2 (1922): 14.
12 Ye, *Seeking Modernity*, 56–59; Azuma, *Between Two Empires*, 3–8, 225–226. See also Paul Kramer, "International Students and U.S. Global Power in the Long Twentieth Century," *Diplomatic History* 33, no. 5 (2009): 775–806.
13 Derek Chang, *Citizens of a Christian Nation: Evangelical Missions and the Problem of Race in the Nineteenth Century* (Philadelphia: University of Pennsylvania Press, 2010), 99–102, 132–135. See also Peggy Pascoe, *Relations of Rescue: The Search for Female Authority in the American West, 1874–1939* (New York: Oxford University Press, 1993) for her insightful look at the connections between white Christian female reformers and immigrant populations in San Francisco and other western cities.
14 See James H. Montgomery and Donald A. McGavran, *The Discipling of a Nation* (Manila: Global Church Growth Bulletin, 1980); Jun Xing, *Baptized in the Fire of Revolution* (Bethlehem, PA: Lehigh University Press, 1996); and Hamish Ion, *American Missionaries, Christian Oyatoi, and Japan, 1859–1873* (Vancouver: University of British Columbia Press, 2002). See also Albert L. Park and David K. Yoo, "Introduction: Modernity and the Materiality of Religion," in *Encountering Modernity: Christianity in East Asia and Asian America*, ed. Albert L. Park and David K. Yoo (Honolulu: University of Hawaii Press, 2014), 9–13.
15 Charlotte Brooks, *Alien Neighbors, Foreign Friends: Asian Americans, Housing, and the Transformation of Urban America* (Chicago: University of Chicago Press, 2009), 47–48. See also Carey McWilliams, *Prejudice: Japanese-Americans, Symbol of Racial Intolerance* (Boston: Little, Brown, 1944); and Carey McWilliams, *California: The Great Exception* (New York: Current Books, 1949), for a then-contemporary view of California's racial issues during the World War II era.
16 See Angelo Ancheta, *Race, Rights, and the Asian American Experience* (New

Brunswick, NJ: Rutgers University Press, 2006), for a discussion of the history and contemporary policies regarding Asian Americans and legal discrimination in the United States.

17 See Kenneth J. Guest, *God in Chinatown: Religion and Survival in New York's Involving Immigrant Community* (New York: NYU Press, 2003); Moses O. Biney, *From Africa to America: Religion and Adaptation among Ghanaian Immigrants in New York* (New York: NYU Press, 2011); Robert J. Priest and Alvaro L. Nieves, *This Side of Heaven: Race, Ethnicity, and Christian Faith* (New York: Oxford University Press, 2006); Richard Alba, Albert J. Raboteau, and Josh DeWind, *Immigration and Religion in America: Comparative and Historical Perspectives* (New York: NYU Press, 2008); Joshua Paddison, *Heathens in America: Religions, Race, and Reconstruction in California* (Berkeley and Los Angeles: Huntington Library Press and University of California Press, 2012); and Jeanette Rodriguez, *Our Lady of Guadalupe: Faith and Empowerment among Mexican-American Women* (Austin: University of Texas Press, 1994). Although Doug Rossinow, a historian of the civil rights movement during the 1960s, has written about the relationships between the YMCA, "liberal Christianity," and student activism, his work is a close case study of the activities of students at the University of Texas–Austin during the postwar period. See Rossinow's *The Politics of Authenticity: Liberalism, Christianity, and the New Left in America* (New York: Columbia University Press, 1998), 54–85.

18 Park and Yoo, "Introduction," 8. See also Timothy Tseng, "Religious Liberalism, International Politics, and Diasporic Realities: The Chinese Students' Christian Association of North America, 1909–1951," *Journal of American–East Asian Relations* 5, no. 3 (1996): 305–330.

19 Park and Yoo, "Introduction," 9.

20 Many books in the existing literature expound the importance to African Americans and other minorities of achieving a level of "respectability" to argue for rights and equality among whites in American history. Glenda Gilmore's *Gender and Jim Crow: Women and the Politics of White Supremacy in North Carolina, 1896–1920* (Chapel Hill: University of North Carolina Press, 1996), Danielle McGuire's *At the Dark End of the Street: Black Women, Rape, and Resistance—A New History of the Civil Rights Movement from Rosa Parks to the Rise of Black Power* (New York: Vintage, 2011), and Karen Ferguson's *Black Politics in New Deal Atlanta* (Chapel Hill: University of North Carolina Press, 2002) offer in-depth analyses on the role of respectability in the politics and gender and activism in the African American civil rights movement. Ellen Wu's recent *The Color of Success: Asian Americans and the Origins of the Model Minority* (Princeton, NJ: Princeton University Press, 2013) and Steffi San Buenaventura's essay "Filipino Religion at Home and Abroad: Historical Roots and Immigrant Transformations," in *Religions in Asian America: Building Faith Communities*, ed. Pyong Gap Min and Jung Ha Kim (Lanham, MD: AltaMira Press, 2002) also offer discussions between the connections of societal and religious respectability and Asian American communities.

21 Park and Yoo, "Introduction," 9.

22 See Josephine Fowler, *Japanese and Chinese Immigrant Activists: Organizing in American and International Communist Movements, 1919–1933* (New Brunswick, NJ: Rutgers University Press, 2007) for a book-length analysis of Chinese and Japanese labor radicals in the United States and their relationship with the Communist Party USA and the Comintern.

23 For discussions of the "long" civil rights movement, see Gilmore, *Gender and Jim Crow* and Jacquelyn Dowd Hall, "The Long Civil Rights Movement and the Political Uses of the Past," *Journal of American History* 91, no. 4 (2005): 1233–1263. See also Randi J. Walker, *Religion and the Public Conscience* (London: John Hunt Publishing, 2012), a study of the role of religion in the rise of a Seattle-based civil rights movement.

24 See Yen Le Espiritu, *Asian American Panethnicity: Bridging Institutions and Identities* (Philadelphia: Temple University Press, 1993); and Wei, *Asian American Movement.*

25 See Gary Okihiro, *Margins and Mainstreams: Asians in American History and Culture* (Seattle: University of Washington Press, 2014); and Natalia Molina, *How Race Is Made in America: Immigration, Citizenship, and the Historical Power of Racial Scripts* (Berkeley: University of California Press, 2014), regarding ethnic and racial identities within the broader constructs of American history.

26 See Nina Mjagkij, *Light in the Darkness: African Americans and the YMCA, 1852–1946* (Louisville: University of Kentucky Press, 2003); Thomas Winter, *Making Men, Making Class: The YMCA and Workingmen, 1877–1920* (Chicago: University of Chicago Press, 2002); and David Setran, *The Student Y: Student Religion in the Era of Secularization* (New York: Palgrave Macmillan, 2007).

27 Walker, *Religion and the Public Conscience,* 100, 105–107.

28 See Nico Slate, *Colored Cosmopolitanism: The Shared Struggle for Freedom in the United States* (Cambridge, MA: Harvard University Press, 2012); and David Yoo, *Contentious Spirits: Religion in Korean American History, 1903–1945* (Redwood City, CA: Stanford University Press, 2010), on the roles of Indian and Korean immigrants in transnational movements.

Chapter 1 "Western People Are Not All Angels": Encountering Racism on the West Coast

1 Henry Yu, "The 'Oriental Problem' in America, 1920–1960: Linking the Identities of Chinese American and Japanese American Intellectuals," in *Claiming America: Constructing Chinese American Identities during the Exclusion Era*, ed. K. Scott Wong and Sucheng Chan (Philadelphia: Temple University Press, 1998), 197–199.

2 Weili Ye, *Seeking Modernity in China's Name: Chinese Students in the United States, 1900–1927* (Redwood City, CA: Stanford University Press, 2001), 105–107, 109. See also Shirley Lim, *A Feeling of Belonging: Asian American Women's Popular Culture* (New York: NYU Press, 2005); David Yoo, *Growing Up Nisei: Race, Generation, and Culture among Japanese Americans of California, 1924–1929* (Urbana: University of Illinois Press, 1999); and Kathleen Yep, *When Basketball Ruled at the Chinese Playground* (Philadelphia: Temple University Press, 2009). Judy Yung's *Unbound Feet: A Social History of Chinese Women in San Francisco* (Berkeley: University of California Press, 1995) also offers a discussion of Chinese female groups and organizations.

3 See Kristin Hoganson's *Consumer's Imperium: The Global Production of American Domesticity* (Chapel Hill: University of North Carolina Press, 2007) and Akira Iriye's *Cultural Internationalism and World Order* (Baltimore: Johns Hopkins University Press, 2000). Jonathan Hansen's discussion of cosmopolitanism and Americanism during the early twentieth century is also useful for understanding the

historical conceptions of these terms in relation to immigration and identity. See Hansen, "True Americanism: Progressive Era Intellectuals and the Problem of Liberal Nationalism," in *Americanism: New Perspectives on the History of an Ideal*, ed. Michael Kazin and Joseph McCartin (Chapel Hill: University of North Carolina Press, 2008), 80–87.

4   Hoganson, *Consumer's Imperium*, 212–215, 220, 232–234.

5   "Guidebook for Foreign Students in the United States," Institute of International Education, Second Series, Bulletin 5 (July 1921), 77.

6   Shelley Sang-Hee Lee, *Claiming the Oriental Gateway: Prewar Seattle and Japanese America* (Philadelphia: Temple University Press, 2012), 13.

7   See also Eiichiro Azuma, "The Pacific Era Has Arrived: Transnational Education among Japanese Americans, 1932–1941," *History of Education Quarterly* 43, no. 1 (Spring 2003): 39–73, for a more in-depth description of the role of Nisei in transpacific relations, specifically during the 1930s and 1940s. Dorothy Fujita Rony's *American Workers, Colonial Power: Philippine Seattle and the Transpacific West, 1919–1941* (Berkeley: University of California Press, 2002) for another example of Seattle's status in an increasingly transpacific world during the early twentieth century.

8   Lee, *Claiming the Oriental Gateway*, 12–13.

9   "University of Arizona," *Filipino Student Bulletin*, October 1923, 6.

10   Discussion: The Amendment of the California Community Property Law—J. W. Bingham, March 1924, folder 7750-CROS, Crossroads Club Files, Stanford University Archives, Stanford University, CA.

11   "Guidebook for Foreign Students," 79.

12   Report for the Year 1911, folder 17, box 1, Record Group 13—Committee on Friendly Relations among Foreign Students Records (hereafter cited as CFRS Records), Yale University Divinity School Library Special Collections, Yale University, New Haven, CT.

13   Nina Mjagkij, *Light in the Darkness: African Americans and the YMCA, 1852–1946* (Louisville: University Press of Kentucky, 1994), 3.

14   During the 1860s, the Chinese immigrants formed their own branches of the YMCA in San Francisco and other areas of California. See Yung, *Unbound Feet*, for more information on Asian branches of the YMCA on the West Coast.

15   Charles Hurrey, "Shortly after the Intervention," 1929, box 190, Charles Hurrey Papers, Kautz Family YMCA Archives, University of Minnesota, Minneapolis. See also David Setran, *The College "Y": Student Religion in the Era of Secularization* (New York: Palgrave Macmillan, 2007), for more discussions of the influence of college YMCAs during the twentieth century.

16   Timothy Tseng, "Religious Liberalism, International Politics, and Diasporic Realities: The Chinese Students' Christian Association of North America, 1909–1951," *Journal of American–East Asian Relations* 5, no. 3 (Fall–Winter 1996): 311.

17   Benedict Anderson, *Imagined Communities: Reflections on the Origin and Spread of Nationalism*, rev. ed. (London: Verso, 2006), 6. See also Lee, *Claiming the Oriental Gateway*, 25–37.

18   Letter from a Chinese Student at Pomona College about Asilomar Conference, *The CSCA Yearbook* (1921–1923), p. 27, file 2, box 1, Archives of the Chinese Students' Christian Association of North America (hereafter cited as CSCA Archives), Yale University Divinity School Library Special Collections.

19 Charles Hurrey, "America's Answer to Ten Thousand Students," *Filipino Student Bulletin*, October 1923, 4.

20 "World Fellowship," *Portal*, November 1925, 4–5; "YWCA Plans Education Week," *Portal*, May 1925, 4–6.

21 Monico C. Calma, "A Bridge for the East and the West," *Filipino Student Bulletin*, November 1933, 1.

22 See Mae Ngai, *Impossible Subjects: Illegal Aliens and the Making of Modern America*, 2nd ed. (Princeton, NJ: Princeton University Press, 2014), for a more in-depth discussion of the variety of anti-Asian reactions to both legal and illegal immigration on the West Coast during the early to mid-twentieth century.

23 Ye, *Seeking Modernity*, 88–92. See also Erika Lee, *At America's Gates: Chinese Immigration during the Exclusion Era, 1882–1943* (Chapel Hill: University of North Carolina Press, 2003); and Erika Lee and Judy Yung, *Angel Island: Immigrant Gateway to America* (New York: Oxford University Press, 2010), for more information on transpacific travels and detainment.

24 Takanaga Hirai, "An Hawaiian Japanese Immigrant-Interview," 1924, item 39, box 24, Survey of Race Relations, Hoover Institution Archives, Stanford University, CA (hereafter cited as SRR).

25 Interview with Dr. F. T. Nakaya, Japanese physician, 1924, item 247, box 28, SRR.

26 Report on Chinese Students in America and Europe, 1931, folder 3, box 45, CFRS.

27 Lee, *At America's Gates*, 128–131, 134–135.

28 Chotoku Toyama, "Life History as a Social Document," item 168, box 25, SRR.

29 See Quintard Taylor, *In Search of the Racial Frontier: African Americans in the West, 1528–1990* (New York: W. W. Norton, 1999), 250–262.

30 Ralph E. Luker, *The Social Gospel in Black and White* (Chapel Hill: University of North Carolina Press, 1991), 70, 110–113.

31 Interview with Dr. F. T. Nakaya, Japanese physician, 1924, item 247, box 38, SRR.

32 Council Minutes, p. 6, folder 5, box 2, YMCA Council Reports, 1923–1927, YMCA Records, Washington State University Archives, Pullman, WA; Council Minutes, p. 3, folder 2, box 3, YMCA Council Reports, 1929–1935, YMCA Records, Washington State University Archives.

33 Council Minutes, p. 3, folder 2, box 3, YMCA Council Reports, 1929–1935, YMCA Records, Washington State University Archives.

34 C. L. Maxfield, "Washington Solves a Problem," *Intercollegian*, November 1924, 37.

35 Hideo Oyama, "Life History as a Social Document," item 60, box 25, SRR.

36 "The Chinese Students' Position of Today," folder 16, box 1, CFRS Records.

37 John Schmoker, "History of the CFR," 80–81, box 4, YMCA International Division, Kautz Family YMCA Archives.

38 Life History of Saka Tsuboi, item 58, box 25, SRR; Interview with Dr. F. T. Nakaya.

39 Oyama, "Life History"; M. Suma, "Paper Written by a Japanese Student in Reply to Questionnaire," 1924, item 48, box 24, SRR; Interview with Dr. F. T. Nakaya.

40 Schmoker, "History of the CFR," 81.

41 Suma, "Paper Written"; Oyama, "Life History."

42 Suma, "Paper Written."

43 "Paper Written by a Japanese Student in Reply to a Questionnaire on Race Relations," item 48, box 24, SRR; Oyama, "Life History."

44 Charles F. Hurrey, "Foreign Students Shock Our Complacency," 9, box 190, Charles Hurrey Papers.

45 Ibid.

46 Luker, *Social Gospel*, 142, 310.

47 Lisa Mar, *Brokering Belonging: Chinese in Canada's Exclusion Era, 1885–1945* (New York: Oxford University Press, 2010), 72–80; Lee, *Oriental Gateway*, 94–98.

48 Y. T. Wu, "The Boomerang of Criticism- A Reply to Mr. Charles Hurrey in Respect to His Views Expressed in an Article Appearing in the Fellowship Notes of the CSCA," *Fellowship Notes*, May 1925, 1–2.

49 Luker, *Social Gospel*, 124–127; Mjagkij, *Light in the Darkness*, 102–111.

50 "Story of the Interracial Movement in the South," *Chinese Christian Student*, February 1930, 3.

51 Sarah Griffith, "Conflicting Dialogues: The Survey of Race Relations and the Fight for Asian American Racial Equality" (PhD diss., University of California at Santa Barbara, 2011), 279.

52 "Christian Oriental Student Conference," *Intercollegian*, November 1924, 19.

53 E. J. Carballo, "To Fellow Members and Readers of the Bulletin," *Filipino Student Bulletin*, December 1924–January 1925, 9.

54 Lillian Kwai, "The Indianapolis Convention: A Personal Impression," *Fellowship Notes*, June 1925, 21.

Chapter 2   A Problem by Any Other Name: Christian Student Associations, the "Second-Generation Problem," and West Coast Racism

1 Walter Mihata, "Americans of Japanese Ancestry," *Japanese Student Christian Bulletin*, May 1925, 4.

2 Eiichiro Azuma, "The Pacific Era Has Arrived: Transnational Education among Japanese Americans, 1932–1941," *History of Education Quarterly* 43, no. 1 (Spring 2003): 42–43. See also Shelley Hang-See Lee, *Claiming the Oriental Gateway: Prewar Seattle and Japanese America* (Philadelphia: Temple University Press, 2012), 25–38.

3 *CSCA General Report* (1927), folder 5, box 1, CSCA Archives.

4 Robert E. Park, "Our Racial Frontier on the Pacific," *Survey Graphic* 56 (May 1926), 194. See also Stanford M. Lyman's "Civilization, Culture, and Color: Changing Foundations of Robert E. Park's Sociology of Race Relations," *International Journal of Politics, Culture, and Society* 3 (1991): 285–287, for a more in-depth discussion of Park's racial frontier from a historical-sociological perspective.

5 William C. Smith, "Preliminary Paper Prepared for Second General Session, June 15–19, 1927—The Second Generation Oriental in America," 21, folder 2, box 10, Pardee Lowe Papers, Hoover Institution Archives, Stanford University.

6 See Henry Yu, *Thinking Orientals: Migration, Contact, and Exoticism in Modern America* (New York: Oxford University Press, 2002); and Lisa Mar, *Brokering Belonging: Chinese in Canada's Exclusion Era, 1885–1945* (New York: Oxford University Press, 2010), for more information on the roles of Asian and Asian American research assistants in conducting larger sociological studies such as the Survey of Race Relations.

7 Lisa Lowe, *Immigrant Acts: On Asian American Cultural Politics* (Durham, NC: Duke University Press, 1996), 8–12.

8   "Interview with Flora Belle Jan, daughter of Proprietor Yet Far Low Chop Suey Restaurant, Fresno, California" (3 pages; Life Histories, Americanization: Accommodation; Chinese; Northern California), p. 2, folder 225, box 28, SRR.

9   Jan to Robert Park, June 1925, in *Unbound Spirit: Letters of Flora Belle Jan*, ed. Fleur Yano and Saralyn Daley (Urbana: University of Illinois Press, 2009), 26.

10 "Interview with Flora Belle Jan," 2.

11 See Robert Park, *Race and Culture* (New York: Free Press, 1964); Robert Park, *The City: Suggestions for the Study of Human Nature in the Urban Environment* (Chicago: University of Chicago Press, 1984); and Robert Park, "Cultural Conflict and the Marginal Man," an introduction to Everett V. Stonequist's *The Marginal Man: A Study in Personality and Culture Conflict* (New York: Russell and Russell, 1961).

12 Robert Park, "Human Migration and the Marginal Man," *American Journal of Sociology* 36, no. 6 (May 1928): 881–893.

13 Eckard V. Toy, "Whose Frontier? The Survey of Race Relations on the Pacific Coast in the 1920s," *Oregon Historical Quarterly* 107, no. 1 (2006): 36–63.

14 See Flora Belle Jan, *Collected Writings of Flora Belle Jan*, ed. Fleur Yano (New York: Xlibris, 2008); and Yano and Daly, *Unbound Spirit*, for more writings and accounts from Jan (a prolific writer of articles, letters, and other pieces on her time in America and later as a married woman in China). Sarah Griffith, "Conflicting Dialogues: The Survey of Race Relations and the Fight for Asian American Racial Equality" (PhD diss., University of California at Santa Barbara, 2011), 117–132.

15 Y. Y. Tsu, "Our Western Department," *Chinese Christian Student*, October 1922, 2–3.

16 Roy Hidemichi Akagi, *The Second Generation Problem—Some Suggestions towards Its Solution* (New York: Japanese Students Christian Association in America, 1926), box 295, Japanese American Research Project, Charles E. Young Research Library, University of California at Los Angeles.

17 Akagi, *Second Generation Problem*, 2.

18 "A Visiting Student—Interview with Tatsuji Suga," item 41, box 24, SRR.

19 "Interview with Ruby Hirose," pp. 2–3, item 159, box 27, SRR.

20 "Development of Aggressive Attitude by American Born Chinese: 1931," in Indifference Folder, box 126b, Pardee Lowe Papers.

21 Florence Chinn Kwan, "Some Rambling Thoughts on Why I Am a Christian," in *Unbound Voices: A Documentary History of Chinese Women in San Francisco*, ed. Judy Yung, 289–296 (Berkeley: University of California Press, 1999), 292.

22 Akagi, *Second Generation Problem*, 11.

23 Ibid.

24 Azuma, "Pacific Era," 45.

25 Griffith, "Conflicting Dialogues," 233.

26 "Pacific Coast Sectional Conference," *Japanese Student Bulletin*, February 1925, 4.

27 Akagi, "Inter-racial Goodwill," *Japanese Student Bulletin*, March 1926, 1.

28 Ibid.; Akagi, *Second Generation Problem*, 16, 10–11.

29 Ibid.

30 See Charlotte Brooks, *Alien Neighbors, Foreign Friends: Asian Americans, Housing, and the Transformation of Urban America* (Chicago: University of Chicago Press, 2009), 42–43. See also Eiichiro Azuma, "Racial Struggle, Immigrant Nationalism, and Ethnic Identity: Japanese and Filipinos in the California Delta," *Pacific Historical Review* 67, no. 2 (May 1998): 163–199; Erika Lee, *At America's Gates: Chinese*

Immigration during the Exclusion Era, 1882–1943 (Chapel Hill: University of North Carolina Press, 2003); and Leslie Bow, *Partly Colored: Asian Americans and Racial Anomaly in the Segregated South* (New York: NYU Press, 2011).

31   Azuma, "Pacific Era," 45.

32   Akagi, *Second Generation*, 11.

33   Chingwah Lee, or Ching Wah Lee, was also a well-known actor, starring in films such as *The Good Earth* (1937) and *Flower Drum Song* (1961). His later activism in San Francisco's Chinatown will be discussed in more detail in chapter 6.

34   "Concluding Luncheon a Success," *Chinese Christian Student*, May 1926, 8.

35   Japanese student to Ms. Snell, item 240, box 28, SRR.

36   George Mears, *Residential Orientals on America's Pacific Coast* (New York: Alfred A. Knopf, 1928), 146.

37   Brooks, *Alien Neighbors*, 88.

38   Alice Fong, "A Challenge to the Chinese-American," *Chinese Christian Student*, November 1932, 5.

39   Ibid.

40   Flora Belle Jan, "An American-Born Looks at Young Chinatown," *Chinese Christian Student*, March 1931, 7.

41   Francis Y. Chang, "An Accommodation Program for Second Generation Chinese," *Journal of Sociology and Social Research* 18 (1934): 541–553, Yuk Ow Research Files, ca. 1930s–1982, Asian American Studies Archive, Ethnic Studies Library, University of California, Berkeley.

42   Chingwah Lee, "The Chinese in Central California," *Chinese Christian Student*, March 1928, 3–7.

43   See Allison Varzally, *Making a Non-White America: Californians Coloring Outside Ethnic Lines, 1925–1955* (Berkeley: University of California Press, 2008).

44   Lee, "Chinese in Central California," 6.

45   "Chinese Students and Their Compatriots in America," *Chinese Christian Student*, March 1929, 7–8.

46   "Chinese Students and Their Compatriots in America: Is Closer Relationship Possible?" *Fellowship Notes of the CSCA*, February 1927, 2.

47   Ye, *Seeking Modernity*, 83.

48   "What Some Japanese Students Think of America," *Japanese Student Bulletin*, April 1931, 4–5.

49   Ibid.

50   "JSCA Movement," *Japanese Student Bulletin*, February 1926, 4.

51   "Miscellaneous Works," *Japanese Student Bulletin*, October 1926, 7.

52   "Chinese Students in West to Meet," *Chinese Christian Student*, November 1931, 5.

53   "Ideals and Objectives of the Filipino Students' Christian Movement," *Filipino Student Bulletin*, October 1927, 4.

54   "Filipino Students Seek Funds for International Club House," *Filipino Student Bulletin*, February 1928, 8.

55   E. J. Carballo, "Filipino Students vs. Chinese and Japanese Students," *Filipino Student Bulletin*, March 1928, 6–7. Here, Carballo is using the immigration term of "Mongoloid" to propose a burgeoning form of panethnic identity.

56   Although consciousness-raising is a term that historians typically use in describing the feminist movement of the late 1960s, I use it here to describe the revolution in thinking of the students. See Sara Evans, *Personal Politics: The Roots of Women's*

Liberation in the Civil Rights Movement and the New Left (New York: Vintage, 1979), 134–135.

57   "Foreign Students at Asilomar," *Japanese Student Bulletin*, March 1927, 5.
58   Ibid.
59   Akagi, *Second Generation*, 17.
60   "Updates from the Evanston Conference," *Japanese Student Bulletin*, May 1929, 3–4.
61   Ye, *Seeking Modernity*, 83–88.
62   "Student Institute of Pacific Relations," *Christian World Education Scrap Book, 1927–1928*, box 5 (Christian World Education, 1927–1929), Student Work Records, Kautz Family YMCA Archives, University of Minnesota.
63   Student Field Councils, Pacific SW 1936–1938, Minutes of Executive Committee Pacific Southwest Field Council and Asilomar Regional Council, YWCA, January 2, 1938, Kautz Family YMCA Archives.
64   *Report: The Federation and International Relations, 1937*, World Student Christian Federation Records (hereafter cited as WSCF Records), Kautz Family YMCA Archives.
65   Charles Hurrey, "Oriental Students in America," *Missionary Review*, 1934, box 058–72, CFRS Records.
66   Report to the Administration Board-Confidential Report, 1937, box 058–72, CFRS Records.
67   Kazuo Kawai to Robert Park, August 13, 1924, item 105, box 266, SRR.

Chapter 3   "We Ask Not for Mercy, but for Justice": Filipino Students and the Battle for Labor and Civil Rights

1   Trinidad Rojo, "Untitled Poem," *Filipino Student Bulletin*, April 1929, 4.
2   Carlos Bulosan's *America Is in the Heart: A Personal History* (Seattle: University of Washington Press, 2014) (originally published in 1946) is the most well-known account of a Filipino laborer's struggles with migration, racism, and work along the Pacific Coast during the interwar years.
3   Antonio Hamay, "Student Opinion: Mr. Marcuelo Is Wrong," *Filipino Student Bulletin*, May 1936, 3.
4   See Dorothy Fujita-Rony, *American Workers, Colonial Power: Philippine Seattle and the Transpacific West, 1919–1941* (Berkeley: University of California Press, 2002); Rick Baldoz, *The Third Asiatic Invasion: Empire and Migration in Filipino America, 1898–1946* (New York: NYU Press, 2011); and Chris Friday, *Organizing Asian American Labor: The Pacific Coast Canned-Salmon Industry, 1870–1942* (Philadelphia: Temple University Press, 1994). The CWFLU was not the only Filipino labor union that played an important role in organization during the interwar period and beyond; however, the CWFLU was, as I argue, a union that explicitly promoted both labor and civil rights for its members.
5   Robert Rodgers Korstad, *Civil Rights Unionism: Tobacco Workers and the Struggle for Democracy in the Mid-Twentieth-Century South* (Chapel Hill: University of North Carolina Press, 2003). See also Vicki Ruiz, *Cannery Women, Cannery Lives: Mexican Women, Unionization, and the California Food Processing Industry, 1930–1950* (Albuquerque: University of New Mexico Press, 1987); Zaragosa Vargas's *Labor Rights Are Civil Rights: Mexican American Workers in Twentieth-Century America* (Princeton, NJ: Princeton University Press, 2005); and Veta Schlimgen,

"Neither Citizens nor Aliens: Filipino 'American Nationals' in the U.S. Empire, 1900–1946" (PhD diss., University of Oregon, 2010) for a more in-depth analysis of the legal status of Filipinos in both the Philippines and the United States.

6 Victorio Velasco, "The Call of the Silver Horde," *Filipino Student Bulletin*, June 1934, 5–6.

7 Max Stern, "The Orientals in the Alaskan salmon industry: First hand observations of Max Stern, Daily News" 1922, pp. 2–3, box 24, item 50, Survey of Race Relations, Hoover Institution Archives, Stanford University.

8 "Common Sense," *Filipino Student Bulletin*, January 1926, 4.

9 Maria Schenk, "Birds of Passage: Perspectives on the Filipino Experience," 4, Maria Schenk Papers, University of Washington Special Collections Department.

10 Ibid.

11 See Catherine Ceniza Choy, *Empire of Care: Nursing and Migration in Filipino American History* (Durham, NC: Duke University Press, 2003).

12 Fujita-Rony, *American Workers*, 53–54; E. V. "Vic" Bacho, *The Long Road: Memoirs of a Filipino Pioneer* (self-published, 1992), 9.

13 Schenk, "Birds of Passage," 14.

14 Benedict Anderson, *Imagined Communities: Reflections on the Origin and Spread of Nationalism*, rev. ed. (New York: Verso, 2006), 1–9.

15 Ibid., 14–15.

16 See Friday, *Organizing*, 56–60, and Gunther Peck, *Reinventing Free Labor: Padrones and Immigrant Workers in the American West, 1880–1930* (New York: Cambridge University Press, 2000) for a more in-depth discussion of labor contractors.

17 Schenk, "Birds of Passage," 14.

18 Delegates' Report, February 23, 1939, folder 19, box 11, CWFLU Records (hereafter cited as CWFLU Records), Special Collections Department, University of Washington; James Moithan, attorney for CWFLU, to Office of the Director for the 19th Region–NLRB, January 11, 1938, folder 14, box 14, Subject Series AFL-CIO Jurisdictional Dispute, CWFLU Records.

19 See Nayan Shah, *Stranger Intimacy: Contesting Race, Sexuality, and the Law in the North American West* (Berkeley: University of California Press, 2012), 90–97; and Stephanie Hinnershitz, "We Ask Not for Mercy, but for Justice: The Cannery Workers' and Farm Laborers' Union and Filipino Civil Rights, 1927–1937," *Journal of Social History* 47, no. 1 (Fall 2013): 132–152.

20 Schenk, "Birds of Passage," 5–6; Delegates' Report, February 23, 1939, folder 19, box 11, CWFLU Records; James Moithan to Office of the Director for the 19th Region–NLRB.

21 Schenk, "Birds of Passage," 14–15.

22 Quoted in Stern, "Orientals," 10; Frank Foster, "Mr. Voter," *Alaska Fishing News*, April 1938, folder 50, box 10, CWFLU Records.

23 Eiichiro Azuma, "Racial Struggle, Immigrant Nationalism, and Ethnic Identity," *Pacific Historical Review* 67, no. 2 (May 1998): 174–181.

24 Schenk, "Birds of Passage," 4. See also Paul Kramer, *The Blood of Government: Race, Empire, the United States, and the Philippines* (Chapel Hill: Universisty of North Carolina Press, 2006), 411–430.

25 Kramer, *Blood of Government*, 407, 409, 412–418.

26 See W.E.B. Du Bois, *The Souls of Black Folk* (Cambridge, MA: University Press, John Wilson and Son, 1903); Paul Gilroy, *The Black Atlantic: Modernity and Double*

Consciousness (Cambridge, MA: Harvard University Press, 1993); and Miriam Jimenez Roman and Juan Flores, eds., *The Afro-Latin@ Reader: History and Culture in the United States* (Durham, NC: Duke University Press, 2010).

27 Luis Quisano, "Preaching the Gospel of Hope," *Filipino Student Bulletin*, March 1935, 5.

28 "Editorial," *Filipino Student Bulletin*, January 1936, 5.

29 E. J. Carballo, "In Appreciation," *Filipino Student Bulletin*, December 1924/January 1925, 3.

30 Manuel Escarrilla, "An Evaluation of Filipino Student Life in America," *Filipino Student Bulletin*, December 1928, 6.

31 "Changing Attitude," *Filipino Student Bulletin*, February/March 1929, 7.

32 Charles Hurrey, "Shortly after the Intervention," p. 16, 1929, box 058, Articles by Charles Hurrey, Kautz Family YMCA Archives.

33 D. H. Ambrosio, "'Failure' Students," *Filipino Student Bulletin*, November 1926, 11.

34 "An Issue Before Us," *Filipino Student Bulletin*, November 1925, 8.

35 Almonte, "The Filipinos in San Francisco," *Filipino Student Bulletin*, April 1924, 2.

36 Emeterio Cruz, "Filipinos Still a Problem," *Chomley Spectator*, July 13, 1929, p.1, folder 3/18–Speeches and Writings of Others, 1935–1964, Victorio Velasco Papers (hereafter cited as Velasco Papers), University of Washington Special Collections.

37 In this case, "brown" refers to Filipinos. Both whites and Filipinos themselves often identified the latter as part of the "brown" race—as Orientals, not as African Americans or blacks. This racial characterization also came from the Americans' referring to the Filipinos as "little brown brothers" from the Pacific.

38 "Editorial," *Chomly Spectator*, July 28, 1929, 5.

39 Natalia Molina, *Fit to Be Citizens? Public Health and Race in Los Angeles, 1879–1939* (Berkeley: University of California Press, 2006), 58–61.

40 History Link Essay: "Filipino Americans in Seattle," Carlene Sobrino Bonnivier Collection, MISC 2-I-Hotel, Asian Pacific Islander Collection, Asian Division, Library of Congress, Washington, DC.

41 Molina, *Fit to Be Citizens*, 67–69.

42 Emeterio Cruz and Jose Blando, "Natural Rights in Danger," *Chomly Spectator*, July 29, 1929, Velasco Papers.

43 Ibid.

44 Schenk, "Birds of Passage," 12.

45 Friday, *Organizing*, 38–39.

46 Schenk, "Birds of Passage," 5.

47 "Our Platform," *Filipino Labor Journal*, 1932, The Filipino American National Historical Society Archives, Seattle, Washington.

48 See Friday, *Organizing*, 163–171.

49 See Michael S. Brown, *Victorio Acosta Velasco: An American Life* (Lanham, MD: University Press of America, 2007), 64–68; and Fujita-Rony, *American Workers*, 166–173.

50 Cabatit had served as "Second President" of the CWFLU under Duyunugan and was also on the board of directors for the University of Washington YMCA.

51 Friday, *Organizing*, 163.

52 August C. Radke, *The Pacific American Fisheries, Inc.: History of a Washington State Salmon Packing Company, 1880–1966* (Jefferson, NC: McFarland, 2002), 149–151.

53 In 1936, the CWFLU reported a breakdown of employees in the Alaska cannery

industry by "nationality" as follows: Whites, 12,995; Natives, 5,758; Filipinos, 3,741; Japanese, 1,181; Chinese, 656; Mexicans, 622; Puerto Ricans, 120; Negroes, 63; and Others (Koreans, Chileans, Peruvians), 46. See Charles E. Jackson to Trinidad Rojo, "Subject: Alaska Fishery Statistics," December 29, 1937, folder 4, box 18, CWFLU Records; Virgil S. Duyungan and Cornelio Mislang to Mr. Joe Dismone, April 24, 1934, folder 3, box 8, CWFLU Records.

54 Dash in original. Petition from Workers of the Astoria and Puget Sound Canning Co. of Excursion Inlet, Alaska, August 31,1937, folder 20, box 9, CWFLU Records.

55 Executive Board Meeting, Joint Session: Emergency Committee and Executive Board Held October 25, 1937, at Union Hall, 84 Union, folder 2, box 1, CWFLU Records; "Reactionaries Raise False Cry of Discrimination," Undated Shop Bulletin, folder 7, box 18, CWFLU Records.

56 The two white CWFLU employees were later expelled from the union for violating the racial code of the constitution. Fred Davidson was the name of one of the white employees charged with racism and discrimination. See also Fred Davidson–20195 to the President of the CWFLU, February 20, 1937, folder 9, box 7, CWFLU Records.

57 Minutes of Special Meeting with Japanese Group, February 11, 1937, folder 4—Minutes, Membership Meeting, Feb–May 1937, box 1, CWFLU records; Andres Bigornia (Recording Secretary) to Secretary Mangawang, February 11, 1937, General Correspondence, Portland Branch, folder 6, box 7, CWFLU Records.

58 Minutes of Special Meeting.

59 Andres Bigornia to Secretary Mangawang, February 19, 1937, General Correspondence, Portland Branch, folder 6, box 7, CWFLU Records.

60 Official Statement, Newsletter dated April 30, 1937, folder 7, box 10, CWFLU records.

61 Ibid.

62 Association of Salmon Packers to Rex Strictland of Public Morals Committee of Olympia, WA, March 27, 1935, folder 2, box 2, CWFLU Records. See also Baldoz, *Third Asiatic Invasion*, 55–59.

63 See also Peggy Pascoe, *What Comes Naturally: Miscegenation Law and the Making of Race in America* (New York: Oxford University Press, 2010), for a more in-depth discussion of the history of anti-miscegenation laws in the United States.

64 Regular membership meeting held on February 28, 1937, folder 4, box 1, CWFLU Records.

65 Gail Nomura, "Within the Law: The Establishment of Filipino Leasing Rights on the Yakima Indian Reservation," *Amerasia* 13, no. 1 (1986–1987): 99–117. In her article, Nomura also discusses the role of Filipino Community of Yakima, Inc., a defense organization led by Roy Baldoz (a Filipino farmer from Washington) in the leasing conflict in Yakima.

66 Mae Ngai, "From Colonial Subject to Undesirable Alien: Filipino Migration, Exclusion, and Repatriation, 1920–1940," in *Re/collecting Early Asian America: Essays in Cultural History*, ed. Josephine D. Lee, Imogene, L. Lim, and Yuko Matsukawa (Philadelphia: Temple University Press, 2002), 111–127.

67 Nomura, "Within the Law," 4–6, 8.

68 "Resolution for a Fair Trial of Nine Filipinos Now Being Tried in Yakima County Accused of Perjury in the Second Degree and Conspiracy Against the Alien Land Law," Delegate Reports, 1937, folder 8, box 8, CWFLU Records; "Special Statement

on Yakima Vigilantism," Yakima Filipinos—Subject Series, folder 8, box 8, CWLU Records.

69 "Resolution for a Fair Trial," Delegate Reports.

70 "Special Statement on Yakima Vigilantism."

71 Ibid.

72 Devra Weber, *Dark Sweat, White Gold: California Farm Workers, Cotton, and the New Deal* (Berkeley: University of California Press, 1994), 4–5.

73 "Plan to Arrest in Labor Trouble," *Spokane Daily Chronicle*, November 18, 1937, 14.

74 Fujita-Rony, *American Workers*, 192. See also Jack K. Masson and Donald L. Guimary, "Pilipinos and Unionization of the Alaskan Canned Salmon Industry," *Amerasia* 8, no. 2 (1981): 25–26.

75 Fujita-Rony, *American Workers*, 192, 202; Masson and Guimary, "Pilipinos and Unionization," 28.

Chapter 4   "A Sweet-and-Sour World": The Second Sino-Japanese War, Christian Citizenship, and Equality

1 Juan Dahilig, "Moderation Beckons Us," *Filipino Student Bulletin*, March 1936, 3.

2 Timothy Tseng, "Religious Liberalism, International Politics, and Diasporic Realities: The Chinese Students' Christian Association of North America, 1909–1951," *Journal of East-Asian Relations* 5, no. 3 (1996): 305–330.

3 See Mary L. Dudziak, *Cold War Civil Rights: Race and the Image of American Democracy* (Princeton, NJ: Princeton University Press, 2002); Thomas Borstelmann, *The Cold War and the Color Line: American Race Relations in the Global Arena* (Cambridge, MA: Harvard University Press, 2003); and Bill V. Mullen and Cathryn Watson, eds., *W.E.B. DuBois on Asia: Crossing the World Color Line* (Jackson: University Press of Mississippi, 2005).

4 See Nico Slate, *Colored Cosmopolitanism: The Shared Struggle for Freedom in the United States and India* (Cambridge, MA: Harvard University Press, 2012); and Glenda Gilmore, *Defying Dixie: The Radical Roots of Civil Rights, 1919–1950* (New York: W. W. Norton, 2009).

5 "A Christian Citizen and His Political Duties," *Ideas and Activities of the CSCA*, 1913, 20–22.

6 Wellington Liu, "The Indianapolis Convention," *CSCA: Makers of New China in College in America*, 1923–1924, 22.

7 "Mobilization Day," *Japanese Student Bulletin*, October 1924, 5.

8 "Towards a New Community," *Student Movement*, ca. 1928, 3–5.

9 Ibid., 5.

10 Ibid.; Liu, "Indianapolis," 22.

11 "WSCF: What Place It Holds among Other Youth Movements, How It Is Tackling the Vital Issues of the Day," *World Education News Service*, 1931.

12 Ryozo Okumura, "The Plight of the Christian Students in Japan," *Japanese Student Bulletin*, October 1926, 6.

13 Ibid.

14 See Cemil Aydin, *The Politics of Anti-Westernism in Asia: Visions of World Order in Pan-Islamic and Pan-Asian Thought* (New York: Columbia University Press, 2007), for more discussion of the rise and evolution of Pan-Asianism and Japan from the nineteenth through twentieth centuries.

15   "Chinese Student Shows How Nationalism and Internationalism May Be Reconciled," *Council of Christian Associations Bulletin*, May 1927, 9.

16   See Arif Dirlik, "The Ideological Foundations of the New Life Movement: A Study in Counterrevolution," *Journal of Asian Studies* 34, no. 4 (August 1975): 948–954, for a more in-depth discussion of Chiang's movement and politics.

17   H. S. Lang, "The Chinese Church and Chinese Nationalism," *Chinese Christian Student*, December 1927, 41.

18   Ibid.

19   Suichi Harada, "Japanese Students See Chinese Affairs," *Japanese Student Bulletin*, April 1927, 4.

20   For a more in-depth discussion of the Manchurian crisis and Sino-Japanese relations prior to 1931, see Yoshihisia Tak Matsusaka, *The Making of Japanese Manchuria, 1904–1932* (Cambridge, MA: Harvard University Press/Harvard University Asian Center, 2003), and Anthony Coogan, *Northeast China and the Origins of Anti-Japanese United Front* (New York: Sage Publications, 1994).

21   Matsusaka, *Japanese Manchuria*, 127–130, 142.

22   Roy Akagi, "China's Violation of Treaties and Agreements in Manchuria," *Japanese Student Bulletin*, February 1931, 9. The JSCA later acknowledged that the Japanese instigated the Mukden Incident in the *Bulletin*.

23   Junichi Naton, "Some Japanese Traits," *Japanese Student Bulletin*, May–June 1934, 2.

24   "Just a Note," *Japanese Student Bulletin*, April 1932, 14.

25   "Chinese Student Advocates Organization for Self-Defense," *Chinese Christian Student*, December 1931, 8.

26   "College Teachers," *Chinese Christian Student*, March 1932, 16–17.

27   Yano and Daly, *Unbound Spirit*, 50–77.

28   Brian Hayashi, *For the Sake of our Brethren: Protestantism among the Japanese in Los Angeles, 1895–1942* (Redwood City, CA: Stanford University Press, 1995), 6–7, 108–127.

29   See Eiichiro Azuma, "The Pacific Era Has Arrived: Transnational Education among Japanese Americans, 1932-1941" *History of Education Quarterly* 43, no. 1 (Spring, 2003): 42–45; and Karen J. Leong and Judy Tzu-Chun Wu, "Filling the Rice Bowls of China: Staging Humanitarian Relief during the Sino-Japanese War," in *Chinese Americans and the Politics of Race and Culture*, ed. Sucheng Chan and Madeline Y. Hsu (Philadelphia: Temple University Press, 2008), 132–153.

30   Favorable Relations, box 127a, Pardee Lowe Papers, Hoover Institution Archives, Stanford University.

31   P. C. Hsu, "The Challenges to Sino-Japanese Liberals," *Chinese Christian Student*, January 1932, 3–4.

32   "We Deplore," *Chinese Christian Student*, March–April 1932, 5.

33   Masahiko Takahashi, "Letter to the Republic of China," *Japanese Student Bulletin*, March 1932, 7.

34   Masatane Mitani, "Editor's Notes—Must China Fight Japan?" *Japanese Student Bulletin*, March 1936, 2.

35   Masatane Mitani, "Japanese Culture vs. Christianity," *Japanese Student Bulletin*, February–March 1935, 3.

36   Ibid., 4; "Propose Sino-Japanese Christian Movement," *Japanese Student Bulletin*, April 1931, 9; CSCA–General Secretary's Report for the Year 1931–1932, CSCA Archives.

37 "Pacific Calls Its Youth to Pacific Area Conference," *Japanese Student Bulletin*, June 1936, 5; "JSCA and CSCA," *Japanese Student Bulletin*, December 1937, 4.

38 "The Oriental Student Christian Conference," *Filipino Student Bulletin*, May 1934, 5.

39 Ibid.

40 Jerome Davis, "Letter to the Editor: Jerome Davis Hopes League Brings Peace," *Chinese Christian Student*, December 1931, 21.

41 Leong and Wu, "Filling the Rice Bowls," 138–151.

42 See Richard Wilson, *When Tigers Fight: The Story of the Sino-Japanese War, 1937–1945* (New York: Viking Press, 1982); Mark Peattie, Edward Drea, and Hans van de Ven, eds., *The Battle for China: Essays on the Military History of the Sino-Japanese War of 1937–1945* (Redwood City, CA: Stanford University Press, 2011), and C. A. Bayly, *Forgotten Wars: Freedom and Revolution in South East Asia* (Cambridge, MA: Belknap Press of Harvard University Press, 2007).

43 United China Relief, "What Others Say," UCLA Chancellor Files, University Archives, Charles E. Young Special Collections Department, University of California at Los Angeles, Los Angeles, CA (hereafter cited as UCLA Chancellor Files).

44 Reprinted in the *Chinese Christian Student*, May 1938, 4.

45 "International Department Favors Embargo Against Japan," *Intercollegian*, 1939. The Y did, however, believe in "continu[ing] to participate in any efforts to keep open the channels of genuine fellowship between the Student Christian Movements" of America, China, and Japan.

46 Charlotte Brooks, *Alien Neighbors, Foreign Friends: Asian Americans, Housing, and the Transformation of Urban America* (Chicago: University of Chicago Press, 2009), 103–105.

47 Report to the National Intercollegiate Christian Council of Student Work (undated), Charles Hurrey Papers.

48 George Kao, "On International Living," *Chinese Christian Student*, October–November 1939, 2.

49 Toru Matsumoto, "Editorial Notes," *Japanese Student Bulletin*, November 1939, 2; see also Alfred Akamatsu, "Beyond the Clouds," *Japanese Student Bulletin*, October 1937, 2.

50 Juan Dahilig, "Moderation Beckons Us," *Filipino Student Bulletin*, March 1936, 3.

51 "Philippine Politics and Filipino Students," *Filipino Student Bulletin*, January 1926, 5.

52 D. H. Ambrosio, "Kicking Against the Pricks," *Filipino Student Bulletin*, November 1928, 7.

53 Albert Park and David Yoo describe a similar phenomenon among Korean students who used Christianity to discuss imperialism and colonization in "Introduction: Modernity and the Materiality of Religion," in *Encountering Modernity: Christianity in East Asia and Asian America* (Honolulu: University of Hawaii Press, 2014), 9–12.

54 "Data Bearing on Policy and Program Decisions," Committee for Friendly Relations among Foreign Students CSCA Archives, Yale University Divinity School Library Special Collections.

55 George Savage, "The Asilomar Convention," *Intercollegian*, February 1938, 157–158.

56 Suichi Harada, "War between Japan and America—An Illusion," *Japanese Student Bulletin*, May–June 1936, 3.

57 David Toong, "How Pacific Coast Organizations Keep Busy," *Chinese Christian Student*, January 1940, 7.

58 "Important Historical Dates for the University of Washington YMCA and YWCA," folder 2, box 1, Young Men's Christian Association, University Branch Records, University of Washington Special Collections; "YW Cabinet Will Hold Discussion," April 1938, folder 2, box 1, Young Men's Christian Association, University Branch Records.

59 "Important Historical Dates"; "News from Around Campus," *Japanese Student Bulletin*, September 1938, 4.

60 "News from Around Campus," 4.

61 "Important Historical Dates."

62 See Michael Denning, *The Cultural Front: The Laboring of American Culture in the Twentieth Century* (New York: Verso, 1998) and Chris Vials, *Realism for the Masses: Aesthetics, Popular Front Pluralism, and U.S. Culture, 1935–1947* (Jackson: University Press of Mississippi, 2009) for more discussions of the broader narrative of the Popular Front and Cultural Front in US history. Carlos Bulosan's *America Is in the Heart: A Personal History* (1946; repr. Seattle: University of Washington Press, 2014) also provides a firsthand account of Filipino labor activism during the Depression and Popular Front era.

63 See Lon Kurashige, *Japanese American Celebration and Conflict: A History of Ethnic Identity and Festival in Los Angeles, 1934–1990* (Berkeley: University of California Press, 2002), 65–67; and David K. Yoo, *Growing Up Nisei: Race, Generation, and Culture among Japanese Americans of California, 1924–1949* (Urbana: University of Illinois Press, 1999), 87–89.

64 Kurashige, *Celebration and Conflict*, 66.

65 Ibid., 66–68; Azuma, "Pacific Era," 60–62.

66 Kay Uchida, "Bridge Across the Pacific," *Japanese Student Bulletin*, March–April 1934, 5.

67 "The Nisei Angle in Far Eastern Situation," *Japanese Student Bulletin*, March–April 1937, 7.

68 Toru Matsumoto, "On America and Japan," *Japanese Student Bulletin*, March 1940, 2–3.

69 Matsumoto, "A Lost Cause?" *Japanese Student Bulletin*, May 1940, 2.

70 Ali-Li-Sung, "Challenge to Chinese Students," *Chinese Christian Student*, January 1941, 5.

71 "Good News from Oregon," *Japanese Student Bulletin*, March–April 1938, 6.

72 General Survey of the Fourth America-Japan Student Conference, August 1937, folder 174, box 30, Record Group 359, UCLA Chancellor Files, University of California at Los Angeles Special Collections.

73 Ed Chin Park, "United States Sustains Non-Recognition Doctrine," *Chinese Christian Student*, April 1940, 6.

74 Hanson Hwang, "Big Doings in Boston," *Chinese Christian Student*, January 1940, 5.

75 "How Pacific Coast Organizations Keep Busy," *Chinese Christian Student*, January 1940, 7.

76 Toru Matsumoto, "Revolution: By Choice," *Japanese Student Bulletin*, January 1941, 2.

77 Toru Matsumoto, "HR 1776," *Japanese Student Bulletin*, January 1941, 1–2.

Chapter 5   Christian Citizenship and Japanese American Incarceration during World War II

1   Throughout this work, I adhere to the 2010 "Power of Words" resolution passed by the Japanese American Citizens League. This resolution seeks to clarify misunderstandings that arise in studying EO 9066 as a result of murky terms—including "internment" and "evacuation"—used to describe the process and experience of removal. Internment is a specific action meant to detain enemy aliens while, as the Power of Words resolution outlines, evacuation refers to government assistance in relocating individuals who are in harm's way of a natural disaster or other threat. Although the US government justified EO 9066 by arguing that the measure was designed for the protection of both the Japanese and non-Japanese along the West Coast, historians have since reevaluated these terms and now identify them as part of government propaganda. Because such government terminology masks the devastating impact of EO 9066 on the Japanese American communities, I use the terms "forced migration" or "forced removal" in reference to the government-mandated evacuation of Japanese from their homes and "imprisoned" or "incarcerated" to indicate that Japanese were held in "prisons" (rather than "camps" or "relocation centers").

2   See John Dower, *War without Mercy: Race and Power in the Pacific* (New York: Pantheon Books, 1986); David K. Yoo, *Growing Up Nisei: Race, Generation, and Culture among Japanese Americans of California, 1924–49* (Urbana: University of Illinois Press, 1999); and Lon Kurashige, *Japanese American Celebration and Conflict: A History of Ethnic Identity and Festival Los Angeles, 1934–1990* (Berkeley: University of California Press, 2002).

3   Ronald Takaki, *Strangers from a Different Shore: A History of Asian Americans* (New York: Little, Brown, and Co., 1989), 379–383.

4   Ibid., 387.

5   See Greg Robinson, *A Tragedy of Democracy: Japanese Confinement in North America* (New York: Columbia University Press, 2009); Greg Robinson, *By Order of the President: FDR and the Internment of Japanese Americans* (Cambridge, MA: Harvard University Press, 2003); Matthew Briones, *Jim and Jap Crow: A Cultural History of 1940s Interracial America* (Princeton: Princeton University Press, 2012); and Cherstin Lyon, *Prisoners and Patriots: Japanese American Wartime Citizenship, Civil Disobedience, and Historical Memory* (Philadelphia: Temple University Press, 2011).

6   Scott Kurashige, *The Shifting Grounds of Race: Black and Japanese Americans in the Making of Multiethnic Los Angeles* (Princeton, NJ: Princeton University Press, 2007), 108–132.

7   See Roger Daniels, *Prisoners without Trial: Japanese Americans in WWII* (New York: Hill and Wang, 2004); Yoshiko Uchida, *Desert Exile: The Uprooting of a Japanese American Family* (Seattle: University of Washington Press, 1982); and John Howard, *Concentration Camps on the Home Front: Japanese Americans in the House of Jim Crow* (Chicago: University of Chicago Press, 2011).

8   "Japanese Students Club Discusses War Problems," *University of Washington Daily*, December 16, 1941, 7.

9   "Campus Japanese Face Evacuation," *University of Washington Daily*, March 4, 1942, 6.

10 Tom Shibutani, "We Hope to Come Back," *Daily Cal*, March 6, 1942, 12.

11 Lyon, *Prisoners and Patriots*, 12–20.

12 Kenji Okuda, "We Must Go," *University of Washington Daily*, April 10, 1942, 12.

13 Daiki Miyagawa, "Guest Editorial," *University of Washington Daily*, March 8, 1942, 7.

14 Oleg Kur, "Letter to the Editor," *University of Washington Daily*, March 3, 1942, 8.

15 Russell Braley, "Reply," *University of Washington Daily*, March 5, 1942, 10.

16 "U Students Urge Nisei Be Retained," *University of Washington Daily*, March 3, 1942, 9.

17 "Japanese Students Living in Berkeley," *Daily Cal*, March 7, 1942, 7.

18 Gordon Hirabayashi Defense Committee, "The Case of Gordon Hirabayashi—The Case of the American People," 1942, folder 3, National Japanese American Student Relocation Council Records (hereafter cited as NJASRC-WA), University of Washington Special Collections.

19 Ibid., 2.

20 History of YWCA from 1939–1941—Report of the Executive Secretary, March 1944, folder 1, YWCA (UW) Records, University of Washington Records. It is unclear exactly what the author of the report meant by "professionally" concerned, although the word appears to imply that the YWCA was devoted to reacting against incarceration from a religious/personal level as much as an organizational level (based on the mission of the YWCA).

21 Gordon Chapman, "The Church and Japanese Evacuation," *Intercollegian*, July 21, 1942, 5.

22 "Third Report on the Japanese Evacuation Situation—Prepared by the Committee on Student Relocation and Distributed by the Regional Office of the Student YMCA and YWCA, Los Angeles," April 15, 1942, folder 3, NJASRC-WA.

23 Edna W. Morris, "Memo on Problems Caused by Evacuation Orders Affecting Japanese and Problems of Organization of the AFSC Work on the Pacific Coast," July, 1942, folder 1, American Friends Service Committee Forms and Procedure (July 1942–October 1942), American Friends Service Committee Records (hereafter cited as AFSC-WA), University of Washington Special Collections.

24 Arthur Jorgensen to Galen Fisher, March 24, 1942, box 66, YMCA Armed Services Records, UW-YMCA University Branch Records.

25 Morris, "Memo on Problems," 10–11.

26 Edmonia Grant, "Fair Play for American Fellow Students of Japanese Descent" (New York: National Commission on Christian Social Reconstruction, 1942), 3.

27 Ibid., 4.

28 "American War Victims," *Intercollegian*, April 1942, 123.

29 Ibid.; Minutes of YMCA Regional Council Meeting (Barton, OR), October 16–18, 1942, Student Regional Council folder, Pacific Northwest, 1941, 1944, 1949, Student Work Records, Kautz Family YMCA Archives, University of Minnesota.

30 Minutes of YMCA Regional Council Meeting.

31 Charlotte Brooks, *Alien Neighbors, Foreign Friends: Asian Americans, Housing, and the Transformation of Urban America* (Chicago: University of Chicago Press, 2009), 4.

32 Minutes of YMCA Regional Council Meeting.

33 See Ellen Wu, *The Color of Success: Asian Americans and the Origins of the Model Minority* (Princeton, NJ: Princeton University Press, 2013), 12–17; and Charlotte

Brooks, "In the Twilight Zone between Black and White: Japanese American Resettlement and Community in Chicago, 1942–1945," *Journal of American History* 86, no. 4 (2000): 1655–1687.

34 Charles Iglehart, Foreign Missions Conference, New York, Committee on Asia–Japanese American Resettlement, May 16, 1943, folder 2:5, AFSC-WA.

35 Ibid.; Information Bulletin No. 8, December 5, 1943, folder 25:2, AFSC-WA.

36 Allan W. Austin, *From Concentration Camp to Campus: Japanese American Students and World War II* (Urbana: University of Illinois Press, 2005), 9–37.

37 Report of the Field Director, delivered at the Council Meeting, September 29, 1943, p. 4, folder 3, NJASRC-WA.

38 WRA Quarterly Report (July 1–Sept. 30, 1942), 2, folder 2–6, American Friends Service Committee Records (hereafter cited as AFSC-UC), Bancroft Library, University of California, Berkeley. The threat of revolt in the camps was a constant concern for the WRA as well as the military. Centers such as Tule Lake in California were primarily for those internees suspected of insurgency or disloyalty to the US.

39 In Robert O'Brien, "Selective Dispersion as a Factor in the Solution of the Nisei Problem Folder," *Social Forces*, 23, no. 2 (December 1944): 146–147.

40 Kenji Okuda to Mary Farquardson, folder 1, Mary Farquardson Papers, University of Washington Special Collections.

41 Sproul to Honorable John H. Tolan, Chairman, Selection Committee of Investigation National Defense Migration, April 7, 1942, folder 2–6, AFSC-UC.

42 University of Tennessee, Knoxville, to the Relocation Council (undated), box 691, Relocation Council Records (hereafter cited as RCR), Hoover Institution Archives, Stanford University; Susquehanna University to Relocation Council (undated), box 691, RCR; University of the South to Reverend George Wieland, August 4, 1942, box 270, RCR; Mary Jean Kennedy, Report from the University of San Francisco (undated), box 679, RCR. See also "Northwestern University Will Bar American Japs from Courses," *Chicago Sun*, April 30, 1942, 4.

43 James E. Edminston to Relocation Council, April 1945, San Jose State College Folder, folder 6, box 3, Pacific Coast Committee on American Principles and Fair Play Records, 1940–1951, BANC MSS C-A 171 (hereafter cited as PCC), Bancroft Library, University of California, Berkeley.

44 Robert Galbraith to Relocation Council, February 9, 1944, folder 3, box 6, PCC.

45 Gary Y. Okihiro, *Storied Lives: Japanese American Students and World War II* (Seattle: University of Washington Press, 1999), 100–101.

46 Ibid., 113–117.

47 Ibid., 100.

48 Wilmina Rowland, "Realism about Relocation—A New SCA," *Intercollegian*, March 1943, 6; "Little Asilomars," *Intercollegian*, January 1944, 136.

49 "Little Asilomars," 136.

50 Okihiro, *Storied Lives*, 90–92; Austin, *From Concentration Camp*, 115–126.

51 Sumiko Fujii to Relocation Council, March 3, 1945, folder 3, box 6, PCC.

52 Letter from Tamio Kitano to Relocation Council, April 5, 1943, folder 3, box 6, PCC.

53 Masaye Nagao from College Park, MO, to Relocation Council, March 24, 1943, folder 3, box 6, PCC.

54 Mary Ono to Relocation Council, May 17, 1943, folder 3, box 6, PCC.

55 Letter from Nagao.
56 Brooks, "In the Twilight Zone," 1660–1670. See also Leslie Bow, *Partly Colored: Asian Americans and Racial Anomaly in the Segregated South* (New York: NYU Press, 2010), for a more in-depth discussion of the encounters and interactions between Japanese and other Asian Americans in the South, both on and off campus.
57 "Hi-Y" was an informal name for the Cornell University branch of the YMCA.
58 Yutaka Kobayoshi from Alfred, NY, to the Relocation Council, April 11, 1943, folder 3, box 6, PCC.
59 Letter from Kobayoshi.
60 Grayce Kaneda to Relocation Council, February 8, 1944, folder 3, box 6, PCC.
61 Other acts liberalizing (to a degree) immigration and naturalization laws affected different Asian groups during and immediately after the war, including Indians and Filipinos in 1946 and Koreans and Japanese in 1952 as a result of the McCarran-Walter/Immigration and Nationality Act. See Cindy I-Fen Cheng, *Citizens of Asian America: Democracy and Race during the Cold War* (New York: NYU Press, 2013), 15–16, 176–177, 180. Donna R. Gabaccia's *Foreign Relations: American Immigration in Global Perspective* (Princeton, NJ: Princeton University Press, 2012) also provides a more in-depth overview of changes in immigration policy before and after World War II.
62 See K. Scott Wong, *Americans First: Chinese Americans and the Second World War* (Cambridge, MA: Harvard University Press, 2005).
63 Wu, *Color of Success*, 11–13.
64 Newsletter from August 18, 1943, Counselor Letters #5, folder 25, Betty Lee Sung Collection (hereafter cited as BLS), Asian American Pacific Islander Collection, Asian Division, Library of Congress, Washington, DC.
65 Daniels, *Prisoners without Trial*, 43–45. For a more in-depth discussion of the role of the WRA in both operating and closing the internment centers as well as assisting Japanese internees with resettlement, see Dillon S. Myer's *Uprooted Americans: The Japanese Americans and the War Relocation Authority during World War II* (Tucson: University of Arizona Press, 1971).
66 Nineteenth Annual Chinese Christian Youth Conference, Zephyr Point, Lake Tahoe, NV, July 22–29, 1945, p. 38, folder 25, BLS.
67 Ibid., 24, 26.
68 See Kurashige, *Shifting Grounds*, 158–185, and Mark Brilliant, *The Color of America Has Changed: How Racial Diversity Shaped Civil Rights in California, 1941–1978* (New York: Oxford University Press, 2010), 140–146.
69 Nineteenth Annual Chinese Christian Youth Conference, 38, 26.
70 "Filipinos Meet; Table Proposal to Exclude Coast Evacuees," *Pacific Citizen*, October 1944, 8.
71 Eiichiro Azuma, *Between Two Empires: Race, History, and Transnationalism in Japanese America* (New York: Oxford University Press, 2005), 187–195.
72 Aquileo Leander Dongallao, "'Pearl of Orient' Is Contemporary with U.S. in Defense of Democracy," *University of Washington Daily*, January 14, 1942, 1, 4.
73 Committee on the Resettlement of Japanese Americans, "The Concern of the Church for Christian and Democratic Treatment of Japanese Americans," April 1944, pp. 15, 15–16, folder 25, box 13, PCC.
74 Quoted in Wu, *Color of Success*, 158.
75 Daniels, *Prisoners without Trial*, 84–86.

76 Wu, *Color of Success;* Briones, *Jim and Jap Crow.* See also Gary Gerstle, *American Crucible: Race and Nation in the Twentieth Century* (Princeton, NJ: Princeton University Press, 2002).

77 Joint Conference on Future of Japanese Church Work Resettlement, Protestant Church Commission for Japanese Service, April 24–26, 1945, carton 3, folder 6, 1945, Japanese American Research Project collection, Charles E. Young Research Library, University of California, Los Angeles.

78 Daniels, *Prisoners without Trial,* 81–83.

79 Toru Matsumoto, "Comments on 'Japs Not Wanted Here,'" *Journal of Social Issues: Race and Prejudice in Everyday Living* (May 1945): 26.

80 Ibid.

81 See Robert G. Lee, *Orientals: Asian Americans in Popular Culture* (Philadelphia: Temple University Press, 1999); and Rosalind S. Chou and Joe R. Feagin, *The Myth of the Model Minority: Asian Americans Facing Racism* (New York: Paradigm Publishers, 2008), for a more in-depth discussion of the model minority myth.

82 Yori Wada, "Beyond the Horizon," *California Alumni Association California Monthly*, December 1943, 1.

Chapter 6   Christian Social Action in the Postwar Era

1 See Martha Biondi, *To Stand and Fight: The Struggle for Civil Rights in Postwar New York City* (Cambridge, MA: Harvard University Press, 2006); and Josh Sides, *L.A. City Limits: African American Los Angeles from the Great Depression to the Present* (Berkeley: University of California Press, 2004).

2 Mark Brilliant, *The Color of America Has Changed: How Racial Diversity Shaped Civil Rights in California, 1941–1978* (New York: Oxford University, 2010), 19–22.

3 Toru Matsumoto, *Beyond Prejudice: A Story of the Church and Japanese Americans* (New York: Friendship Press, 1946), xiii. I will discuss this work in more detail later in this chapter.

4 Ibid., xiii.

5 Ibid., 136–137.

6 Shana Bernstein, *Bridges of Reform: Interracial Civil Rights Activism in Twentieth-Century Los Angeles* (New York: Oxford University Press, 2011), 96–97, 99.

7 See Charles Marsh, *God's Long Summer: Stories of Faith and Civil Rights* (Princeton, NJ: Princeton University Press, 2008); Johnny E. Williams, *African American Religion and the Civil Rights Movement in Arkansas* (Jackson: University Press of Mississippi, 2008); Mary R. Sawyer, *Black Ecumenism: Implementing the Demands of Justice* (Valley Forge, PA: Trinity Press International, 1994); Wallace D. Best, *Passionately Human, No Less Divine: Religion and Culture in Black Chicago, 1915–1952* (Princeton, NJ: Princeton University Press, 2005); John T. McGreevy, *Parish Boundaries: The Catholic Encounter with Race in the Twentieth-Century Urban North* (Chicago: University of Chicago Press, 2006); and Charles M. Payne, *I've Got the Light of Freedom: The Organizing Tradition and the Mississippi Freedom Struggle* (Berkeley: University of California Press, 1995), for more information on religion and the African American civil rights movement.

8 Matthew Briones, *Jim and Jap Crow: A Cultural History of 1940s Interracial America* (Princeton, NJ: Princeton University Press, 2012), 12, 153, 186, 207, 235.

9 Ellen Wu, *The Color of Success: Asian Americans and the Origins of the Model Minority* (Princeton, NJ: Princeton University Press, 2013), 243–290.

10 Kevin Allen Leonard, *The Battle for Los Angeles: Racial Ideology and World War II* (Albuquerque: University of New Mexico Press, 2006), 148–199.

11 Greg Robinson, *After Camp: Portraits in Midcentury Japanese American Life and Politics* (Berkeley: University of California Press, 2012), 224–227.

12 "CA Intercollegiate Nisei Organization Disbands," *San Francisco County Examiner*, January 1959. See also Daryl Maeda, *Chains of Babylon: The Rise of Asian America* (Minneapolis: University of Minnesota Press, 2009), 49.

13 Maeda, *Chains*, 49–50.

14 "Nisei Organization Disbands"; Maeda, *Chains*, 50.

15 Maeda, *Chains*, 49–50.

16 "Nisei Organization Disbands."

17 "*Saturday Evening Post* Featuring Article by Hayakawa," 1955, box 445, Samuel Hayakawa Papers, Hoover Institution Archives, Stanford University.

18 Lon Kurashige, *Japanese American Celebration and Conflict: A History of Ethnic Identity and Festival in Los Angeles, 1934–1990* (Berkeley: University of California Press, 2002), 148–149.

19 Brilliant, *Color of America*, 41–48.

20 See Madeline Y. Hsu, "Befriending the Yellow Peril: Chinese Students and Intellectuals and the Liberalization of U.S. Immigration Laws, 1950–1965," *Journal of American East Asian Relations* 16, no. 3 (2009): 139–162; and Madeline Y. Hsu, "Domesticating the Yellow Peril: Students and Changing Perceptions of the Indigestibility of Chinese immigrants, 1905–1950," in *Transpacific Interactions: The United States and China, 1880–1950*, ed. Vanessa Kuennemann and Ruth Mayer (New York: Palgrave Macmillan, 2009), 105–122, for a more in-depth discussion of Chinese students in America and "cultural ambassadorship" through postwar programs such as the Fulbright educational exchange system.

21 Hsu, "Befriending the Yellow Peril," 139–141.

22 Timothy Tseng, "Religious Liberalism, International Politics, and Diasporic Realities: The Chinese Students' Christian Association of North America, 1909–1915," *Journal of American East-Asian Relations* 5, no. 3 (1996): 305–330.

23 *CSCA Western Conference Bulletin*, June 1948, 6.

24 Ibid.

25 Tom Moore, "National Intercollegiate Council Message," *Chinese Press*, August 1948, 7.

26 Ibid.

27 Nina Mjagkij, *Light in the Darkness: African Americans and the YMCA, 1852–1946* (Louisville: University of Kentucky Press, 2003), 115–118, 122–123.

28 Ronald Takaki, *Strangers from a Different Shore: A History of Asian Americans* (New York: Little, Brown, 1989), 415.

29 See J. B. Schmoker, "Committee on Friendly Relations among Foreign Students," box 4, CFRS Records. At the College Park branch of the National Archives, there are copies of the *Chinese Student Bulletin* from the late 1940s obtained by the FBI and investigated for potential evidence of communist infiltration. See also Record Group 59, General Records of the Department of State, Office of the Assistant Secretary of State for Public Affairs—Subject Files, 1949–1953, box 1, National Archives and Records Administration II, College Park, MD.

30 Atha Fong, "Chingwah Lee: San Francisco Chinatown's Renaissance Man," *Chinese America: History & Perspectives* (2011): 38.

31 Ibid.

32 "Notes taken at a meeting called by Galen Fisher on August 11 at 12:30pm at the Institute of Pacific Relations in San Francisco to discuss the Fall program of the Committee on American Principles and Fair Play–Comments section," folder 1:5—Committee Records–General Membership Minutes, 1942–1944, PCC.

33 "Release, AM Monday for January 8th, 1945," p. 1, folder 1:9—Committee Records, General Membership, "Conference on Interracial Relations," PCC.

34 Ibid.

35 See chapter 2 for a more in-depth description of Lee's earlier activities with the CSCA while a student at Berkeley.

36 "Release, AM Monday for January 8th," 1.

37 "Cooperation of Other Minorities with Evacuees," p. 1, folder 1:10—Committee Records–General Membership, PCC.

38 "Resolutions from Interracial Conference," p. 1, folder 1:10—Committee Records-General Membership, PCC.

39 Ibid.

40 Cindy I-Fen Cheng, *Citizens of Asian America: Democracy and Race during the Cold War* (New York: NYU Press, 2013), 117–147, 149–155.

41 Fong, "Chingwah Lee," 44–46.

42 Ibid., 44–47.

43 Daryl Joji Maeda, *Rethinking the Asian American Movement* (New York: Routledge, 2011), 86–92, 95.

44 See Huping Ling, *Chinese St. Louis: From Enclave to Cultural Community* (Philadelphia: Temple University Press, 2004); Mary Rose Wong, *Sweet Cakes, Long Journey: The Chinatowns of Portland* (Seattle: University of Washington Press, 2004); and Min Zhou, *Chinatown: The Socioeconomic Potential of an Urban Enclave* (Philadelphia: Temple University Press, 1992), for more information on the changing nature of Chinatowns in the United States.

45 Matsumoto, *Beyond Prejudice*, 12–15.

46 Ibid., xiii.

47 Ibid.

48 Ibid.

49 "Christian Youth Council Session Planned in N.Y.," *Afro-American*, October 1946, 14.

50 Robinson, *After Camp*, 258–263.

51 "Christian Youth Council," 14.

52 Matsumoto, *Beyond Prejudice*, 140–141.

53 Ibid., 141; Mary Sawyer, *Black Ecumenism: Implementing the Demands of Justice* (New York: Trinity Press International, 1994), 42–43.

54 "History of the Christian Friends for Racial Equality–1950," 3, folder 3—Speeches and Writings of Others, 1935–1946, box 3, Velasco Papers.

55 Johanna McClees [Phillips], "Christian Friends for Racial Equality: A Unique Approach to Race and Religious Relations in Seattle 1942–1970" (BA thesis, University of Washington, 2000), University of Washington Special Collections, 15.

56 "History of the Christian Friends," 5.

57 McClees, "Christian Friends," 15.

58   "History of the Christian Friends," 5; see also Quintard Taylor, *The Forging of a Black Community: Seattle's Central District from 1870 through the Civil Rights Era* (Seattle: University of Washington Press, 1994).

59   Bernstein, *Bridges of Reform*, 103–107.

60   Ibid., 7.

61   McClees, "Christian Friends," 16–23; "History of the Christian Friends," 10–11, 11, 6–7.

62   Randi J. Walker, *Religion and the Public Conscience* (London: John Hunt Publishing, 2012), 164–168.

63   Victorio Velasco, "No Rest for the Weary," *Daily*, November 1950, 6.

64   Ibid.

65   "We Are Indebted," *Racial Equality Bulletin*, May 1952, 3. The *Racial Equality Bulletin* was the monthly publication of the CFRE.

66   McClees, "Christian Friends," 13.

67   Walker, *Religion and the Public Conscience*, 143–146.

68   "History of the Christian Friends," 14.

69   "Excerpts from the Report of the Citizens' Advisory Committee on Minority Housing, Seattle, 12/1962," folder 7—Reports, 1955–1963, box 7, Velasco Papers; Kurashige, *Shifting Grounds*, 178–181.

70   "Excerpts from the Report."

71   Ibid.

72   "History of the Christian Friends," 23.

73   Ibid., 24.

74   McClees, "Christian Friends," 38.

75   See Wu, *Color of Success*; Brooks, *Alien Neighbors*; Cheng, *Citizens of Asian America*; and David M. P. Freund, *Colored Property: State Police and White Racial Politics in Suburban America* (Chicago: University of Chicago Press, 2010).

76   McClees, "Christian Friends," 32–37. See also David Farber, *The Age of Great Dreams: America in the 1960s* (New York: Hill and Wang, 1994); Robert Cohen, *Freedom's Orator: Mario Savio and the Radical Legacy of the 1960s* (New York: Oxford University Press, 2009); Robert Cohen, *The Free Speech Movement: Reflections on Berkeley in the 1960s* (Berkeley: University of California Press, 2002); Joshua Bloom, *Blacks against Empire: The History and Politics of the Black Panther Party* (Berkeley: University of California Press, 2013); and Sonia Song-Ha Lee, *Building a Latino Civil Rights Movement: Puerto Ricans, African Americans, and the Pursuit of Racial Justice in New York* (Chapel Hill: University of North Carolina Press, 2014).

77   Amy Uyematsu, "The Emergence of Yellow Power in America," *Gidra* (October 1969), reprinted in *Roots: An Asian American Reader*, ed. Amy Tachiki (Berkeley: University of California Press, 1971).

78   See Grace Lee Boggs and Scott Kurashige, *The Next American Revolution: Sustainable Activism for the Twenty-First Century* (Berkeley: University of California Press, 2012); Diane C. Fujino, *Heartbeat of Struggle: The Revolutionary Life of Yuri Kochiyama* (Minneapolis: University of Minnesota Press, 2005); Steven G. Louie and Glenn K. Omatsu, *Asian Americans: The Movement and the Moment* (Los Angeles: UCLA Asian American Studies Center Press, 2002); and Laura Pulido, *Black, Brown, Yellow, and Left: Radical Activism in Los Angeles* (Berkeley: University of California Press, 2006).

79 Cohen, *Free Speech Movement*, 62, 537–547.
80 "History of the Christian Friends," 24; McClees, "Christian Friends," 38.
81 Victorio Velasco, "From the Anti-Discrimination Committee," *Racial Equality Bulletin*, April 25, 1966, 3; McClees, "Christian Friends," 38.

Conclusion

1 Yen Le Espiritu, *Asian American Panethnicity: Bridging Institutions and Identities* (Philadelphia: Temple University Press, 1992), 25, 20–21, 25.

Selected Bibliography

Manuscript and Archival Collections

American Friends Service Committee Records. Special Collections Department. University of Washington.

Asian-American Pacific Islander Collection. Library of Congress, Washington, DC.

Board of Regents Reports and Minutes. Washington State University Archives, Pullman.

Cannery Workers' and Farm Laborers' Union Records. Special Collections Department. University of Washington.

Chinese Students' Christian Association Records (Record Group 16). Yale University Divinity School Library Special Collections, Yale University.

Committee for Friendly Relations among Foreign Students History Records. Kautz Family YMCA Archives. University of Minnesota.

Filipino Labor Papers. Filipino American National Historical Society Archives, Seattle.

Japanese American Research Project Collection, Charles E. Young Research Library. University of California, Los Angeles.

National Japanese American Student Relocation Council Letters. Bancroft Library. University of California, Berkeley.

National Japanese American Student Relocation Council Records. Special Collections Department. University of Washington

Publications and Ephemera Collection. Stanford University Archives.

Records of the U.S. Cultural Program with China: 1917–1976 (Record Group 59). National Archives and Records Administration, College Park, MD.

Relocation Council Records. Hoover Institution Archives. Stanford University.

Student Organization Record Books. San Jose State University Archives.

Survey of Race Relations, Hoover Institution Archives. Stanford University.

UCLA Chancellor Files. Charles E. Young Research Library. University of California, Los Angeles.

UW-YMCA University Branch Records. University Archives. University of Washington.

Victorio Velasco Papers. Special Collections Department. University of Washington.

Yuk Ow Research Files. Ethnic Studies Library. University of California, Berkeley.

Published Sources

Akagi, Roy Hidemichi. *The Second Generation Problem—Some Suggestions towards Its Solu-tion.* New York: Japanese Students Christian Association in America, 1926.

Alba, Richard, Albert J. Raboteau, and Josh DeWind. *Immigration and Religion in America: Comparative and Historical Perspectives.* New York: NYU Press, 2008.

Alidio, Kimberly. "Between Civilizing Mission and Ethnic Assimilation: Racial Discourse, U.S. Colonial Education, and Filipino Ethnicity, 1901–1946." PhD diss., University of Michigan, 2001.

Allen, Austin. *From Concentration Camp to Campus: Japanese American Students and WWII.* Urbana: University of Illinois Press, 2007.

Altschul, Craig. *Pearls: The Fred Hoshiyama Story.* New York: Marshall Jones, 2010.

Ancheta, Angelo. *Race, Rights, and the Asian American Experience.* New Brunswick, NJ: Rutgers University Press, 2006.

Anderson, Benedict. *Imagined Communities: Reflections on the Origin and Spread of Nation-alism,* rev. ed. New York: Verso, 2006.

Asian Community Center Archive Group. *Stand Up: An Archive Collection of the Bay Area Asian American Movement, 1968–1974.* Berkeley, CA: Eastwind Books of Berkeley, 2009.

Austin, Allan W. *From Concentration Camp to Campus: Japanese American Students and World War II.* Urbana: University of Illinois Press, 2005.

Azuma, Eiichiro. *Between Two Empires: Race, History, and Transnationalism in Japanese America.* New York: Oxford University Press, 2005.

———. "The Pacific Era Has Arrived: Transnational Education among Japanese Americans, 1932–1941." *History of Education Quarterly* 43, no. 1 (Spring 2003): 39–73.

———. "Racial Struggle, Immigrant Nationalism, and Ethnic Identity: Japanese and Filipinos in the California Delta." *Pacific Historical Review* 67, no. 2 (May 1998): 163–199.

Bacho, E. V. "Vic." *The Long Road: Memoirs of a Filipino Pioneer.* Self-published, 1992.

Baldoz, Rick. *The Third Asiatic Invasion: Empire and Migration in Filipino America, 1898–1946.* New York: NYU Press, 2011.

Bayless, Pamela. *The YMCA at 150: A History of the YMCA of Greater New York, 1852–2002.* New York: Fordham University Press, 2002.

Bayly, C. A. *Forgotten Wars: Freedom and Revolution in South East Asia.* Cambridge, MA: Belknap Press of Harvard University Press, 2007.

Bennett, David H. *The Party of Fear: The American Far Right from Nativism to the Militia Movement.* New York: Vintage Books, 1995.

Bernstein, Shana. *Bridges of Reform: Interracial Civil Rights Activism in Twentieth-Century Los Angeles.* New York: Oxford University Press, 2011.

Best, Wallace. *Passionately Human, No Less Divine: Religion and Culture in Black Chicago, 1915–1952.* Princeton: Princeton University Press, 2005.

Biney, Moses O. *From Africa to America: Religion and Adaptation among Ghanaian Immi-grants in New York.* New York: NYU Press, 2011.

Borstelmann, Thomas. *The Cold War and the Color Line: American Race Relations in the Global Arena.* Cambridge, MA: Harvard University Press, 2003.

Bow, Leslie. *Partly Colored: Asian Americans and Racial Anomaly in the Segregated South.* New York: NYU Press, 2010.

Brilliant, Mark. *The Color of America Has Changed: How Racial Diversity Shaped Civil Rights in California, 1941–1978.* New York: Oxford University Press, 2010.

Briones, Matthew. *Jim and Jap Crow: A Cultural History of 1940s Interracial America*. Princeton, NJ: Princeton University Press, 2012.

Brooks, Charlotte. *Alien Neighbors, Foreign Friends: Asian Americans, Housing, and the Transformation of Urban America*. Chicago: University of Chicago Press, 2009.

Brown, Michael S. *Victorio Acosta Velasco: An American Life*. Lanham, MD: University Press of America, 2007.

Bu, Liping. *Making the World Like Us: Education, Cultural Expansion, and the American Century*. Westport, CT: Praeger Press, 2003.

Carson, Clayborn. *In Struggle: SNCC and the Black Awakening of the 1960s*. Cambridge, MA: Harvard University Press, 2005.

Chaing, Yung Chang. "Chinese Students Educated in the United States and the Emergence of Chinese Orientalism in the Early Twentieth Century." *Taiwan Journal of East Asian Studies* 1, no. 2 (December 2004): 37–76.

———. "Chinese Students in America in the Early Twentieth Century: Preliminary Reflections on a Research Topic." *Chinese Studies in History* 36, no. 3 (2003): 38–62.

Chang, Derek. *Citizens of a Christian Nation: Evangelical Missions and the Problem of Race in the Nineteenth Century*. Philadelphia: University of Pennsylvania Press, 2010.

Cheng, Cindy I-Fen. *Citizens of Asian America: Democracy and Race during the Cold War*. New York: NYU Press, 2013.

Chou, Rosalind S., and Joe R. Feagin. *The Myth of the Model Minority: Asian Americans Facing Racism*. New York: Paradigm Publishers, 2008.

Choy, Catherine Ceniza. *Empire of Care: Nursing and Migration in Filipino American History*. Durham, NC: Duke University Press, 2003.

Conte, James. "Overseas Study in the Meiji Period: Japanese Students in America, 1867–1902." PhD diss., Princeton University, 1977.

Coogan, Anthony. *Northeast China and the Origins of Anti-Japanese United Front*. New York: Sage Publications, 1994.

Daniels, Roger. *Prisoners without Trial: Japanese Americans in WWII*. New York: Hill and Wang, 2004.

Davidann, Jon Thares. *A World of Crisis and Progress*. Bethlehem, PA: Lehigh University Press, 1998.

Dower, John. *War without Mercy: Race and Power in the Pacific*. New York: Pantheon Books, 1986.

Dudziak, Mary. *Cold War Civil Rights: Race and the Image of American Democracy*. Princeton, NJ: Princeton University Press, 2002.

Elfenbein, Jessica. *The Making of a Modern City: Philanthropy, Civic Culture, and the Baltimore YMCA*. Gainesville: University Press of Florida, 2001.

Espiritu, Yen Le. *Asian American Panethnicity: Bridging Institutions and Identities*. Philadelphia: Temple University Press, 1992.

Flores, Juan, and Miriam Jimenez Roman. "Triple Consciousness? Approaches to Afro-Latino Culture in the United States." *Latin American and Caribbean Ethnic Studies* 4, no. 3 (2009): 319–328.

Fong, Atha. "Chingwah Lee: San Francisco Chinatown's Renaissance Man." *Chinese America: History & Perspectives* (2011): 37–48.

Fowler, Josephine. *Japanese and Chinese Immigrant Activists: Organizing in American and International Communist Movements, 1919–1933*. New Brunswick, NJ: Rutgers University Press, 2007.

Friday, Chris. *Organizing Asian American Labor: The Pacific Coast Canned-Salmon Industry, 1870–1942.* Philadelphia: Temple University Press, 1994.

Fujita-Rony, Dorothy. *American Workers, Colonial Power: Philippine Seattle and the Transpacific West, 1919–1941.* Berkeley: University of California Press, 2002.

Gerstle, Gary. *American Crucible: Race and Nation in the Twentieth Century.* Princeton, NJ: Princeton University Press, 2002.

Gilmore, Glenda. *Defying Dixie: The Radical Roots of Civil Rights, 1919–1950.* New York: W. W. Norton, 2009.

———. *Gender and Jim Crow: Women and the Politics of White Supremacy in North Carolina, 1896–1920.* Chapel Hill: University of North Carolina Press, 1996.

Gilroy, Paul. *The Black Atlantic: Modernity and Double Consciousness.* Cambridge, MA: Harvard University Press, 1993.

Goldman, Jennifer. "Color and Conscience: Student Internationalism in the United States and the Challenges of Race and Nationality, 1896–1965." PhD diss., University of California, Berkeley, 2009.

Grant, Edmonia. *American Minority People during World War II.* New York: American Missionary Association, 1945.

Greene, Julie. *The Canal Builders: Making America's Empire at the Panama Canal.* New York: Penguin Press, 2009.

Griffith, Sarah. "Conflicting Dialogues: The Survey of Race Relations and the Fight for Asian American Racial Equality." PhD diss., University of California, Santa Barbara, 2011.

Guest, Kenneth J. *God in Chinatown: Religion and Survival in New York's Evolving Immigrant Community.* New York: NYU Press, 2003.

Guyotte, Roland, and Barbara Posadas. "Unintentional Immigrants: Chicago's Filipino Foreign Students Become Settlers, 1900–1941." *Journal of American Ethnic History* 9, no. 2 (1990): 26–48.

Hall, Jacquelyn Dowd. "The Long Civil Rights Movement and the Political Uses of the Past." *Journal of American History* 91, no. 4 (March 2005): 1233–1263.

Han, Yelong. "An Untold Story: American Policy towards Chinese Students in the United States, 1949–1955." *Journal of American–East Asian Relations* 2, no. 1 (1993): 77–99.

Hargrave, Thomas, Jr. *Private Differences—General Good: A History of the YMCA of Metropolitan Washington.* Washington, DC: YMCA of Metropolitan Washington, 1985.

Higginbotham, Evelyn Brooks. *Righteous Discontent: The Women's Movement in the Black Baptist Church, 1880–1920.* Cambridge, MA: Harvard University Press, 1994.

Higham, John. *Strangers in the Land: Patterns of American Nativism, 1860–1925.* New Brunswick, NJ: Rutgers University Press, 2002.

Hofstadter, Richard. *The Paranoid Style in American Politics.* New York: Vintage, 2008.

Hoganson, Kristin. *Consumer's Imperium: The Global Production of American Domesticity.* Chapel Hill: University of North Carolina Press, 2007.

Hopkins, C. Howard. *History of the YMCA in North America.* New York: Association Press, 1951.

———. *John R. Mott, 1865–1955: A Biography.* New York: Eerdmans Publishing, 1980.

Howard, John. *Concentration Camps on the Home Front: Japanese Americans in the House of Jim Crow.* Chicago: University of Chicago Press, 2008.

Hsu, Madeline Y. "Befriending the Yellow Peril: Chinese Students and Intellectuals and the Liberalization of U.S. Immigration Laws, 1950–1965." *Journal of American–East Asian Relations* 16, no. 3 (November 2009): 139–162.

————. *Dreaming of Gold, Dreaming of Home: Transnationalism and Migration between the United States and South China, 1882–1943*. Stanford, CA: Stanford University Press, 2000.

Institute of International Education. *Guidebook for Foreign Students in the United States*. New York: Institute of International Education, 1921.

Ion, Hamish. *American Missionaries, Christian Oyatoi, and Japan, 1859–1873*. Vancouver, BC: University of British Columbia Press, 2002.

Iriye, Akira. *Cultural Internationalism and World Order*. Baltimore: Johns Hopkins University Press, 2000.

Japanese Students' Christian Association. *Japanese Students' Christian Association Directory in North America and Hawaii, 1925–1926*. New York: Japanese Students' Christian Association in North America, 1927.

Joseph, Gilbert, Catherine Legrand, and Ricardo Salvatore, eds. *Close Encounters of Empire: Writing the Cultural History of U.S.–Latin American Relations*. Durham, NC: Duke University Press, 1998.

Jun, Helen Heran. *Race for Citizenship: Black Orientalism and Asian Uplift from Pre-Emancipation to Neoliberal America*. New York: NYU Press, 2011.

Kawai, Kazuo. *Japan's American Interlude*. Chicago: University of Chicago Press, 1979.

Klure, Laura. *Let's Be Doers: A History of the YMCA of Riverside, California, 1906–1992*. Riverside, CA: YMCA Publications, 1992.

Korstad, Robert Rodgers. *Civil Rights Unionism: Tobacco Workers and the Struggle for Democracy in the Mid-Twentieth-Century South*. Chapel Hill: University of North Carolina Press, 2003.

Kramer, Paul. *The Blood of Government: Race, Empire, the United States, and the Philippines*. Chapel Hill: University of North Carolina Press, 2006.

————. "International Students and US Global Power in the Long Twentieth Century." *Diplomatic History* 33, no. 5 (2009): 775–806.

Kurashige, Lon. *Japanese American Celebration and Conflict: A History of Ethnic Identity and Festival in Los Angeles, 1934–1990*. Berkeley: University of California Press, 2002.

Kurashige, Scott. *The Shifting Grounds of Race: Black and Japanese Americans in the Making of Multiethnic Los Angeles*. Princeton, NJ: Princeton University Press, 2007.

Kwan, Florence Chinn. "Some Rambling Thoughts on Why I Am a Christian." In *Unbound Feet: A Documentary History of Chinese Women in San Francisco*, edited by Judy Yung, 289–296. Berkeley: University of California Press, 1999.

Lawcock, Lawrence. "Filipino Students in the United States and the Filipino Independence Movement, 1900–1935." PhD diss., University of California, Berkeley, 1975

Lawsin, Emily. "Pensionados, Paisonos, and Pinoys: An Analysis of the Filipino Student Bulletin, 1922–1939." *Filipino American National Historical Society Journal* 4 (1996): 33–50.

Lee, Erika. *At America's Gates: Chinese Immigration during the Exclusion Era, 1882–1943*. Chapel Hill: University of North Carolina Press, 2003.

Lee, Robert G. *Orientals: Asian Americans in Popular Culture*. Philadelphia: Temple University Press, 1999.

Lee, Shelley Sang-Hee. *Claiming the Oriental Gateway: Prewar Seattle and Japanese America*. Philadelphia: Temple University Press, 2012.

Leonard, Kevin Allen. *The Battle for Los Angeles: Racial Ideology and World War II*. Albuquerque: University of New Mexico Press, 2006.

Ling, Huping. "A History of Chinese Female Students in the United States, 1880s–1990s." *Journal of American Ethnic History* 16, no. 3 (1997): 81–109.

Liu, Haiming. "The Identity Formation of American-Born Chinese in the 1930s: A Review of Lei Jieqiong's (Kit King Louis) Master's Thesis." *Journal of Chinese Overseas* 3, no. 1 (May 2007): 97–121.

Lowe, Lisa. *Immigrant Acts: On Asian American Cultural Politics.* Durham, NC: Duke University Press, 1996.

Luker, Ralph E. *The Social Gospel in Black and White.* Chapel Hill: University of North Carolina Press, 1991.

Lyman, Stanford M. "Civilization, Culture, and Color: Changing Foundations of Robert E. Park's Sociology of Race Relations." *International Journal of Politics, Culture, and Society* 3 (1991): 285–300.

Lyon, Cherstin. *Prisoners and Patriots: Japanese American Wartime Citizenship, Civil Disobedience, and Historical Memory.* Philadelphia: Temple University Press, 2011.

Maeda, Daryl. *Chains of Babylon: The Rise of Asian America.* Minneapolis: University of Minnesota Press, 2009.

——. *Rethinking the Asian American Movement.* New York: Routledge, 2011.

Mar, Lisa. *Brokering Belonging: Chinese in Canada's Exclusion Era, 1885–1945.* New York: Oxford University Press, 2010.

Masson, Jack K., and Donald L. Guimary. "Pilipinos and Unionization of the Alaskan Canned Salmon Industry." *Amerasia* 8, no. 2 (1981): 1–30.

Matsumoto, Toru. *Beyond Prejudice: A Story of the Church and Japanese Americans.* New York: Friendship Press, 1946.

——. *A Brother Is a Stranger.* New York: John Day, 1946.

Matsusaka, Yoshihisa Tak. *The Making of Japanese Manchuria, 1904–1932.* Cambridge, MA: Harvard University Press/Harvard University Asian Center, 2003.

McClees, Johana. "Christian Friends for Racial Equality: A Unique Approach to Religious and Race Relations in Seattle, 1942–1970." BA thesis, University of Washington, 1999.

Mears, George. *Residential Orientals on America's Pacific Coast.* New York: Harcourt, Brace, 1928.

Mjagkij, Nina. *Light in the Darkness: African Americans and the YMCA, 1852–1946.* Louisville: University of Kentucky Press, 1994.

——. *Men and Women Adrift: The YMCA and the YWCA in the City.* New York: NYU Press, 1997.

Molina, Natalia. *Fit to Be Citizens? Public Health and Race in Los Angeles, 1879–1939.* Berkeley: University of California Press, 2006.

Montgomery, James H., and Donald A. McGavaran. *The Disciplining of a Nation.* Manila: Global Church Growth Bulletin, 1980.

Mullen, Bill. *Afro Orientalism.* Minneapolis: University of Minnesota Press, 2004.

Myer, Dillon S. *Uprooted Americans: The Japanese Americans and the War Relocation Authority during World War II.* Tucson: University of Arizona Press, 1971.

Neptune, Harvey. *Caliban and the Yankees: Trinidad and the United States Occupation.* Chapel Hill: University of North Carolina Press, 2007.

Ngai, Mae. *Impossible Subjects: Illegal Aliens and the Making of Modern America.* Princeton, NJ: Princeton University Press, 2005.

Ninkovich, Frank. *The Diplomacy of Ideas: U.S. Foreign Policy and Cultural Relations, 1938–1950.* New York: Cambridge University Press, 1981.

Nomura, Gail. "Within the Law: The Establishment of Filipino Leasing Rights on the Yakima Indian Reservation." *Amerasia* 13, no. 1 (1986–1987): 99–117.

Okihiro, Gary Y. *Storied Lives: Japanese Students and WWII*. Seattle: University of Washington Press, 1999.

Paddison, Joshua. *Heathens in America: Religions, Race, and Reconstruction in California*. Berkeley: Huntington Library and University of California Press, 2012.

Park, Albert L., and David Y. Koo, eds. *Encountering Modernity: Christianity in East Asia and Asian America*. Honolulu: University of Hawaii Press, 2014.

Park, Robert E. *The City: Suggestions for the Study of Human Nature in the Urban Environment*. Chicago: University of Chicago Press, 1984.

———. "Human Migration and the Marginal Man." *American Journal of Sociology* 36, no. 6 (May 1928): 881–893.

———. "Our Racial Frontier on the Pacific." *Survey Graphic* 56 (May 1926): 56–72.

———. *Race and Culture*. New York: Free Press, 1964.

Pascoe, Peggy. *What Comes Naturally: Miscegenation Law and the Making of Race in America*. New York: Oxford University Press, 2010.

Peattie, Mark, Edward Drea, and Hans van de Ven, eds. *The Battle for China: Essays on the Military History of the Sino-Japanese War of 1937–1945*. Stanford, CA: Stanford University Press, 2011.

Peck, Gunther. *Reinventing Free Labor: Padrones and Immigrant Workers in the American West, 1880–1930*. New York: Cambridge University Press, 2000.

Pfaelzer, Jean. *Driven Out: The Forgotten War against Chinese Americans*. Berkeley: University of California Press, 2007.

Priest, Robert J., and Alvaro L. Nieves. *This Side of Heaven: Race, Ethnicity, and Christian Faith*. New York: Oxford University Press, 2006.

Pulido, Laura. *Black, Brown, Yellow, and Left: Radical Activism in Los Angeles*. Berkeley: University of California Press, 2006.

Radke, August C. *The Pacific American Fisheries, Inc.: History of a Washington State Salmon Packing Company, 1800–1966*. Jefferson, NC: McFarland, 2002.

Renada, Mary A. *Taking Haiti: Military Occupation and the Culture of U.S. Imperialism*. Chapel Hill: University of North Carolina Press, 2000.

Rhoads, Edward. "In the Shadow of Yung Wing: Zeng Laishum and the Chinese Education Mission to the United States." *Pacific Historical Review* 74, no. 1 (2005): 19–38.

Robinson, Greg. *After Camp: Portraits in Midcentury Japanese American Life and Politics*. Berkeley: University of California Press, 2012.

———. *By Order of the President: FDR and the Internment of Japanese Americans*. Cambridge, MA: Harvard University Press, 2003.

———. *A Tragedy of Democracy: Japanese Confinement in North America*. New York: Columbia University Press, 2009.

Rodriguez, Jeanette. *Our Lady of Guadalupe: Faith and Empowerment among Mexican-American Women*. Austin: University of Texas Press, 1994.

Rossinow, Doug. *The Politics of Authenticity: Liberalism, Christianity, and the New Left in America*. New York: Columbia University Press, 1998.

Ruiz, Vicki. *Cannery Women, Cannery Lives: Mexican Women, Unionization, and the California Food Processing Industry, 1930–1950*. Albuquerque: University of New Mexico Press, 1987.

San Miguel, Guadalupe. *Brown, Not White: School Integration and the Chicano Movement in Houston*. College Station: Texas A&M University Press, 2005.

Sawyer, Mary. *Black Ecumenism: Implementing the Demands of Justice*. New York: Trinity Press International, 1994.

Scheiner, Irwin. *Christian Converts and Social Protest in Meiji Japan*. Berkeley: University of California Press, 1970.

Schlimgen, Veta. "Neither Citizens nor Aliens: Filipino 'American Nationals' in the U.S. Empire, 190–1946." PhD diss., University of Oregon, 2010.

Schwartz, Eugene G. *American Students Organize: Founding the National Student Association after World War II*. New York: Praeger Press, 2006.

Selby, Gary. *Martin Luther King and the Rhetoric of Freedom: The Exodus Narrative in America's Struggle for Civil Rights*. Waco, TX: Baylor University Press, 2008.

Setran, David. *The Student Y: Student Religion in the Era of Secularization*. New York: Palgrave Macmillan, 2007.

Shah, Nayan. *Contagious Divides: Epidemics and Race in San Francisco's Chinatown*. Berkeley: University of California Press, 2001.

———. *Stranger Intimacy: Contesting Race, Sexuality, and the Law in the North American West*. Berkeley: University of California Press, 2012.

Slate, Nico. *Colored Cosmopolitanism: The Shared Struggle for Freedom in the United States and India*. Cambridge, MA: Harvard University Press, 2012.

Smith, William. *The Second Generation Oriental in America*. Honolulu: Institute of Pacific Relations, 1927.

Stonequist, Everett V. *The Marginal Man: A Study in Personality and Culture Conflict*. New York: Russell and Russell, 1961.

Strong, Edward K. *The Second-Generation Japanese Problem*. Stanford, CA: Stanford University Press, 1934.

Takaki, Ronald. *Strangers from a Different Shore: A History of Asian Americans*. New York: Little, Brown, 1989.

Taylor, Quintard. *The Forging of a Black Community: Seattle's Central District from 1870 through the Civil Rights Era*. Seattle: University of Washington Press, 1994.

———. *In Search of the Racial Frontier: African Americans in the West, 1528–1990*. New York: W. W. Norton 1999.

Teodoro, Noel. "Pensionados and Workers: The Filipinos in the United States, 1903–1956." *Asian and Pacific Migration Journal* 8, no. 1 (1999): 157–178.

Thompson, Larry Clinton. *William Scott Ament and the Boxer Rebellion: Heroism, Hubris, and the Ideal Missionary*. Jefferson, NC: McFarland Publishing, 2009.

Tseng, Timothy. "Religious Liberalism, International Politics, and Diasporic Realities: The Chinese Students' Christian Association of North America, 1909–1951." *Journal of American East–Asian Relations* 5, no. 3 (1996): 305–330.

Uchida, Yoshiko. *Desert Exile: The Uprooting of a Japanese American Family*. Seattle: University of Washington Press, 1982.

Ueda, Reed. "The Changing Path to Citizenship: Ethnicity and Naturalization during World War II." In *The War in American Culture: Society and Consciousness during World War II*, edited by Lewis A. Erenberg and Susan E. Hirsch. Chicago: University of Chicago Press, 1996.

Vargas, Zaragosa. *Labor Rights Are Civil Rights: Mexican American Workers in Twentieth-Century America*. Princeton, NJ: Princeton University Press, 2005.

Varzally, Allison. *Making a Non-White America: Californians Coloring Outside Ethnic Lines, 1925–1955*. Berkeley: University of California Press, 2008.

Walker, Randi J. *Religion and the Public Conscience*. London: John Hunt Publishing, 2012.

Walton, Whitney. "Internationalism and the Junior Year Abroad: American Students in France in the 1920s and 1930s." *Diplomatic History* 29, no. 2 (2005): 255–278.

Wang, Chih-ming. *Transpacific Articulations: Student Migration and the Remaking of Asian America.* Honolulu: University of Hawaii Press, 2013.

Weber, Devra. *Dark Sweat, White Gold: California Farm Workers, Cotton, and the New Deal.* Berkeley: University of California Press, 1994.

Wei, William. *The Asian American Movement.* Philadelphia: Temple University Press, 1993.

Williams, Johnny E. *African American Religion and the Civil Rights Movement in Arkansas.* Jackson: University of Mississippi Press, 2008.

Wilson, Richard. *When Tigers Fight: The Story of the Sino-Japanese War, 1937–1945.* New York: Viking Press, 1982.

Winter, Thomas. *Making Men, Making Class: The YMCA and Workingmen, 1877–1920.* Chicago: University of Chicago Press, 2002.

Wong, K. Scott. *Americans First: Chinese Americans and the Second World War.* Cambridge, MA: Harvard University Press, 2005.

Wu, Ellen. *The Color of Success: Asian Americans and the Origins of the Model Minority.* Princeton, NJ: Princeton University Press, 2013.

Xing, Jun. *Baptized in the Fire of Revolution.* Bethlehem, PA: Lehigh University Press, 1996.

Yano, Fleur, and Saralyn Daly, eds. *Unbound Spirit: Letters of Flora Belle Jan.* Urbana: University of Illinois Press, 2009.

Ye, Weili. *Seeking Modernity in China's Name: Chinese Students in the United States, 1900–1927.* Stanford, CA: Stanford University Press, 2001.

Yoo, David K. *Contentious Spirits: Religion in Korean American History, 1903–1945.* Stanford, CA: Stanford University Press, 2010.

———. *Growing Up Nisei: Race, Generation, and Culture among Japanese Americans of California, 1924–49.* Urbana: University of Illinois Press, 1999.

Yu, Henry. *Thinking Orientals: Migration, Contact, and Exoticism in Modern America.* New York: Oxford University Press, 2002.

Yung, Judy, Gordon Chang, and Mark Him Lai. *Chinese American Voices: From the Gold Rush to the Present.* Berkeley: University of California Press, 2006.

Zia, Helen. *Asian American Dreams: The Emergence of an American People.* New York: Farrar, Straus, and Giroux, 2001.

Zolberg, Aristide. *A Nation by Design: Immigration Policy in the Fashioning of America.* Cambridge, MA: Harvard University Press, 2008.

Index

Abella, Sebastian, 72, 93, 94

activism: Asian American, 4; black, 175; Christian-based, 2, 3, 8, 9, 12; civil rights, 143; community, 162–173; concerning Executive Order 9066 (incarceration of Japanese Americans), 148–153; defining, 122; divergent paths to, 162–173; early, 13; emergence from World War II, 173; emergence in Filipino Students' Christian Movement (FSCM), 84–97; among foreign and American-born members of Christian associations, 47, 48; interracial, 4; intraethnic, 2; labor, 72, 112; legal, 175, 178, 204; limits to, 13; panethnic, 13; political, 12, 68, 69; in postwar era, 175–211; radical, 13, 207; social, 11; student, 178, 217*n17*; union, 92; use of education and fellowship in, 190

Adler, Curtiss, 146, 147

African Americans: Colored Works Division (YMCA) and, 31; importance of achieving "respectability" to argue for equality, 217*n20*; migration to West Coast for wartime employment, 140, 175; "talented tenth," 37; tensions with Nisei, 160; use of nonviolent protest, 176

Agricultural Laborers' Association, 81

Akagi, Roy, 48, 49, 52, 53, 54, 115

Alfred University (New York), 161

Alien Land Law (Washington), 97, 98

Al-Li-Sing, 135

Almonte, A., 84

Alonzo, Frank, 90

Ambrosio, Dominador, 72, 83, 128

America-Japan Student Conference (Stanford University, 1937), 136

American Civil Liberties Union (ACLU): membership representative of various groups, 176; presents civil disobedience case to Supreme Court, 148

American Committee for Non-Participation in Japanese Aggression, 124

American Federation of Labor (AFL), 91, 102

American Friends Service Committee (AFSC), 149, 154; discourages detainees from returning to West Coast, 171, 172; notes that all constitutional guarantees were endangered by Evacuation Orders, 150; presents civil disobedience case to Supreme Court, 148

American Legion, 141

American Students Association, 183

Anderson, Benedict, 77

anti-miscegenation laws. *See* marriage

Arai, Clarence, 93, 94, 95, 96

About the Author

STEPHANIE HINNERSHITZ is an assistant professor in the History Department at Valdosta State University in Valdosta, Georgia. She received her PhD in American history from the University of Maryland in 2013 and specializes in immigration, Asian American, and social history of the United States during the twentieth century.

CPSIA information can be obtained at www.ICGtesting.com
Printed in the USA
LVOW06s1413021115

460746LV00001B/17/P